Ford
Diesel
Engine
Owners
Workshop
Manual

Matthew Minter

Models covered

This manual covers the Ford 1608 cc (1.6 litre) and 1753 cc (1.8 litre) Diesel engines used in the Ford Fiesta, Ford Escort and Ford Orion

Does not cover Turbo-Diesel engine or P100/Sierra applications

(1172-2V6)

ABCDE
FGHIJ
KLMN

2

Haynes Publishing Group
Sparkford Nr Yeovil
Somerset BA22 7JJ England

Haynes Publications, Inc
861 Lawrence Drive
Newbury Park
California 91320 USA

Acknowledgements

Thanks are due to Douglas Seaton Ltd, of Yeovil, for the loan of the cars used in the preparation of this manual. Certain illustrations are the copyright of the Ford Motor Company, and are used with their permission. Duckhams Oils provided lubrication data. Thanks are also due to Sykes-Pickavant who supplied some of the workshop tools, and to all those people at Sparkford who helped in the production of the manual.

© **Haynes Publishing Group 1993**

A book in the **Haynes Owners Workshop Manual Series**

Printed by J. H. Haynes & Co. Ltd, Sparkford, Nr Yeovil Somerset BA22 7JJ, England

ISBN 1 85010 907 9

British Library Cataloguing in Publication Data
A catalogue record for this book is available from the British Library

Restoring and Preserving our Motoring Heritage

Few people can have had the luck to realise their dreams to quite the same extent and in such a remarkable fashion as John Haynes, Founder and Chairman of the Haynes Publishing Group.

Since 1965 his unique approach to workshop manual publishing has proved so successful that millions of Haynes Manuals are now sold every year throughout the world, covering literally thousands of different makes and models of cars, vans and motorcycles.

A continuing passion for cars and motoring led to the founding in 1985 of a Charitable Trust dedicated to the restoration and preservation of our motoring heritage. To inaugurate the new Museum, John Haynes donated virtually his entire private collection of 52 cars.

Now with an unrivalled international collection of over 210 veteran, vintage and classic cars and motorcycles, the Haynes Motor Museum in Somerset is well on the way to becoming one of the most interesting Motor Museums in the world.

A 70 seat video cinema, a cafe and an extensive motoring bookshop, together with a specially constructed one kilometre motor circuit, make a visit to the Haynes Motor Museum a truly unforgettable experience.

Every vehicle in the museum is preserved in as near as possible mint condition and each car is run every six months on the motor circuit.

Enjoy the picnic area set amongst the rolling Somerset hills. Peer through the William Morris workshop windows at cars being restored, and browse through the extensive displays of fascinating motoring memorabilia.

From the 1903 Oldsmobile through such classics as an MG Midget to the mighty 'E' Type Jaguar, Lamborghini, Ferrari Berlinetta Boxer, and Graham Hill's Lola Cosworth, there is something for everyone, young and old alike, at this Somerset Museum.

Haynes Motor Museum

Situated mid-way between London and Penzance, the Haynes Motor Museum is located just off the A303 at Sparkford, Somerset (home of the Haynes Manual) and is open to the public 7 days a week all year round, except Christmas Day and Boxing Day.

Contents

Front three-quarter view of Ford 1.6 Diesel engine. Camshaft drivebelt cover has been removed

1 Camshaft sprocket
2 Inlet manifold
3 Engine oil filler cap
4 Lifting eye
5 Coolant hose connections
   (coolant pump inlet)
6 Injector (one of four)
7 Injection pipes

8 Crankcase ventilation hose
9 Fuel pipes
10 Engine oil dipstick
11 Temperature gauge sender
12 Vacuum pump
13 Thermostat elbow
14 Radiator fan switch
15 Flywheel

16 Cold start device
17 Fuel injection pump
18 Alternator
19 Alternator/water pump
   drivebelt
20 Crankshaft pulley
21 Injection pump sprocket

22 Water pump pulley
23 Mounting bracket
24 Coolant hose connection
   (heater)
25 Camshaft drivebelt
26 Camshaft drivebelt tensioner
27 Coolant hose connection
   (bleed)

About this manual

Its aim

The aim of this manual is to help you get the best value from your vehicle. It can do so in several ways. It can help you decide what work must be done (even should you choose to get it done by a garage), provide information on routine maintenance and servicing, and give a logical course of action and diagnosis when random faults occur. However, it is hoped that you will use the manual by tackling the work yourself. On simpler jobs it may even be quicker than booking the car into a garage and going there twice, to leave and collect it. Perhaps most important, a lot of money can be saved by avoiding the costs a garage must charge to cover its labour and overheads.

The manual has drawings and descriptions to show the function of the various components so that their layout can be understood. Then the tasks are described and photographed in a step-by-step sequence so that even a novice can do the work.

Unlike most Haynes manuals, which cover a particular vehicle in different trim levels and engine sizes, this book covers one engine and its associated equipment as fitted to a range of vehicles. Items which are common to Diesel and petrol models – eg bodywork, transmission and running gear – are not covered in this book.

Its arrangement

The manual is divided into eight Chapters, each covering a logical sub-division of the engine and its systems. The Chapters are each divided into Sections, numbered with single figures, eg 5; and the Sections into paragraphs (or sub-sections), with decimal numbers following on from the Section they are in, eg 5.1, 5.2, 5.3 etc.

It is freely illustrated, especially in those parts where there is a detailed sequence of operations to be carried out. There are two forms of illustration: figures and photographs. The figures are numbered in sequence with decimal numbers, according to their position in the Chapter – eg Fig. 6.4 is the fourth drawing/illustration in Chapter 6. Photographs carry the same number (either individually or in related groups) as the Section or sub-section to which they relate.

There is an alphabetical index at the back of the manual as well as a contents list at the front. Each Chapter is also preceded by its own individual contents list.

References to the 'left' or 'right' of the vehicle are in the sense of a person in the driver's seat facing forwards.

Unless otherwise stated, nuts and bolts are removed by turning anti-clockwise, and tightened by turning clockwise.

Vehicle manufacturers continually make changes to specifications and recommendations, and these, when notified, are incorporated into our manuals at the earliest opportunity.

We take great pride in the accuracy of information given in this manual, but vehicle manufacturers make alterations and design changes during the production run of a particular vehicle of which they do not inform us. No liability can be accepted by the authors or publishers for loss, damage or injury caused by any errors in, or omissions from, the information given.

Introduction to the Ford 1.6 & 1.8 Diesel engines

This engine, the smallest Diesel in Ford's range, has been available since 1984. It is fitted to the front wheel drive passenger vehicles and light vans – Fiesta, Escort and Orion. Like the equivalent petrol engines it is mounted transversely. The engine is a completely new design, unlike those offered by some other manufacturers which are simply 'conversions' of existing petrol engines.

On paper the outputs of the 1.6 and 1.8 Diesel engines fall between those of Ford's 1.1 and 1.3 petrol engines. On the road it is no slouch, only a certain amount of clatter at idle betraying its presence to the driver. It is almost impossible to stall, and satisfactory progress can be made in heavy traffic using the first two gears without touching the throttle. The Diesel's fuel economy benefits are well known; to these can be added longer engine life, and (at present) a higher resale value, than petrol-engined equivalents.

Routine maintenance tasks are few and easily carried out. Access is limited for some repair operations. Certain jobs will require the purchase or construction of special tools; this apart, the engine is easy to work on and displays many thoughtful design features.

The fuel injection equipment is made by Bosch on early 1.6 engines, with a CAV RotoDiesel system being fitted from July 1986. 1.8 engines are fitted with either Bosch or CAV RotoDiesel systems. Note that when a vehicle's fuel system is manufactured by CAV RotoDiesel (which is part of the Lucas group) system components and replacement parts may be found marked with any of the following names: 'Lucas', 'Lucas CAV', 'CAV', 'ConDiesel' or 'RotoDiesel'. While the major components may not be user-serviceable (whichever system is fitted to a particular vehicle), provided that all fuel system maintenance procedures are carried out correctly and at the specified intervals, no problems should be encountered during normal use.

Outside the engine bay, the vehicles to which this engine is fitted are much the same in Diesel and petrol versions. For complete coverage of a particular vehicle, the appropriate manual for petrol-engined vehicles will be needed as well.

General dimensions, weights and capacities

Dimensions (typical)
Overall length:
Fiesta 1.6	3.647 m (11 ft 11.6 in)
Fiesta 1.8	3.791 m (12 ft 5.4 in)
Escort (Hatchback)	3.970 to 4.056 m (13 ft 0.3 in to 13 ft 3.7 in)
Escort (Estate)	4.034 to 4.128 m (13 ft 2.8 in to 13 ft 6.5 in)
Escort (Van)	4.219 m (13 ft 10.1 in)
Orion	4.194 m (13 ft 9.1 in)

Overall width (including mirrors):
Fiesta 1.6	1.709 to 1.725 m (5 ft 7.3 in to 5 ft 7.9 in)
Fiesta 1.8 (excluding mirrors)	1.605 m (5 ft 3.2 in)
Escort (all models)	1.844 m (6 ft 0.6 in)
Orion	1.844 m (6 ft 0.6 in)

Overall height:
Fiesta 1.6	1.334 m (4 ft 4.5 in)
Fiesta 1.8	1.389 m (4 ft 6.7 in)
Escort (Hatchback)	1.402 m (4 ft 7.2 in)
Escort (Estate)	1.400 m (4 ft 7.1 in)
Escort (Van)	1.568 m (5 ft 1.7 in)
Orion	1.407 m (4 ft 7.4 in)

Weights (typical)
Kerb weights (approx):
Fiesta 1.6 (except Van)	860 kg (1896 lb)
Fiesta 1.6 (Van)	850 kg (1874 lb)
Fiesta 1.8 (except Van)	895 kg (1973 lb)
Fiesta 1.8 (Van)	955 kg (2106 lb)
Escort (Hatchback)	925 to 950 kg (2040 to 2095 lb)
Escort (Estate)	950 to 970 kg (2095 to 2139 lb)
Escort (Van)	930 to 940 kg (2051 to 2073 lb)
Orion	950 kg (2095 lb)
Roof rack load (all models)	75 kg (165 lb) max
Tow-bar vertical load (all models)	25 to 50 kg (55 to 110 lb)

Trailer weight limit:
Fiesta	800 kg (1764 lb)
Escort	900 kg (1985 lb)
Orion	900 kg (1985 lb)
Gross vehicle weight	See VIN plate (under bonnet)

Capacities (approx)
Engine oil, drain and refill (1.6):
With filter	5.0 litres (8.8 pints)
Without filter	4.5 litres (7.9 pints)

Engine oil, drain and refill (1.8):
With filter	4.5 litres (7.9 pints)
Without filter	4.1 litres (7.2 pints)

Cooling system:
Fiesta	8.5 litres (15.0 pints)
Escort/Orion	9.3 litres (16.4 pints)

Fuel tank:
Fiesta 1.6 (up to August 1984)	34 litres (7.5 gallons)
Fiesta 1.6 (August 1984 on)	40 litres (8.8 gallons)
Fiesta 1.8	42 litres (9.2 gallons)
Escort (except Van) and Orion	48 litres (10.6 gallons)
Escort Van	50 litres (11.0 gallons)
Transmission oil, drain and refill	3.1 litres (5.5 pints)

Buying spare parts

Only Ford spare parts should be used if the vehicle (or engine) is still under warranty. The use of other makes of parts may invalidate the warranty if a claim has to be made. In any case, only buy parts of reputable make. 'Pirate' parts, often of unknown origin, may not meet the maker's standards either dimensionally or in material quality.

Large items or sub-assemblies – eg cylinder heads, starter motors, injection pumps – may be available on an 'exchange' basis. Consult a Ford dealer for availability and conditions. Dismantled or badly damaged units may not be accepted in exchange.

When buying engine parts, be prepared to quote the engine number. This is stamped into the flywheel end of the block, just above the clutch bellhousing. For purchases of a more general nature, the vehicle identification number (VIN) may be needed; this is stamped on a plate secured to the engine bay front crossmember.

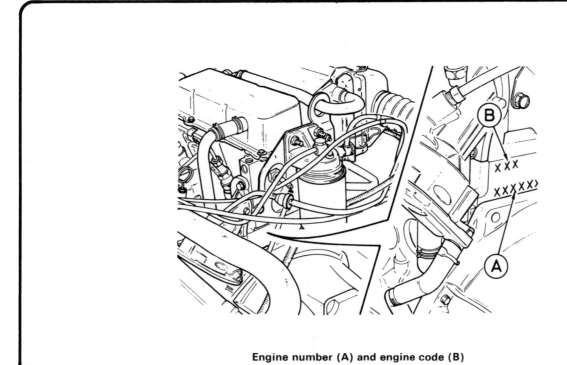

Engine number (A) and engine code (B)

General repair procedures

Whenever servicing, repair or overhaul work is carried out on the car or its components, it is necessary to observe the following procedures and instructions. This will assist in carrying out the operation efficiently and to a professional standard of workmanship.

Joint mating faces and gaskets

Where a gasket is used between the mating faces of two components, ensure that it is renewed on reassembly, and fit it dry unless otherwise stated in the repair procedure. Make sure that the mating faces are clean and dry with all traces of old gasket removed. When cleaning a joint face, use a tool which is not likely to score or damage the face, and remove any burrs or nicks with an oilstone or fine file.

Make sure that tapped holes are cleaned with a pipe cleaner, and keep them free of jointing compound if this is being used unless specifically instructed otherwise.

Ensure that all orifices, channels or pipes are clear and blow through them, preferably using compressed air.

Oil seals

Whenever an oil seal is removed from its working location, either individually or as part of an assembly, it should be renewed.

The very fine sealing lip of the seal is easily damaged and will not seal if the surface it contacts is not completely clean and free from scratches, nicks or grooves. If the original sealing surface of the component cannot be restored, the component should be renewed.

Protect the lips of the seal from any surface which may damage them in the course of fitting. Use tape or a conical sleeve where possible. Lubricate the seal lips with oil before fitting and, on dual lipped seals, fill the space between the lips with grease.

Unless otherwise stated, oil seals must be fitted with their sealing lips toward the lubricant to be sealed.

Use a tubular drift or block of wood of the appropriate size to install the seal and, if the seal housing is shouldered, drive the seal down to the shoulder. If the seal housing is unshouldered, the seal should be fitted with its face flush with the housing top face.

Screw threads and fastenings

Always ensure that a blind tapped hole is completely free from oil, grease, water or other fluid before installing the bolt or stud. Failure to do this could cause the housing to crack due to the hydraulic action of the bolt or stud as it is screwed in.

When tightening a castellated nut to accept a split pin, tighten the nut to the specified torque, where applicable, and then tighten further to the next split pin hole. Never slacken the nut to align a split pin hole unless stated in the repair procedure.

When checking or retightening a nut or bolt to a specified torque setting, slacken the nut or bolt by a quarter of a turn, and then retighten to the specified setting.

Locknuts, locktabs and washers

Any fastening which will rotate against a component or housing in the course of tightening should always have a washer between it and the relevant component or housing.

Spring or split washers should always be renewed when they are used to lock a critical component such as a big-end bearing retaining nut or bolt.

Locktabs which are folded over to retain a nut or bolt should always be renewed.

Self-locking nuts can be reused in non-critical areas, providing resistance can be felt when the locking portion passes over the bolt or stud thread.

Split pins must always be replaced with new ones of the correct size for the hole.

Special tools

Some repair procedures in this manual entail the use of special tools such as a press, two or three-legged pullers, spring compressors etc. Wherever possible, suitable readily available alternatives to the manufacturer's special tools are described, and are shown in use. In some instances, where no alternative is possible, it has been necessary to resort to the use of a manufacturer's tool and this has been done for reasons of safety as well as the efficient completion of the repair operation. Unless you are highly skilled and have a thorough understanding of the procedure described, never attempt to bypass the use of any special tool when the procedure described specifies its use. Not only is there a very great risk of personal injury, but expensive damage could be caused to the components involved.

Tools and working facilities

Introduction

A selection of good tools is a fundamental requirement for anyone contemplating the maintenance and repair of a motor vehicle. For the owner who does not possess any, their purchase will prove a considerable expense, offsetting some of the savings made by doing-it-yourself. However, provided that the tools purchased meet the relevant national safety standards and are of good quality, they will last for many years and prove an extremely worthwhile investment.

To help the average owner to decide which tools are needed to carry out the various tasks detailed in this manual, we have compiled three lists of tools under the following headings: *Maintenance and minor repair*, *Repair and overhaul*, and *Special*. The newcomer to practical mechanics should start off with the *Maintenance and minor repair* tool kit and confine himself to the simpler jobs around the vehicle. Then, as his confidence and experience grow, he can undertake more difficult tasks, buying extra tools as, and when, they are needed. In this way, a *Maintenance and minor repair* tool kit can be built-up into a *Repair and overhaul* tool kit over a considerable period of time without any major cash outlays. The experienced do-it-yourselfer will have a tool kit good enough for most repair and overhaul procedures and will add tools from the *Special* category when he feels the expense is justified by the amount of use to which these tools will be put.

It is obviously not possible to cover the subject of tools fully here. For those who wish to learn more about tools and their use there is a book entitled *How to Choose and Use Car Tools* available from the publishers of this manual.

Maintenance and minor repair tool kit

The tools given in this list should be considered as a minimum requirement if routine maintenance, servicing and minor repair operations are to be undertaken. We recommend the purchase of combination spanners (ring one end, open-ended the other); although more expensive than open-ended ones, they do give the advantages of both types of spanner.

    Combination spanners - 10, 11, 12, 13, 14 & 17 mm
    Adjustable spanner - 9 inch
    Set of feeler gauges
    Brake bleed nipple spanner
    Screwdriver - 4 in long x $1/4$ in dia (flat blade)
    Screwdriver - 4 in long x $1/4$ in dia (cross blade)
    Combination pliers - 6 inch
    Hacksaw (junior)
    Tyre pump
    Tyre pressure gauge
    Oil can
    Fine emery cloth (1 sheet)
    Wire brush (small)
    Funnel (medium size)
    Chain or strap wrench

Repair and overhaul tool kit

These tools are virtually essential for anyone undertaking any major repairs to a motor vehicle, and are additional to those given in the *Maintenance and minor repair* list. Included in this list is a comprehensive set of sockets. Although these are expensive they will be found invaluable as they are so versatile - particularly if various drives are included in the set. We recommend the $1/2$ in square-drive type, as this can be used with most proprietary torque wrenches. If you cannot afford a socket set, even bought piecemeal, then inexpensive tubular box spanners are a useful alternative.

The tools in this list will occasionally need to be supplemented by tools from the *Special* list.

    Sockets (or box spanners) to cover range in previous list, plus
    27 mm/$1^1/16$ in for injectors
    Reversible ratchet drive (for use with sockets)
    Extension piece, 10 inch (for use with sockets)

    Universal joint (for use with sockets)
    Torque wrench (for use with sockets)
    'Mole' wrench - 8 inch
    Ball pein hammer
    Soft-faced hammer, plastic or rubber
    Screwdriver - 6 in long x $5/16$ in dia (flat blade)
    Screwdriver - 2 in long x $5/16$ in square (flat blade)
    Screwdriver - $1^1/2$ in long x $1/4$ in dia (cross blade)
    Screwdriver - 3 in long x $1/8$ in dia (electricians)
    Pliers - electricians side cutters
    Pliers - needle nosed
    Pliers - circlip (internal and external)
    Cold chisel - $1/2$ inch
    Scriber
    Scraper
    Centre punch
    Pin punch
    Hacksaw
    Valve grinding tool
    Steel rule/straight-edge
    Allen keys
    'Torx' drive keys (Ford type)
    Dial test indicator and stand (photo)
    Camshaft drivebelt tension gauge
    Selection of files
    Wire brush (large)
    Axle-stands
    Jack (strong trolley or hydraulic type)
    Light with extension lead

Dial test indicator being used to set the injection timing

Special tools

The tools in this list are those which are not used regularly, are expensive to buy, or which need to be used in accordance with their manufacturers' instructions. Unless relatively difficult mechanical jobs are undertaken frequently, it will not be economic to buy many of these tools. Where this is the case, you could consider clubbing together with friends (or joining a motorists' club) to make a joint purchase, or borrowing the tools against a deposit from a local garage or tool hire specialist.

The following list contains only those tools and instruments freely available to the public, and not those special tools produced by the vehicle manufacturer specifically for its dealer network. You will find occasional references to these manufacturers' special tools in the text of this manual. Generally, an alternative method of doing the job without the vehicle manufacturers' special tool is given. However, sometimes, there is no alternative to using them. Where this is the case and the relevant tool cannot be bought or borrowed, you will have to entrust the work to a franchised garage.

> *Valve spring compressor*
> *Piston ring compressor*
> *Balljoint separator*
> *Universal hub/bearing puller*
> *Impact screwdriver*
> *Micrometer and/or vernier gauge*
> *Universal electrical multi-meter*
> *Cylinder compression gauge (suitable for Diesel)*
> *Lifting tackle*
> *Trolley jack*

Buying tools

For practically all tools, a tool factor is the best source since he will have a very comprehensive range compared with the average garage or accessory shop. Having said that, accessory shops often offer excellent quality tools at discount prices, so it pays to shop around.

There are plenty of good tools around at reasonable prices, but always aim to purchase items which meet the relevant national safety standards. If in doubt, ask the proprietor or manager of the shop for advice before making a purchase.

Care and maintenance of tools

Having purchased a reasonable tool kit, it is necessary to keep the tools in a clean serviceable condition. After use, always wipe off any dirt, grease and metal particles using a clean, dry cloth, before putting the tools away. Never leave them lying around after they have been used. A simple tool rack on the garage or workshop wall, for items such as screwdrivers and pliers is a good idea. Store all normal wrenches and sockets in a metal box. Any measuring instruments, gauges, meters, etc, must be carefully stored where they cannot be damaged or become rusty.

Take a little care when tools are used. Hammer heads inevitably become marked and screwdrivers lose the keen edge on their blades from time to time. A little timely attention with emery cloth or a file will soon restore items like this to a good serviceable finish.

Working facilities

Not to be forgotten when discussing tools, is the workshop itself. If anything more than routine maintenance is to be carried out, some form of suitable working area becomes essential.

It is appreciated that many an owner mechanic is forced by circumstances to remove an engine or similar item, without the benefit of a garage or workshop. Having done this, any repairs should always be done under the cover of a roof.

Wherever possible, any dismantling should be done on a clean, flat workbench or table at a suitable working height.

Any workbench needs a vice: one with a jaw opening of 4 in (100 mm) is suitable for most jobs. As mentioned previously, some clean dry storage space is also required for tools, as well as for lubricants, cleaning fluids, touch-up paints and so on, which become necessary.

Another item which may be required, and which has a much more general usage, is an electric drill with a chuck capacity of at least 5/16 in (8 mm). This, together with a good range of twist drills, is virtually essential for fitting accessories such as mirrors and reversing lights.

Last, but not least, always keep a supply of old newspapers and clean, lint-free rags available, and try to keep any working area as clean as possible.

Spanner jaw gap comparison table

Jaw gap (in)	Spanner size
0.250	$\frac{1}{4}$ in AF
0.276	7 mm
0.313	$\frac{5}{16}$ in AF
0.315	8 mm
0.344	$\frac{11}{32}$ in AF; $\frac{1}{8}$ in Whitworth
0.354	9 mm
0.375	$\frac{3}{8}$ in AF
0.394	10 mm
0.433	11 mm
0.438	$\frac{7}{16}$ in AF
0.445	$\frac{3}{16}$ in Whitworth; $\frac{1}{4}$ in BSF
0.472	12 mm
0.500	$\frac{1}{2}$ in AF
0.512	13 mm
0.525	$\frac{1}{4}$ in Whitworth; $\frac{5}{16}$ in BSF
0.551	14 mm
0.563	$\frac{9}{16}$ in AF
0.591	15 mm
0.600	$\frac{5}{16}$ in Whitworth; $\frac{3}{8}$ in BSF
0.625	$\frac{5}{8}$ in AF
0.630	16 mm
0.669	17 mm
0.686	$\frac{11}{16}$ in AF
0.709	18 mm
0.710	$\frac{3}{8}$ in Whitworth; $\frac{7}{16}$ in BSF
0.748	19 mm
0.750	$\frac{3}{4}$ in AF
0.813	$\frac{13}{16}$ in AF
0.820	$\frac{7}{16}$ in Whitworth; $\frac{1}{2}$ in BSF
0.866	22 mm
0.875	$\frac{7}{8}$ in AF
0.920	$\frac{1}{2}$ in Whitworth; $\frac{9}{16}$ in BSF
0.938	$\frac{15}{16}$ in AF
0.945	24 mm
1.000	1 in AF
1.010	$\frac{9}{16}$ in Whitworth; $\frac{5}{8}$ in BSF
1.024	26 mm
1.063	$1\frac{1}{16}$ in AF; 27 mm
1.100	$\frac{5}{8}$ in Whitworth; $\frac{11}{16}$ in BSF
1.125	$1\frac{1}{8}$ in AF
1.181	30 mm
1.200	$\frac{11}{16}$ in Whitworth; $\frac{3}{4}$ in BSF
1.250	$1\frac{1}{4}$ in AF
1.260	32 mm
1.300	$\frac{3}{4}$ in Whitworth; $\frac{7}{8}$ in BSF
1.313	$1\frac{5}{16}$ in AF
1.390	$\frac{13}{16}$ in Whitworth; $\frac{15}{16}$ in BSF
1.417	36 mm
1.438	$1\frac{7}{16}$ in AF
1.480	$\frac{7}{8}$ in Whitworth; 1 in BSF
1.500	$1\frac{1}{2}$ in AF
1.575	40 mm; $\frac{15}{16}$ in Whitworth
1.614	41 mm
1.625	$1\frac{5}{8}$ in AF
1.670	1 in Whitworth; $1\frac{1}{8}$ in BSF
1.688	$1\frac{11}{16}$ in AF
1.811	46 mm
1.813	$1\frac{13}{16}$ in AF
1.860	$1\frac{1}{8}$ in Whitworth; $1\frac{1}{4}$ in BSF
1.875	$1\frac{7}{8}$ in AF
1.969	50 mm
2.000	2 in AF
2.050	$1\frac{1}{4}$ in Whitworth; $1\frac{3}{8}$ in BSF
2.165	55 mm
2.362	60 mm

Conversion factors

Length (distance)

Inches (in)	X	25.4	= Millimetres (mm)	X	0.0394	= Inches (in)
Feet (ft)	X	0.305	= Metres (m)	X	3.281	= Feet (ft)
Miles	X	1.609	= Kilometres (km)	X	0.621	= Miles

Volume (capacity)

Cubic inches (cu in; in³)	X	16.387	= Cubic centimetres (cc; cm³)	X	0.061	= Cubic inches (cu in; in³)
Imperial pints (Imp pt)	X	0.568	= Litres (l)	X	1.76	= Imperial pints (Imp pt)
Imperial quarts (Imp qt)	X	1.137	= Litres (l)	X	0.88	= Imperial quarts (Imp qt)
Imperial quarts (Imp qt)	X	1.201	= US quarts (US qt)	X	0.833	= Imperial quarts (Imp qt)
US quarts (US qt)	X	0.946	= Litres (l)	X	1.057	= US quarts (US qt)
Imperial gallons (Imp gal)	X	4.546	= Litres (l)	X	0.22	= Imperial gallons (Imp gal)
Imperial gallons (Imp gal)	X	1.201	= US gallons (US gal)	X	0.833	= Imperial gallons (Imp gal)
US gallons (US gal)	X	3.785	= Litres (l)	X	0.264	= US gallons (US gal)

Mass (weight)

Ounces (oz)	X	28.35	= Grams (g)	X	0.035	= Ounces (oz)
Pounds (lb)	X	0.454	= Kilograms (kg)	X	2.205	= Pounds (lb)

Force

Ounces-force (ozf; oz)	X	0.278	= Newtons (N)	X	3.6	= Ounces-force (ozf; oz)
Pounds-force (lbf; lb)	X	4.448	= Newtons (N)	X	0.225	= Pounds-force (lbf; lb)
Newtons (N)	X	0.1	= Kilograms-force (kgf; kg)	X	9.81	= Newtons (N)

Pressure

Pounds-force per square inch (psi; lbf/in²; lb/in²)	X	0.070	= Kilograms-force per square centimetre (kgf/cm²; kg/cm²)	X	14.223	= Pounds-force per square inch (psi; lbf/in²; lb/in²)
Pounds-force per square inch (psi; lbf/in²; lb/in²)	X	0.068	= Atmospheres (atm)	X	14.696	= Pounds-force per square inch (psi; lbf/in²; lb/in²)
Pounds-force per square inch (psi; lbf/in²; lb/in²)	X	0.069	= Bars	X	14.5	= Pounds-force per square inch (psi; lbf/in²; lb/in²)
Pounds-force per square inch (psi; lbf/in²; lb/in²)	X	6.895	= Kilopascals (kPa)	X	0.145	= Pounds-force per square inch (psi; lbf/in²; lb/in²)
Kilopascals (kPa)	X	0.01	= Kilograms-force per square centimetre (kgf/cm²; kg/cm²)	X	98.1	= Kilopascals (kPa)
Millibar (mbar)	X	100	= Pascals (Pa)	X	0.01	= Millibar (mbar)
Millibar (mbar)	X	0.0145	= Pounds-force per square inch (psi; lbf/in²; lb/in²)	X	68.947	= Millibar (mbar)
Millibar (mbar)	X	0.75	= Millimetres of mercury (mmHg)	X	1.333	= Millibar (mbar)
Millibar (mbar)	X	0.401	= Inches of water (inH₂O)	X	2.491	= Millibar (mbar)
Millimetres of mercury (mmHg)	X	0.535	= Inches of water (inH₂O)	X	1.868	= Millimetres of mercury (mmHg)
Inches of water (inH₂O)	X	0.036	= Pounds-force per square inch (psi; lbf/in²; lb/in²)	X	27.68	= Inches of water (inH₂O)

Torque (moment of force)

Pounds-force inches (lbf in; lb in)	X	1.152	= Kilograms-force centimetre (kgf cm; kg cm)	X	0.868	= Pounds-force inches (lbf in; lb in)
Pounds-force inches (lbf in; lb in)	X	0.113	= Newton metres (Nm)	X	8.85	= Pounds-force inches (lbf in; lb in)
Pounds-force inches (lbf in; lb in)	X	0.083	= Pounds-force feet (lbf ft; lb ft)	X	12	= Pounds-force inches (lbf in; lb in)
Pounds-force feet (lbf ft; lb ft)	X	0.138	= Kilograms-force metres (kgf m; kg m)	X	7.233	= Pounds-force feet (lbf ft; lb ft)
Pounds-force feet (lbf ft; lb ft)	X	1.356	= Newton metres (Nm)	X	0.738	= Pounds-force feet (lbf ft; lb ft)
Newton metres (Nm)	X	0.102	= Kilograms-force metres (kgf m; kg m)	X	9.804	= Newton metres (Nm)

Power

Horsepower (hp)	X	745.7	= Watts (W)	X	0.0013	= Horsepower (hp)

Velocity (speed)

Miles per hour (miles/hr; mph)	X	1.609	= Kilometres per hour (km/hr; kph)	X	0.621	= Miles per hour (miles/hr; mph)

Fuel consumption*

Miles per gallon, Imperial (mpg)	X	0.354	= Kilometres per litre (km/l)	X	2.825	= Miles per gallon, Imperial (mpg)
Miles per gallon, US (mpg)	X	0.425	= Kilometres per litre (km/l)	X	2.352	= Miles per gallon, US (mpg)

Temperature

Degrees Fahrenheit = (°C x 1.8) + 32

Degrees Celsius (Degrees Centigrade; °C) = (°F - 32) x 0.56

*It is common practice to convert from miles per gallon (mpg) to litres/100 kilometres (l/100km), where mpg (Imperial) x l/100 km = 282 and mpg (US) x l/100 km = 235

Safety first!

Professional motor mechanics are trained in safe working procedures. However enthusiastic you may be about getting on with the job in hand, do take the time to ensure that your safety is not put at risk. A moment's lack of attention can result in an accident, as can failure to observe certain elementary precautions.

There will always be new ways of having accidents, and the following points do not pretend to be a comprehensive list of all dangers; they are intended rather to make you aware of the risks and to encourage a safety-conscious approach to all work you carry out on your vehicle.

Essential DOs and DON'Ts

DON'T rely on a single jack when working underneath the vehicle. Always use reliable additional means of support, such as axle stands, securely placed under a part of the vehicle that you know will not give way.

DON'T attempt to loosen or tighten high-torque nuts (e.g. wheel hub nuts) while the vehicle is on a jack; it may be pulled off.

DON'T start the engine without first ascertaining that the transmission is in neutral and the parking brake applied.

DON'T suddenly remove the filler cap from a hot cooling system – cover it with a cloth and release the pressure gradually first, or you may get scalded by escaping coolant.

DON'T attempt to drain oil until you are sure it has cooled sufficiently to avoid scalding you.

DON'T grasp any part of the engine or exhaust without first ascertaining that it is sufficiently cool to avoid burning you.

DON'T allow brake fluid or antifreeze to contact vehicle paintwork.

DON'T syphon toxic liquids such as fuel, brake fluid or antifreeze by mouth, or allow them to remain on your skin.

DON'T inhale dust – it may be injurious to health (see *Asbestos* below).

DON'T allow any spilt oil or grease to remain on the floor – wipe it up straight away, before someone slips on it.

DON'T use ill-fitting spanners or other tools which may slip and cause injury.

DON'T attempt to lift a heavy component which may be beyond your capability – get assistance.

DON'T rush to finish a job, or take unverified short cuts.

DON'T allow children or animals in or around an unattended vehicle.

DO wear eye protection when using power tools such as drill, sander, bench grinder etc, and when working under the vehicle.

DO use a barrier cream on your hands prior to undertaking dirty jobs – it will protect your skin from infection as well as making the dirt easier to remove afterwards; but make sure your hands aren't left slippery. Note that long-term contact with used engine oil can be a health hazard.

DO keep loose clothing (cuffs, tie etc) and long hair well out of the way of moving mechanical parts.

DO remove rings, wristwatch etc, before working on the vehicle – especially the electrical system.

DO ensure that any lifting tackle used has a safe working load rating adequate for the job.

DO keep your work area tidy – it is only too easy to fall over articles left lying around.

DO get someone to check periodically that all is well, when working alone on the vehicle.

DO carry out work in a logical sequence and check that everything is correctly assembled and tightened afterwards.

DO remember that your vehicle's safety affects that of yourself and others. If in doubt on any point, get specialist advice.

IF, in spite of following these precautions, you are unfortunate enough to injure yourself, seek medical attention as soon as possible.

Asbestos

Certain friction, insulating, sealing, and other products – such as brake linings, clutch linings, gaskets, etc – contain asbestos. *Extreme care must be taken to avoid inhalation of dust from such products since it is hazardous to health.* If in doubt, assume that they *do* contain asbestos.

Fire

Remember at all times that fuel is highly flammable. Never smoke, or have any kind of naked flame around, when working on the vehicle. But the risk does not end there – a spark caused by an electrical short-circuit, by two metal surfaces contacting each other, by careless use of tools, or even by static electricity built up in your body under certain conditions, can ignite fuel vapour, which in a confined space is highly explosive.

Always disconnect the battery earth (ground) terminal before working on any part of the fuel or electrical system, and never risk spilling fuel on to a hot engine or exhaust.

It is recommended that a fire extinguisher of a type suitable for fuel and electrical fires is kept handy in the garage or workplace at all times.

Note: *Any reference to a 'torch' appearing in this manual should always be taken to mean a hand-held battery-operated electric lamp or flashlight. It does NOT mean a welding/gas torch or blowlamp.*

Fumes

Certain fumes are highly toxic and can quickly cause unconsciousness and even death if inhaled to any extent. Fuel vapour comes into this category, as do the vapours from certain solvents such as trichloroethylene. Any draining or pouring of such volatile fluids should be done in a well ventilated area.

When using cleaning fluids and solvents, read the instructions carefully. Never use materials from unmarked containers – they may give off poisonous vapours.

Never run the engine of a motor vehicle in an enclosed space such as a garage. Exhaust fumes contain carbon monoxide which is extremely poisonous; if you need to run the engine, always do so in the open air or at least have the rear of the vehicle outside the workplace.

If you are fortunate enough to have the use of an inspection pit, never drain or pour fuel, and never run the engine, while the vehicle is standing over it; the fumes, being heavier than air, will concentrate in the pit with possibly lethal results.

The battery

Never cause a spark, or allow a naked light, near the vehicle's battery. It will normally be giving off a certain amount of hydrogen gas, which is highly explosive.

Always disconnect the battery earth (ground) terminal before working on the fuel or electrical systems.

If possible, loosen the filler plugs or cover when charging the battery from an external source. Do not charge at an excessive rate or the battery may burst.

Take care when topping up and when carrying the battery. The acid electrolyte, even when diluted, is very corrosive and should not be allowed to contact the eyes or skin.

If you ever need to prepare electrolyte yourself, always add the acid slowly to the water, and never the other way round. Protect against splashes by wearing rubber gloves and goggles.

When jump starting a car using a booster battery, for negative earth (ground) vehicles, connect the jump leads in the following sequence: First connect one jump lead between the positive (+) terminals of the two batteries. Then connect the other jump lead first to the negative (–) terminal of the booster battery, and then to a good earthing (ground) point on the vehicle to be started, at least 18 in (45 cm) from the battery if possible. Ensure that hands and jump leads are clear of any moving parts, and that the two vehicles do not touch. Disconnect the leads in the reverse order.

Mains electricity and electrical equipment

When using an electric power tool, inspection light etc, always ensure that the appliance is correctly connected to its plug and that, where necessary, it is properly earthed (grounded). Do not use such appliances in damp conditions, and, again, beware of creating a spark or applying excessive heat in the vicinity of fuel or fuel vapour. Also ensure that the appliances meet the relevant national safety standards.

Diesel fuel

Diesel injection pumps supply fuel at very high pressure, and extreme care must be taken when working on the fuel injectors and fuel pipes. It is advisable to place an absorbent cloth around the union before slackening a fuel pipe, and *never expose the hands or any part of the body to injector spray, as the high working pressure can cause the fuel to penetrate the skin, with possibly fatal results.*

Routine maintenance

The maintenance schedules below are basically those recommended by the manufacturer. Servicing intervals are determined by mileage or time elapsed – this is because fluids and systems deteriorate with age as well as with use. Follow the time intervals if the appropriate mileage is not covered within the specified period.

Vehicles operating under adverse conditions may need more frequent maintenance. 'Adverse conditions' include climatic extremes,

full-time towing or taxi work, driving on unmade roads, and a high proportion of short journeys. The use of inferior fuel (such as may be found in some foreign countries) can cause early degradation of the engine oil. Consult a Ford dealer for advice on these points.

Some of the tasks called up will be described in detail in the approriate manual for petrol-engined vehicles.

Under-bonnet view of a 1.6 litre Fiesta Diesel – other 1.6 litre models are similar

1	Windscreen washer reservoir
2	Camshaft drivebelt cover
3	Engine oil filler cap
4	Suspension turret
5	Expansion tank filler cap
6	Cooling system bleed hose
7	Throttle cable
8	Air cleaner cover
9	Bonnet catch
10	Air intake hose
11	Crankcase ventilation hoses
12	Windscreen wiper motor
13	Brake master cylinder reservoir
14	Fuel filter head
15	Battery
16	Radiator top hose
17	Radiator fan shroud
18	Servo non-return valve
19	Cooling system bleed screw
20	Vacuum pump
21	Engine oil dipstick
22	Thermostat housing
23	Injection pipes
24	Injection pump
25	Water pump connector

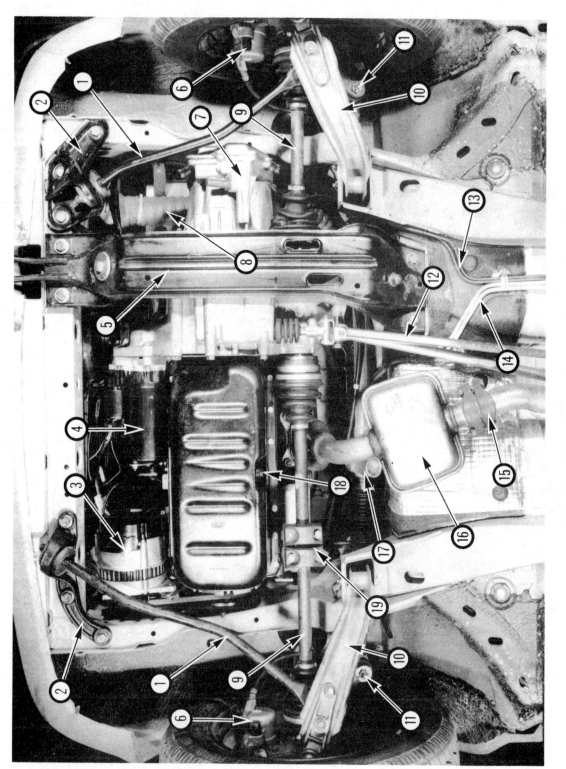

Under-view of the front end of a 1.6 litre Fiesta Diesel

1 Tie-bars
2 Tie-bar brackets
3 Alternator
4 Starter motor

5 Transmission bearer
6 Brake calipers
7 Transmission
8 Air cleaner intake

9 Driveshafts
10 Track control arms
11 Steering balljoints
12 Gearshift linkage

13 Brake pipes
14 Fuel pipes
15 Exhaust flanged joint
16 Front silencer

17 Steering gear
18 Sump drain plug
19 Driveshaft weights

Weekly, before a long journey, or every 250 miles (400 km)

Check engine oil level; top up if necessary (Chapter 1, Section 2)
Check coolant level and top up if necessary (Chapter 2, Section 2)
Top up screen washer reservoir(s)
Check brake fluid level; top up if necessary and determine reason for fall
Check tyre pressures (cold) and correct if necessary – see Chapter 6 Specifications
Check operation of exterior lights, signals, horn etc

Every 6000 miles (10 000 km) or six months – whichever comes first

Renew engine oil and oil filter (Chapter 1, Section 4)
1.6 litre engine – check tension and condition of water pump/alternator drivebelt (Chapter 2, Section 11)
Drain water from fuel filter (Chapter 3, Section 4 and/or Chapter 8, Section 5, Part A)
Inspect brake pad lining thickness
Inspect tyres thoroughly for tread wear and damage
Inspect brake shoe lining thickness
Check tightness of wheel nuts or bolts
Check idle speed and adjust if necessary (Chapter 3, Section 5)
Check all hoses, pipes etc for leaks or damage; make good as necessary
Check operation of brake vacuum pump and servo (Chapter 5, Section 2)
Check operation of instruments, warning lights etc

Every 12 000 miles (20 000 km) or 12 months – whichever comes first

In addition to the work in the previous schedule
Lubricate catches, door check straps etc
Clean battery terminals (Chapter 7, Section 2)
1.8 litre engines – check tension and condition of auxiliary drivebelt(s) – eg alternator, power-assisted steering pump (Chapter 2, Section 11 and Chapter 8, Section 4)
Check steering and suspension linkages, balljoints and gaiters for wear and damage
Check driveshaft gaiters for damage
Check transmission oil level (Chapter 4, Section 2)

Check exhaust system for corrosion and condition of mountings (Chapter 3, Section 18)
Lubricate handbrake linkage, check adjustment
Check rear hub bearing adjustment
Inspect underbody and panels for corrosion or other damage
Check smoke emission visually (Chapter 3, Section 19)

Every 24 000 miles (40 000 km) or two years – whichever comes first

In addition to the work in the previous schedules
Renew air cleaner element (Chapter 3, Section 3)
Renew fuel filter element (Chapter 3, Section 4)
1.6 litre engines – check valve clearances; adjust if necessary (Chapter 1, Section 7)

Every 36 000 miles (60 000 km) or two years – whichever comes first

Renew coolant (Chapter 2, Sections 4, 5, 6 and 14)

Every 36 000 miles (60 000 km) or three years – whichever comes first

In addition to the work in the previous schedules
1.8 litre engines – renew camshaft and fuel injection pump drivebelts (Chapter 8, Section 3)
1.6 litre engines – consider renewing camshaft drivebelt on a precautionary basis (Chapter 1, Section 2, referring to Section 6 for details of procedure)
Renew braking system hydraulic fluid by bleeding; consider renewing braking system flexible hoses on a precautionary basis
Check front wheel alignment

Every 48 000 miles (80 000 km)

In addition to the work in the previous schedules
1.8 litre engines – check the valve clearances; adjust if necessary (Chapter 8, Section 3, Part B and Chapter 1, Section 7)

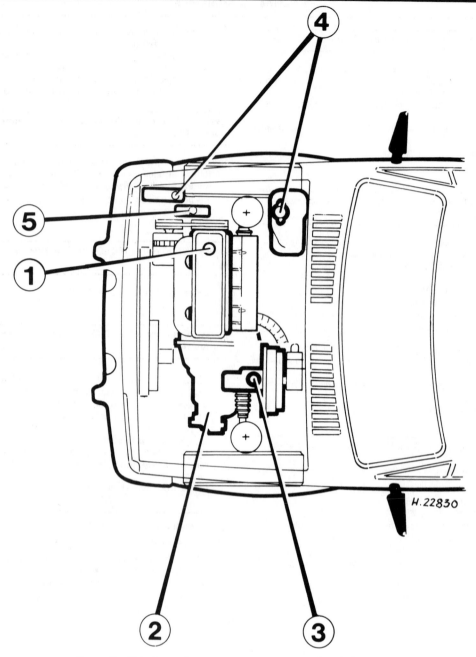

H.22830

Recommended lubricants and fluids

Component or system	Lubricant type/specification	Duckhams recommendation
1 Engine	Multigrade engine oil, viscosity range SAE 10W/30 to 20W/50, to specification API SG/CD or better	Duckhams Diesel, QXR or Hypergrade
2 Manual transmission	Hypoid gear oil, viscosity SAE 80EP, to Ford specification SQM 2C 9008 A	Duckhams Hypoid 80
3 Brake fluid reservoir	Hydraulic fluid to Ford specification SAM 6C 9103 A Amber	Duckhams Universal Brake and Clutch Fluid
4 Cooling system	Antifreeze to Ford specification ESD-M97B-49A	Duckhams Universal Antifreeze and Summer Coolant
5 Power-assisted steering	Fluid to Ford specification ESP-M2C 166-H	Duckhams Uni-Matic or D-Matic

Fault diagnosis

Introduction

The vehicle owner who does his or her own maintenance according to the recommended schedules should not have to use this section of the manual very often. Modern component reliability is such that, provided those items subject to wear or deterioration are inspected or renewed at the specified intervals, sudden failure is comparatively rare. Faults do not usually just happen as a result of sudden failure, but develop over a period of time. Major mechanical failures in particular are usually preceded by characteristic symptoms over hundreds or even thousands of miles. Those components which do occasionally fail without warning are often small and easily carried in the vehicle.

With any fault finding, the first step is to decide where to begin investigations. Sometimes this is obvious, but on other occasions a little detective work will be necessary. The owner who makes half a dozen haphazard adjustments or replacements may be successful in curing a fault (or its symptoms), but he will be none the wiser if the fault recurs and he may well have spent more time and money than was necessary. A calm and logical approach will be found to be more satisfactory in the long run. Always take into account any warning signs or abnormalities that may have been noticed in the period preceding the fault – power loss, high or low gauge readings, unusual noises or smells, etc – and remember that failure of components such as fuses may only be pointers to some underlying fault.

The pages which follow here are intended to help in cases of failure to start or breakdown on the road. There is also a Fault Diagnosis Section at the end of each Chapter which should be consulted if the preliminary checks prove unfruitful. Whatever the fault, certain basic principles apply. These are as follows:

Verify the fault. This is simply a matter of being sure that you know what the symptoms are before starting work. This is particularly important if you are investigating a fault for someone else who may not have described it very accurately.

Don't overlook the obvious. For example, if the vehicle won't start, is there fuel in the tank? (Don't take anyone else's word on this particular point, and don't trust the fuel gauge either!) If an electrical fault is indicated, look for loose or broken wires before digging out the test gear.

Cure the disease, not the symptom. Substituting a flat battery with a fully charged one will get you off the hard shoulder, but if the underlying cause is not attended to, the new battery will go the same way.

Don't take anything for granted. Particularly, don't forget that a 'new' component may itself be defective (especially if it's been rattling round in the boot for months), and don't leave components out of a fault diagnosis sequence just because they are new or recently fitted. When you do finally diagnose a difficult fault, you'll probably realise that all the evidence was there from the start.

Electrical faults

Electrical faults can be more puzzling than straightforward mechanical failures, but they are no less susceptible to logical analysis if the basic principles of operation are understood. Vehicle electrical wiring exists in extremely unfavourable conditions – heat, vibration and chemical attack – and the first things to look for are loose or corroded connections and broken or chafed wires, especially where the wires pass through holes in the bodywork or are subject to vibration.

All metal-bodied vehicles in current production have one pole of the battery 'earthed', ie connected to the vehicle bodywork, and in nearly all modern vehicles it is the negative (–) terminal. The various electrical components – motors, bulb holders etc – are also connected to earth, either by means of a lead or directly by their mountings. Electric current flows through the component and then back to the battery via the bodywork. If the component mounting is loose or corroded, or if a good path back to the battery is not available, the circuit will be incomplete and malfunction will result. The engine and/or gearbox are also earthed by means of flexible metal straps to the body or subframe; if these straps are loose or missing, starter motor, generator and other trouble may result.

Assuming the earth return to be satisfactory, electrical faults will be due either to component malfunction or to defects in the current supply. If supply wires are broken or cracked internally this results in an open-circuit, and the easiest way to check for this is to bypass the suspect wire temporarily with a length of wire having a crocodile clip or suitable connector at each end. Alternatively, a 12V test lamp can be used to verify the presence of supply voltage at various points along the wire and the break can be thus isolated.

If a bare portion of a live wire touches the bodywork or other earthed metal part, the electricity will take the low-resistance path thus formed back to the battery: this is known as a short-circuit. Hopefully a short-circuit will blow a fuse, but otherwise it may cause burning of the insulation (and possibly further short-circuits) or even a fire. This is why it is inadvisable to bypass persistently blowing fuses with silver foil or wire.

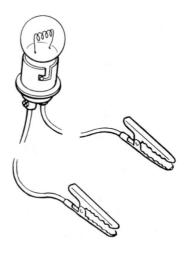

Simple test lamp is useful for tracing electrical faults

Spares and tool kit

Most vehicles are supplied only with sufficient tools for wheel changing; the *Maintenance and minor repair* tool kit detailed in *Tools and working facilities,* with the addition of a hammer, is probably sufficient for those repairs that most motorists would consider attempting at the roadside. In addition a few items which can be fitted without too much trouble in the event of a breakdown should be carried. Experience and available space will modify the list below, but the following may save having to call on professional assistance:

Drivebelt(s) – emergency type may suffice
Spare fuses
Set of principal light bulbs
Tin of radiator sealer and hose bandage
Exhaust bandage
Roll of insulating tape
Length of soft iron wire
Length of electrical flex
Torch or inspection lamp (can double as test lamp)
Battery jump leads
Tow-rope
Litre of engine oil
Sealed can of hydraulic fluid
Emergency windscreen
Worm drive clips
Tube of filler paste

If spare fuel is carried, a can designed for the purpose should be used to minimise risks of leakage and collision damage. A first aid kit and a warning triangle, whilst not at present compulsory in the UK, are obviously sensible items to carry in addition to the above.

When touring abroad it may be advisable to carry additional spares which, even if you cannot fit them yourself, could save having to wait while parts are obtained. The items below may be worth considering:

Clutch and throttle cables
Cylinder head gasket
Alternator brushes
Tyre valve core
Fuel injector(s) and heat protection washers

One of the motoring organisations will be able to advise on availability of fuel etc in foreign countries.

Engine will not start

Engine fails to turn when starter operated

Flat battery (recharge, use jump leads, or push start)
Battery terminals loose or corroded
Battery earth to body defective
Engine earth strap loose or broken
Starter motor (or solenoid) wiring loose or broken
Starter switch faulty
Major mechanical failure (seizure)
Starter or solenoid internal fault (see Chapter 7)

Starter motor turns engine slowly

Partially discharged battery (recharge, use jump leads, or push start)
Battery terminals loose or corroded
Battery earth to body defective
Engine earth strap loose
Starter motor (or solenoid) wiring loose
Starter motor internal fault (see Chapter 7)

Starter motor spins without turning engine

Flywheel gear teeth damaged or worn
Starter motor mounting bolts loose
Starter motor reduction gears stripped (when applicable)

Engine turns normally but fails to start

No fuel in tank
Wax formed in fuel (in very cold weather)
Exhaust system blocked
Poor compression (see Chapter 1)

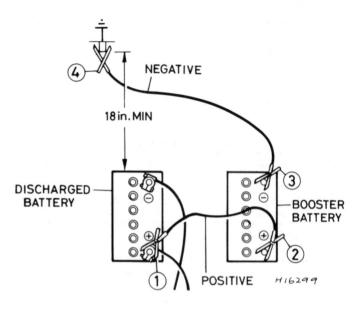

Jump start lead connections for negative earth vehicles – connect leads in order shown

Fuel system or preheater fault (see Chapter 3)
Major mechanical failure

Engine fires but will not run

Preheater fault (see Chapter 3)
Wax formed in fuel (in very cold weather)
Other fuel system fault (see Chapter 3)

Engine cuts out and will not restart

Engine misfires before cutting out – fuel fault

Fuel tank empty
Fuel filter blocked (check for delivery)
Fuel tank filler vent blocked (suction will be evident on releasing cap)
Other fuel system fault (see Chapter 3)

Engine cuts out – other causes

Serious overheating
Major mechanical failure (eg camshaft drive)

Engine overheats

Alternator (no-charge) warning light illuminated

Slack or broken drivebelt – retension or renew (Chapter 2)

Charge warning light not illuminated

Coolant loss due to internal or external leakage (see Chapter 2)
Thermostat defective
Low oil level
Brakes binding
Radiator clogged externally or internally
Electric cooling fan not operating correctly
Engine waterways clogged

Note: *Do not add cold water to an overheated engine or damage may result*

Low engine oil pressure

Gauge reads low or warning light illuminated with engine running

Oil level low or incorrect grade
Defective gauge or sender unit
Wire to sender unit earthed
Engine overheating
Oil filter clogged or bypass valve defective
Oil pressure relief valve defective
Oil pick-up strainer clogged
Oil pump worn or mountings loose
Worn main or big-end bearings

Note: *Low oil pressure in a high-mileage engine at tickover is not necessarily a cause for concern. Sudden pressure loss at speed is far more significant. In any event, check the gauge or warning light sender before condemning the engine.*

Engine noises

To inexperienced ears the Diesel engine sounds alarming even when there is nothing wrong with it. Try to have unusual noises expertly diagnosed before making renewals or repairs.

Whistling or wheezing noises

Leaking vacuum hose
Leaking manifold gasket
Blowing head gasket

Tapping or rattling

Incorrect valve clearances
Worn valve gear
Worn timing gears or belt
Broken piston ring (ticking noise)

Knocking or thumping

Unintentional mechanical contact (eg fan blades)
Worn drivebelt
Peripheral component fault (generator, water pump etc)
Fuel pump sucking air
Fuel contaminated
Fuel injector(s) leaking or sticking – see Chapter 3
Worn big-end bearings (regular heavy knocking, perhaps less under load)
Worn main bearings (rumbling and knocking, perhaps worsening under load)
Piston slap (most noticeable when cold)

Chapter 1 Engine

For modifications, and information applicable to later models, see Supplement at end of manual

Contents

Specifications

General

Engine type	Four-cylinder in-line, four-stroke, overhead camshaft, compression ignition
Maker's designation:	
Fiesta	LTB
Escort and Orion	LTA
Maker's type reference	S
Bore and stroke (nominal)	80.0 x 80.0 mm (3.150 x 3.150 in)
Cubic capacity	1608 cc (98.09 cu in)
Compression ratio	21.5 : 1
Compression pressure (at starter motor cranking speed)	28 to 34 bar (406 to 493 lbf/in²)
Maximum power	40 kW (54 bhp) @ 4800 rpm
Maximum torque	95 Nm (70 lbf ft) @ 3000 rpm
Maximum speed:	
Continuous	4800 rpm
Intermittent	5350 rpm
Firing order	1 - 3 - 4 - 2 (No 1 at pulley end)

Cylinder block

Main bearing bore diameter	57.683 to 57.696 mm (2.2710 to 2.2715 in)
Cylinder bore diameter:	
Class A	80.000 to 80.015 mm (3.1496 to 3.1502 in)
Class B	80.015 to 80.030 mm (3.1502 to 3.1508 in)
Class C	80.160 to 80.175 mm (3.1559 to 3.1565 in)
Class D	80.175 to 80.190 mm (3.1565 to 3.1571 in)
Class E (first rebore)	80.500 to 80.515 mm (3.1693 to 3.1699 in)
Class F (second rebore)	81.000 to 81.015 mm (3.1890 to 3.1896 in)

Crankshaft

Main bearing journal diameter:	
Standard	53.970 to 53.990 mm (2.1248 to 2.1256 in)
Undersize (production or repair)	53.720 to 53.740 mm (2.1150 to 2.1157 in)
Big-end bearing journal diameter:	
Standard	48.970 to 48.990 mm (1.9280 to 1.9287 in)
Undersize (production or repair)	48.720 to 48.740 mm (1.9181 to 1.9189 in)
Centre main bearing width:	
Standard	31.690 to 31.750 mm (1.2476 to 1.2500 in)
Oversize (production or repair)	32.070 to 32.130 mm (1.2626 to 1.2650 in)
Bearing shell identification:	
Standard	None
Undersize	Green
Main bearing clearance	0.015 to 0.062 mm (0.0006 to 0.0024 in)
Big-end bearing clearance	0.016 to 0.070 mm (0.0006 to 0.0028 in)
Crankshaft endfloat	0.093 to 0.306 mm (0.0037 to 0.0121 in)
Connecting rod endfloat (between crank webs)	0.125 to 0.325 mm (0.0049 to 0.0128 in)
Torque needed to rotate fitted crankshaft (without connecting rods or pistons	10 Nm (7 lbf ft) max

Pistons

Diameter (measured at 90° to gudgeon pin bore):	
Class A	79.960 to 79.975 mm (3.1480 to 3.1486 in)
Class B	79.975 to 79.990 mm (3.1486 to 3.1492 in)
Class C	80.120 to 80.135 mm (3.1543 to 3.1549 in)
Class D	80.135 to 80.150 mm (3.1549 to 3.1555 in)
Class E (first rebore)	80.461 to 80.479 mm (3.1678 to 3.1685 in)
Class F (second rebore)	80.961 to 80.979 mm (3.1874 to 3.1881 in)
Clearance in bores (new):	
Classes A to D	0.025 to 0.055 mm (0.0010 to 0.0022 in)
Classes E and F	0.021 to 0.054 mm (0.0008 to 0.0021 in)
Piston protrusion at TDC	0.430 to 0.860 mm (0.0169 to 0.0339 in)

Piston rings

Clearance in groove:	
Top compression	0.070 to 0.102 mm (0.0028 to 0.0040 in)
Second compression	0.050 to 0.082 mm (0.0020 to 0.0032 in)
Oil control	0.030 to 0.065 mm (0.0012 to 0.0026 in)
End gap (fitted):	
Top compression	0.30 to 0.50 mm (0.012 to 0.020 in)
Second compression	0.20 to 0.40 mm (0.008 to 0.016 in)
Oil control	0.20 to 0.45 mm (0.008 to 0.018 in)

Camshaft

Cam lift:	
Inlet	8.4 mm (0.331 in)
Exhaust	9.0 mm (0.354 in)
Endfloat	0.10 to 0.24 mm (0.0039 to 0.0095 in)
Bearing journal diameter	27.96 to 27.98 mm (1.1008 to 1.1016 in)
Bearing clearance	0.020 to 0.079 mm (0.0008 to 0.0031 in)

Valve timing

Inlet opens	10° BTDC
Inlet closes	38° ABDC
Exhaust opens	49° BBDC
Exhaust closes	11° ATDC

Valve clearances (cold)

Inlet	0.235 to 0.365 mm (0.009 to 0.014 in)
Exhaust	0.435 to 0.565 mm (0.017 to 0.022 in)

Valves, springs and tappets

Valve length:	
Inlet	107.25 to 107.35 mm (4.2224 to 4.2264 in)
Exhaust	108.55 to 108.65 mm (4.2736 to 4.2776 in)
Valve head diameter:	
Inlet	34.80 to 35.00 mm (1.3701 to 1.3780 in)
Exhaust	30.90 to 31.10 mm (1.2165 to 1.2244 in)
Valve stem diameter – standard:	
Inlet	7.965 to 7.980 mm (0.3136 to 0.3142 in)
Exhaust	7.945 to 7.960 mm (0.3128 to 0.3134 in)
Valve stem diameter – first oversize:	
Inlet	8.228 to 8.243 mm (0.3239 to 0.3245 in)
Exhaust	8.208 to 8.223 mm (0.3231 to 0.3237 in)

Valve stem diameter – second oversize:
    Inlet .... 8.428 to 8.443 mm (0.3318 to 0.3324 in)
    Exhaust .... 8.408 to 8.423 mm (0.3310 to 0.3316 in)
Tappet diameter:
    Standard .... 34.950 to 34.975 mm (1.3760 to 1.3770 in)
    Oversize .... 35.450 to 35.475 mm (1.3957 to 1.3967 in)
Shim thicknesses available .... 3.00 to 4.75 mm (0.1181 to 0.1870 in) in
                                                                increments of 0.05 mm (0.0020 in)
Valve spring free length .... 43 mm (1.69 in) approx

Cylinder head gasket

Thickness identification:
    Standard bores .... 1 to 5 teeth
    Oversize bores .... 1 to 5 holes
Selection according to piston protrusion:
    0.430 to 0.620 mm (0.0169 to 0.0244 in) .... 1 tooth or hole
    0.621 to 0.680 mm (0.0245 to 0.0268 in) .... 2 teeth or holes
    0.681 to 0.740 mm (0.0268 to 0.0291 in) .... 3 teeth or holes
    0.741 to 0.800 mm (0.0292 to 0.0315 in) .... 4 teeth or holes
    0.801 to 0.860 mm (0.0315 to 0.0339 in) .... 5 teeth or holes

Cylinder head

Distortion limit .... 0.15 mm (0.006 in) overall
Camshaft bearing bore diameter:
    Standard .... 30.500 to 30.525 mm (1.2008 to 1.2018 in)
    Oversize .... 30.575 to 30.600 mm (1.2037 to 1.2047 in)
Tappet bore diameter:
    Standard .... 35.000 to 35.030 mm (1.3780 to 1.3791 in)
    Oversize .... 35.500 to 35.530 mm (1.3976 to 1.3988 in)
Valve guide bore diameter:
    Standard .... 8.000 to 8.025 mm (0.3150 to 0.3159 in)
    First oversize .... 8.263 to 8.288 mm (0.3253 to 0.3263 in)
    Second oversize .... 8.463 to 8.488 mm (0.3332 to 0.3342 in)
Valve stem clearance in guide:
    Inlet .... 0.020 to 0.060 mm (0.0008 to 0.0024 in)
    Exhaust .... 0.040 to 0.080 mm (0.0016 to 0.0032 in)
Swirl chamber seat dimensions (see Section 11) – standard:
    Diameter A .... 30.500 to 30.530 mm (1.2008 to 1.2020 in)
    Diameter B .... 26.860 to 26.990 mm (1.0575 to 1.0626 in)
    Dimension C .... 3.998 to 4.034 mm (0.1574 to 0.1588 in)
Swirl chamber seat dimensions – oversize:
    Diameter A .... 30.800 to 30.830 mm (1.2126 to 1.2138 in)
    Diameter B .... 27.160 to 27.290 mm (1.0893 to 1.0744 in)
    Dimension C .... 4.248 to 4.284 mm (0.1672 to 0.1687 in)
Swirl chamber projection .... 0.001 to 0.042 mm (0.0004 to 0.00165 in)
Valve seat dimensions (see Section 11) – standard:
    Diameter A, inlet .... 36.500 to 36.530 mm (1.4370 to 1.4382 in)
    Depth B, inlet .... 8.70 to 8.90 mm (0.3425 to 0.3504 in)
    Diameter A, exhaust .... 33.000 to 33.030 mm (1.2992 to 1.3004 in)
    Depth B, exhaust .... 9.20 to 9.40 mm (0.3622 to 0.3701 in)
Valve seat dimensions – Class A oversize (production or service):
    Diameter A .... + 0.20 mm (0.0079 in) on standard
    Depth B .... + 0.30 mm (0.0118 in) on standard
Valve seat dimensions – second oversize (service only):
    Diameter A .... + 0.40 mm (0.0158 in) on standard
    Depth B .... + 0.60 mm (0.0236 in) on standard

Camshaft drivebelt

Tension, cold (using tester 21 - 113 – see text):
    When refitting .... 8.5 to 10.5
    Checking in service .... 1.0 to 8.0

Lubrication system

Oil type/specification.. Refer to 'Recommended lubricants and fluids'

Oil filter.. Champion C101 or C151
Oil capacity (drain and refill):
    Excluding filter .... 4.5 litre (7.9 pint) approx
    Including filter .... 5.0 litre (8.8 pint) approx
Oil pressure (engine hot):
    At 900 rpm .... 1.3 to 3.0 bar (19 to 44 lbf/in²)
    At 2000 rpm .... 3.0 to 6.0 bar (44 to 87 lbf/in²)
Oil pressure relief valve setting .... 4.0 to 6.0 bar (58 to 87 lbf/in²)
Oil pump tolerances .... Not specified

Torque wrench settings

	Nm	lbf ft
Main bearing caps*:		
Stage 1	24 to 30	18 to 22
Stage 2	Further 71° to 79°	
Connecting rod cap bolts*:		
Stage 1	20 to 30	15 to 22
Stage 2	Further 50° to 60°	
Stage 3	Further 20° to 30°	
Crankshaft rear oil seal housing bolts	16 to 20	12 to 15
Timing case to cylinder block:		
M6	8 to 10	6 to 7
M8	18 to 22	13 to 16
Oil pump to timing case	7 to 10	5 to 7
Oil pump pick-up pipe to timing case	8 to 10	6 to 7
Oil pump pick-up pipe bracket to block	16 to 20	12 to 15
Sump bolts	6 to 9	4 to 7
Flywheel bolts*:		
Stage 1	24 to 30	18 to 22
Stage 2	Further 35° to 45°	
Stage 3	Further 35° to 45°	
Fuel injection pump to timing case	18 to 22	13 to 16
Fuel injection pump bracket to block	18 to 22	13 to 16
Idler gear bolt	45 to 50	33 to 37
Fuel injection pump shaft nut	40 to 50	30 to 37
Timing cover bolts	8 to 10	6 to 7
Injection pump sprocket bolts	18 to 22	13 to 16
Water pump to block	20 to 25	15 to 18
Water pump pulley bolts	7 to 10	5 to 7
Crankshaft pulley bolt*:		
Stage 1	20 to 30	15 to 22
Stage 2	Further 140° to 150°	
Cylinder head bolts*:		
Stage 1	20 to 30	15 to 22
Stage 2	76 to 92	56 to 68
Stage 3 (after at least 2 minutes)	Further 80° to 90°	
Camshaft drivebelt rear cover plate bolts:		
M6	8 to 10	6 to 7
M8	18 to 22	13 to 16
Camshaft drivebelt tensioner bolt	27 to 33	20 to 24
Camshaft sprocket bolt	27 to 33	20 to 24
Vacuum pump bolts	18 to 22	13 to 16
Camshaft cover bolts	8 to 11	6 to 8
Thermostat housing bolts	18 to 22	13 to 16
Fuel filter bracket to head	20 to 25	15 to 18
Manifolds to head:		
Nuts	10 to 16	7 to 12
Bolts	18 to 22	13 to 16
Lifting eyes to head	18 to 22	13 to 16
Camshaft bearing caps	18 to 22	13 to 16
Oilway blanking plugs	19 to 25	14 to 18
TDC setting hole plug	20 to 25	15 to 18
Sump drain plug	21 to 28	16 to 21
Gearshift stabiliser to transmission	55	41
Lower arm balljoint pinch-bolt:		
Fiesta	30	22
Escort/Orion	58	43
Lower arm pivot bolt:		
Fiesta	45	33
Escort/Orion	60	44
Tie-bar brackets (Fiesta)	50	37
Anti-roll bar brackets (Escort/Orion)	50	37
Transmission mountings	See Chapter 4 Specifications	
Engine mounting (suggested – not specified)	50	37

* Bolts should be renewed every time after slackening

1 General description

The Diesel engine fitted to the smallest vehicles in the Ford range is of four-cylinder overhead camshaft design. The engine is mounted transversely, in line with the transmission. Both the block and the cylinder head are of iron.

Drive to the camshaft is by means of a toothed belt. The belt is driven by a sprocket bolted to the injection pump gear, and (apart from an idler/tensioner pulley) has no other loads. Solid cam followers (tappets) are used, these being considered preferable to hydraulic tappets on grounds of reduced drag. Valve clearance adjustment is by means of selective shims. The cam lobes bear directly on the shims and tappets, which in turn bear directly on the valves. The camshaft runs in five renewable shell bearings.

The rotary injection pump is gear-driven from the crankshaft nose via an idler gear. The idler gear is split, and its two halves spring-loaded against each other, to reduce noise and backlash. The timing gears are enclosed in a case, the rear of which carries the oil pump and oil filter.

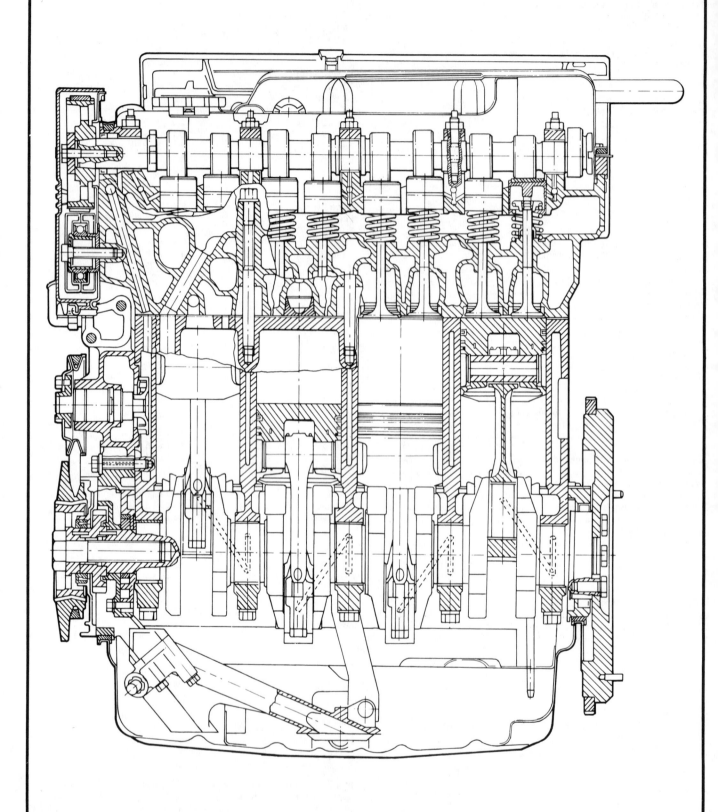

Fig. 1.1 Sectional view of Ford 1.6 Diesel engine (Sec 1)

The oil pump is driven directly by flats on the crankshaft; the lubricating system is conventional.

The crankshaft runs in five main bearings, of the usual shell type. Endfloat is controlled by separate thrust washers at the centre bearing. A large pulley on the crankshaft nose acts as a vibration damper, and drives the alternator and the water pump by means of a V-belt.

Pistons, gudgeon pins and connecting rods are carefully selected to be of matching weight; connecting rods are also graded by length. The gudgeon pins are fully floating in the pistons and rods; they are retained by circlips. The big-ends of the rods are horizontally split and carry shell bearings.

Crankcase ventilation is by means of a hose which connects the camshaft cover to the inlet manifold. Within the manifold the crankcase fumes are piped into each inlet duct, so ensuring lubrication of the inlet valves. A non-return valve prevents crankcase pressurization taking place. Another hose connects the camshaft cover to the lower crankcase.

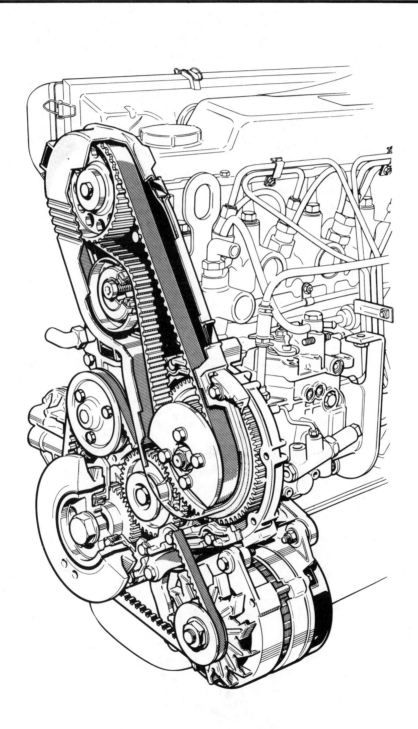

Fig. 1.2 Part cutaway view of pulley end of engine (Sec 1)

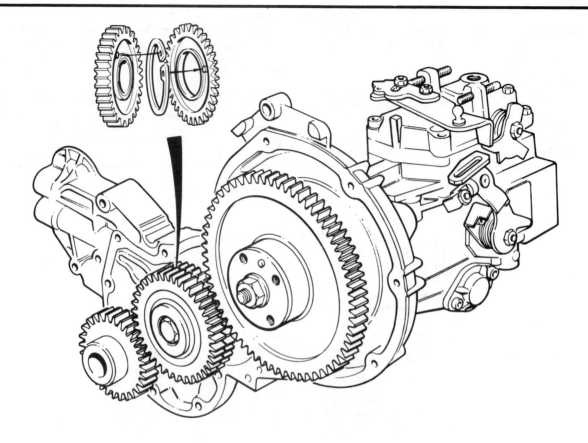

Fig. 1.3 Timing gears, showing split spring-loaded idler (Sec 1)

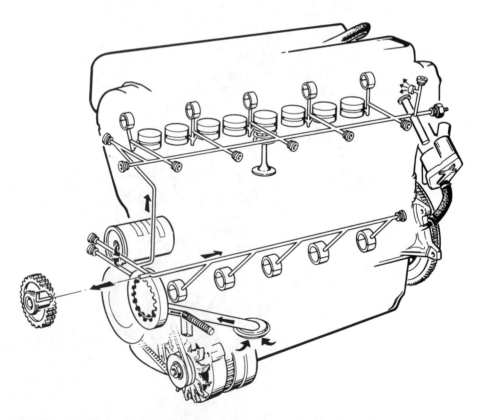

Fig. 1.4 Lubrication circuit – arrows show direction of oil flow (Sec 1)

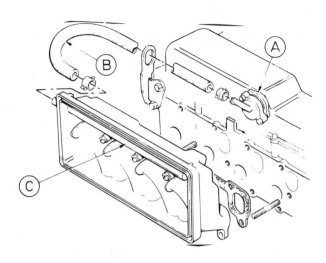

Fig. 1.5 Part of the crankcase ventilation system (Sec 1)

A *Non-return valve*   C *Distribution pipe*
B *Hose*

2 Maintenance and inspection

1 The engine oil level should be checked weekly, before a long journey, or every 250 miles (400 km) – more frequently if experience shows this to be necessary. The vehicle must be parked on level ground and the engine must have been stopped for a couple of minutes to allow oil in circulation to return to the sump. Open and prop the bonnet and proceed as follows.

2 Withdraw the dipstick from its tube, wipe the end on a piece of clean rag, re-insert it fully and then withdraw it again. Read the oil level on the end of the dipstick: it should lie between the MAX and MIN marks (photo).

3 It is not necessary to top up the engine oil until the level reaches the MIN mark on the dipstick, but on no account allow the level to fall any lower. The amount of oil needed to top up from MIN to MAX is approximately 1 litre (1.8 pints). Do not overfill.

4 When topping-up is necessary, use clean engine oil of the specified type, preferably of the same make and grade as that already in the engine. Top up via the oil filler cap on the camshaft cover (photo). Allow time for the oil to run down to the sump before rechecking the level on the dipstick. When the level is correct, refit the oil filler cap and mop up any oil spilt.

5 All engines use some oil, depending on the degree of wear and the pattern of use. Oil which is not being lost through external leaks is entering the cylinders and being burnt. A compression test (see Section 33) can help to establish whether oil burning is due to leakage past the valve stems or the pistons.

6 Models equipped with the auxiliary warning system have a dashboard warning light which illuminates when the oil level is low. The prudent operator will also check the level occasionally using the dipstick.

7 Change the engine oil and renew the oil filter at the intervals specified in Routine Maintenance. Refer to Section 4. At the same time, inspect the engine carefully for leaks of oil, fuel or coolant; repair or rectify leaking or damaged components without delay.

8 At alternate service intervals, check the valve clearances and adjust if necessary. Refer to Section 7.

9 Although this task is not specified by Ford for the 1.6 litre engine, in view of the extensive damage that can occur if a drivebelt should break or slip while the engine is running, it is certainly worth renewing the camshaft drivebelt on a precautionary basis at the interval given in Routine Maintenance for the 1.8 litre engine; refer to Section 6 for details. At the very least a check of the belt's condition should be made, say every 24 000 miles/40 000 km, as described in Section 5; renew the drivebelt if there is the slightest doubt about its condition.

10 Inspect the crankcase ventilation hoses periodically. Clean the hoses if they are blocked with sludge or 'mayonnaise'. Renew the hoses if they are cracked or broken, and their clips if they are in poor condition (photo). Also clean the non-return valve on the camshaft cover.

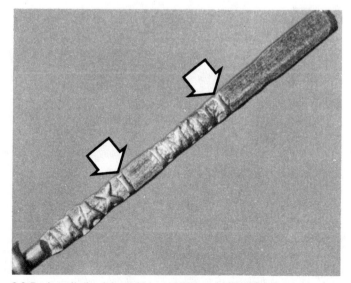

2.2 Engine oil dipstick markings – MAX and MIN lines arrowed

2.4 Topping up the engine oil

2.10 A crankcase ventilation hose

3 Major operations possible with the engine in the vehicle

1 The cylinder head and sump can both be removed from the engine in situ; the pistons and connecting rods can therefore be removed also.

2 Any operation which involves slackening the crankshaft pulley bolt cannot be carried out with the engine in place unless the necessary special tools are purchased or made. Refer to Section 13 for more details.

3 Subject to undoing the pulley bolt, the timing cover, timing case and oil pump can all be removed with the engine installed. It must be said that access is not good and the procedures are lengthy.

4 All the engine oil seals can be dealt with in situ; some are easier than others.

5 The engine must be removed for attention to the crankshaft, main bearings and cylinder block.

6 In practice it will probably be quicker and more satisfactory to remove the engine for most major tasks.

4 Engine oil and oil filter – renewal

1 The engine oil should be drained just after a run, when the contaminants which it carries are still in suspension.

2 Park the vehicle on level ground. Position a drain pan of adequate capacity beneath the sump. Wipe clean around the sump drain plug, then unscrew and remove it (photo). Be careful to avoid scalding if the oil is very hot. Do not lose the drain plug washer.

3 Remove the oil filler cap to speed up the draining process. Allow the oil to drain for at least 15 minutes. Inspect the drain plug washer and renew it if necessary.

4 When draining is complete, refit the drain plug and tighten it to the specified torque.

5 Refit the engine with the specified quantity and grade of fresh oil.

6 Before the engine is run again, renew the oil filter as follows.

7 Position the drain pan underneath the oil filter (located on the rear of the engine, inboard of the timing case). Unscrew the filter and remove it. A chain or strap wrench will probably be needed to undo the filter; failing this, a screwdriver can be driven through the filter and used as a lever to unscrew it. Be prepared for considerable oil spillage in this case. Some spillage is inevitable as the filter is withdrawn (photo).

8 Wipe clean around the filter seat on the engine and check that no sealing rings have been left behind. Smear the sealing ring on the new filter with engine oil or grease, then screw the filter into position. Unless instructed otherwise by the filter maker, tighten the filter **by hand only** (photo). Usually, tightening by two-thirds of a turn beyond the point where the sealing ring contacts the seat is sufficient.

9 Check that the engine has been refilled with oil and that the level is at least up to the MIN mark on the dipstick, then start the engine. The oil pressure warning light will take a few seconds to go out as the filter fills with oil: do not rev the engine until the light has gone out.

10 With the engine running, check for leaks around the filter base and the drain plug. Tighten further if necessary. Stop the engine and check again for leaks.

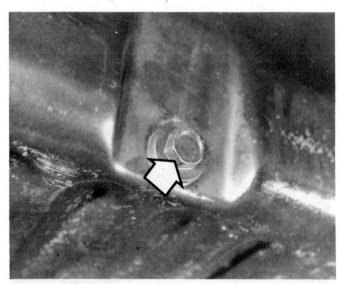

4.2 Sump drain plug (arrowed)

4.7 Using a chain wrench to unscrew the oil filter

4.8 Fitting a new oil filter

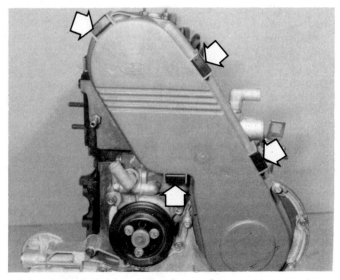

5.2 Camshaft drivebelt cover clips (arrowed)

11 Allow a couple of minutes for the oil to return to the sump, then recheck the level on the dipstick and top up if necessary. The new filter will absorb approximately 0.5 litre (nearly a pint) of oil.

12 Put the old oil into a sealed container and dispose of it safely.

5 Camshaft drivebelt – inspection and checking tension

1 Disconnect the battery earth (negative) lead.

2 Unclip and remove the drivebelt cover (photo).

3 Inspect the belt for cracks, fraying and damage to the teeth. Pay particular attention to the roots of the teeth. A belt which is damaged must be renewed. An oil-soaked belt must also be renewed, and the source of oil contamination dealt with; similarly, the drivebelt must be renewed if flooded with Diesel fuel.

4 To measure the belt tension, Ford tool No. 21 - 113 or equivalent will be needed. Refer also to Section 6, paragraph 15.

5 Turn the engine in the normal direction of rotation, and through at least 90°, until the timing mark on the injection pump sprocket is 25° past the mark on the timing cover (Fig. 1.6). (The engine may be turned by raising a front wheel clear of the ground, engaging a gear and turning the wheel. It will be easier if the glow plugs are removed.) In this position No 1 cylinder is at TDC on compression.

6 Turn the engine anti-clockwise to bring the sprocket mark back into alignment with the mark on the timing cover.

7 Fit the belt tension gauge (tool No 21 - 113) to the longest run of the belt, following the instructions supplied with the gauge. Read the belt tension and compare it with the value given in the Specifications.

8 If adjustment is necessary, proceed as described in Section 6.

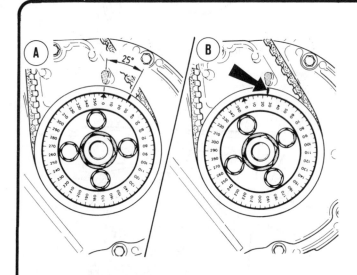

Fig. 1.6 Injection pump sprocket positions relative to pump timing mark (arrowed) (Sec 5)

A TDC No 1 cylinder
B Position for checking drivebelt tension

Fig. 1.7 Tension gauge fitted to the camshaft drivebelt (Sec 5)

5.9 Securing a drivebelt cover clip

6.3 Removing the camshaft cover

9   When the belt tension is correct, remove the tension gauge and refit the belt cover (photo). Reconnect the battery earth lead.

6   Camshaft drivebelt – removal, refitting and tensioning

1   Two special tools will have to be bought or made for this operation: they are needed to position the crankshaft and camshaft accurately at TDC, No 1 firing. Refer to Section 9 for more details.

2   Disconnect the battery earth (negative) lead.

3   Release the breather hoses and remove the camshaft cover (photo). It is secured by ten bolts. Recover the washers and reinforcing strips, noting their location. Remove the gasket, sealing strip and plug; obtain new ones for reassembly if necessary.

4   Unclip and remove the camshaft drivebelt cover.

5   Turn the engine in the normal direction of rotation until the timing mark on the injection pump sprocket is aligned with the mark on the timing cover.

6   Remove the plug from the crankcase and insert the TDC setting pin (see Section 9). Carefully turn the engine further until the crankshaft web contacts the pin.

7   Insert the camshaft setting tool so that it is a snug fit in the camshaft tail. See Section 9 for details.

8   Counterhold the camshaft sprocket and slacken its bolt.

9   Slacken the drivebelt tensioner pivot bolt. This bolt is of the Torx type, so the appropriate key will be needed to deal with it. Access is restricted with the engine installed; the key must be of the angled type.

10 Mark the running direction of the drivebelt if it is to be re-used. Slip the belt off the sprockets and remove it.

11 Do not rotate the camshaft or crankshaft with the belt removed. Piston/valve contact may occur.

12 Make sure that the camshaft sprocket is free to turn. Break the taper if necessary by tapping the sprocket with a wooden or plastic mallet.

13 Commence refitting by placing the belt over the sprockets, observing the running direction if it is a used belt. Tension the belt

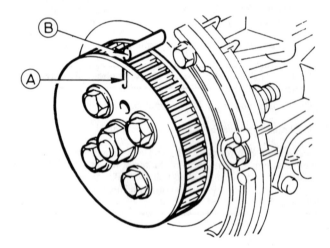

Fig. 1.8 Injection pump timing marks (Sec 6)

A   Sprocket mark   B   Timing cover mark

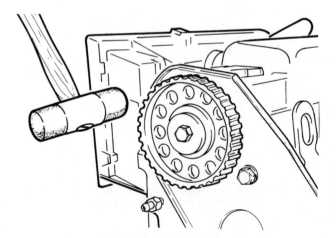

Fig. 1.9 Tap the sprocket with a mallet to break the taper
(Sec 6)

6.13A Camshaft drivebelt correctly fitted

6.13B Tensioning the camshaft drivebelt

initially by levering the tensioner anti-clockwise and nipping up the pivot bolt (photos). An Allen key will be required to lever the tensioner.

14 Fit the belt tension gauge (tool No. 21 - 113) to the longest run of the belt, following the instructions supplied with the gauge. Read the belt tension and compare it with the value given in the Specifications. Adjust if necessary by slackening the tensioner pivot bolt, moving the tensioner and retightening the bolt. **The camshaft sprocket must be free on its taper during tensioner movement.**

15 In the absence of the proper belt tension gauge, correct tension can be estimated by attempting to twist the belt, with finger and thumb, in the middle of its longest run. A correctly tensioned belt should not be capable of being twisted more than 90° by anyone of average strength. A belt which is too tight will hum or honk in use; a slack belt may wear rapidly or even jump sprocket teeth. It is wise to have the tension checked by a Ford dealer if the belt has been set up by rule of thumb.

16 When the belt tension is correct, tighten the tensioner pivot bolt to the specified torque.

17 Counterhold the camshaft sprocket and tighten the sprocket bolt to the specified torque.

18 Remove the camshaft setting tool and the TDC setting pin. Refit the setting hole plug and tighten it to the specified torque. Refit the camshaft drivebelt cover.

19 Refit the camshaft cover, if necessary using a new gasket, sealing strip and plug (photos). Secure with the bolts, washers and reinforcing strips (photos). Tighten the bolts progressively to the specified torque.

20 Refit the breather hoses.

21 Reconnect the battery earth lead.

6.19A Camshaft cover sealing strip (arrowed)

6.19B Camshaft cover sealing plug

6.19C Reinforcing strip (arrowed) – pulley end, rear side

6.19D Reinforcing strip (arrowed) – pulley end, front side

6.19E Reinforcing strip (arrowed) – flywheel end. This one is marked TOP

Fig. 1.10 Injection pump stop solenoid (arrowed) (Sec 7)

7 Valve clearances – checking and adjustment

1   Release the breather hoses and remove the camshaft cover. It is secured by 10 bolts. Recover the washers and the reinforcing strips, noting their locations. Remove the gasket, sealing strip and plug; obtain new ones for reassembly if necessary.

2   Turn the engine in the normal direction of rotation until two cam lobes for any one cylinder are pointing upwards (relative to the engine) at the same angle. It is permissible to 'bounce' the engine round on the starter motor for this procedure, but disconnect the fuel shut-off solenoid first.

3   Measure the clearance between the bases of the two cam lobes and the underlying shims using feeler blades (photo). Record the thickness of blade(s) required to give a firm sliding fit. The desired clearances are given in the Specifications. Note that the clearances for inlet and exhaust valves are different. From the pulley end of the engine, the valve sequence is:

I - E - I - E - I - E - I - E

7.3 Measuring a valve clearance

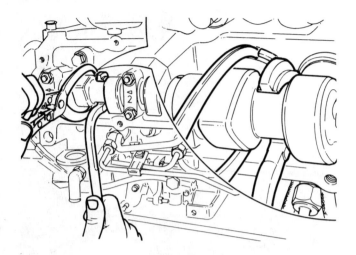

Fig. 1.11A Maker's tools for tappet depression and shim extraction (Sec 7)

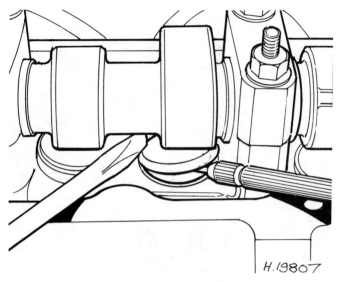

Fig. 1.11B Depressing the tappet with a screwdriver and removing the shim (Sec 7)

4   If adjustment is required, turn the engine in the normal direction of rotation through approximately 90°, to bring the pistons to mid-stroke. (If this is not done, the pistons at TDC will prevent the tappets being depressed, and damage may result.) Depress the tappets, and then either shim can be withdrawn if the peak of the cam doesn't prevent access. The Ford tools for this operation are Nos. 21 - 106 and 21 - 107, but with care and patience a C-spanner or screwdriver can be used to depress the tappet and the shim can be flicked out with a small screwdriver.

5   If the valve clearance was too small, a thinner shim must be fitted. If the clearance was too large, a thicker shim must be fitted. The thickness of the shim (in mm) is engraved on the side facing away from the camshaft (photo). If the marking is missing or illegible, a micrometer will be needed to establish shim thickness.

6   When the shim thickness and the valve clearance are known, the required thickness of the new shim can be calculated as follows.

Sample calculation – clearance too small

Desired clearance (A)	=	0.50 mm
Measured clearance (B)	=	0.35 mm
Shim thickness found (C)	=	3.95 mm
Shim thickness required (D)	=	C + B – A = 3.80 mm

Sample calculation – clearance too large

Desired clearance (A)	=	0.30 mm
Measured clearance (B)	=	0.40 mm
Shim thickness found (C)	=	4.05 mm
Shim thickness required (D)	=	C + B – A = 4.15 mm

7   With the correct shim fitted, release the tappet depressing tool. Turn the engine back so that the cam lobes are again pointing upwards and check that the clearance is now correct.

8   Repeat the process for the remaining valves, turning the engine each time to bring a pair of cam lobes upwards.

9   It will be helpful for future adjustment if a record is kept of the thickness of shim fitted at each position. The shims required can be purchased in advance once the clearances and the existing shim thicknesses are known.

10   It is permissible to interchange shims between tappets to achieve the correct clearances, but it is not advisable to turn the camshaft with any shims removed, since there is a risk that the cam lobe will jam in the empty tappet.

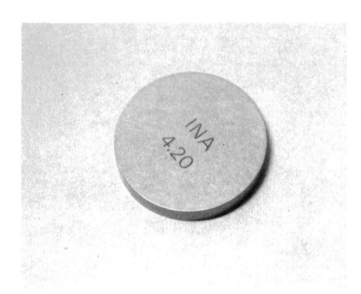

7.5 Shim thickness marking

11   When all the clearances are correct, refit the camshaft cover, using a new gasket etc if necessary. Fit the bolts with washers and reinforcing strips. Tighten the bolts progressively to the specified torque.

12   Secure the breather hoses.

13   If it was disconnected, reconnect the fuel shut-off solenoid.

8   Camshaft – removal and refitting

1   Remove the camshaft drivebelt as described in Section 6, paragraphs 1 to 6 and 8 to 10.

2   Remove the camshaft sprocket bolt and washer (photo). Release the sprocket from its taper by tapping it with a wooden or plastic mallet and remove it.

3   Remove the drivebelt tensioner (one Torx bolt) and the drivebelt backplate (secured by two hex head bolts) (photos).

8.2 Removing the camshaft sprocket bolt and washer

8.3A Undoing the drivebelt tensioner bolt

8.3B Drivebelt backplate securing bolts (arrowed)

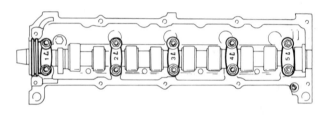

Fig. 1.12 Camshaft bearing caps – note numbers and arrows
(Sec 8)

4   Undo the nuts of bearing caps Nos 2 and 4. Remove these caps and
their shells. Keep the shells with their caps if they are to be re-used.
Note that the caps are numbered and carry an arrow pointing to the
pulley end of the engine.

5   Slacken the nuts of bearing caps Nos. 1, 3 and 5 one turn at a time,
working from end to end so that the camshaft is released gradually.
Remove the bearing caps and shells, again keeping the shells with their
caps if necessary.

6   Lift out the camshaft with its oil seal. Recover the lower half
bearing shells, keeping them in order if necessary.

7   If purchasing new bearing shells, note that either standard or
oversize outside diameter shells may have been fitted in production.
Oversize shells are identified by a green mark.

8   Commence refitting by placing the lower half bearing shells (the
ones with the oil holes) in position (photo). Lubricate the shells.

9   Make sure that all tappets, shims and the vacuum pump plunger are
in place. Remove the old oil seal, if not already done, and place the

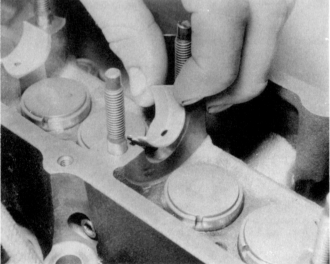

8.8 Fitting a camshaft lower bearing shell

camshaft on the lower half bearings (photo). Position the camshaft
with the groove in the tail parallel with the head top face and the larger
semi-circular segment uppermost (Fig. 1.13).

10 Clean any old sealant from No 1 bearing cap. Fit the upper bearing
shells to their caps and lubricate them (photo). Coat the mating
surfaces of No 1 cap with sealant (to Ford spec SPM - 4G - 9112 -
F/G) in the areas shown in Fig. 1.14 (photo).

8.9 Fitting the camshaft

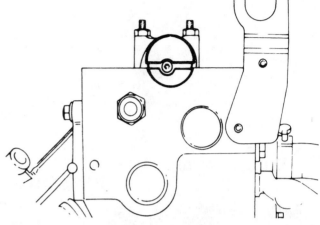

Fig. 1.13 Camshaft tail position with camshaft correctly fitted (Sec 8)

8.10A Fitting a camshaft upper bearing shell to its cap

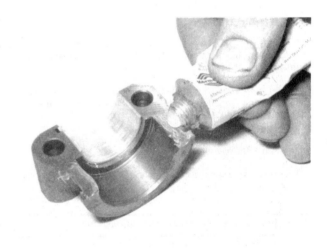

8.10B Applying sealant to No 1 bearing cap

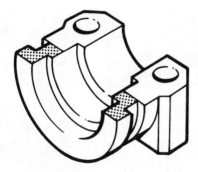

Fig. 1.14 Camshaft No 1 bearing cap – coat shaded area with sealant (Sec 8)

11 Fit bearing caps and shells Nos 1, 3 and 5, making sure that they are the right way round. Tighten the cap nuts, half a turn at a time, in the sequence No 3 – No 1 – No 5. Carry on until the caps are seated.

12 Fit caps and shells Nos 2 and 4, tapping them down with a mallet if necessary to seat them. Fit their nuts.

13 Tighten all the bearing cap nups to the specified torque (photo).

14 Insert the camshaft setting tool into the groove on the tail so that it is a snug fit. See Section 9 for details.

15 Fit a new oil seal to the camshaft nose as described in Section 13. (There is a temptation to fit this seal to the camshaft before it is installed, but to do so risks pinching or cocking the seal as the bearing cap is tightened).

16 Lubricate the cam lobes liberally with engine oil, or with special cam lube if supplied with a new camshaft.

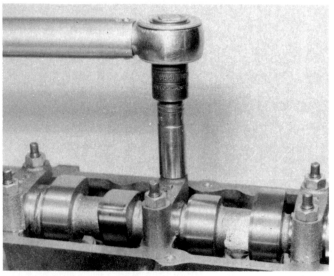

8.13 Tightening a camshaft bearing cap nut

17 Refit the drivebelt backplate. Secure it with the two bolts, applying a little sealant to their threads. Refit the drivebelt tensioner, but do not tighten its pivot bolt yet.

18 Refit the camshaft sprocket, washer and bolt. The taper must be clean and dry. Only tighten the bolt by hand, so that the sprocket can still move on its taper.

19 Refit and tension the camshaft drivebelt as described in Section 6, paragraph 13 onwards.

20 Observe any running-in instructions which may be supplied with a new camshaft.

9 Valve timing – checking and adjustment

1   Valve timing is more complicated than on similar petrol engines because there are no camshaft or crankshaft timing marks. The camshaft sprocket is not keyed to the shaft, so no permanent mark can be made there. Two special tools must therefore be made or bought.

2   Because the camshaft is driven from the injection pump sprocket, the pump timing must be correct before the valve timing is checked. See Chapter 3, Section 7.

3   There is one pair of timing marks on the injection pump sprocket and timing cover. When the pump timing is correct, these marks are aligned at 50° BTDC, No 1 on compression.

4   If the valve timing has been lost, be careful when turning the crankshaft and camshaft in case piston/valve contact occurs.

Using Ford special tools
5   Remove the camshaft drivebelt cover. Turn the crankshaft until the injection pump sprocket timing mark is aligned with the pointer on the timing case.

6   Remove the TDC setting hole plug from the front of the crankcase (just below the injection pump) (photo). Screw in the TDC setting pin, tool No. 21 - 104.

7   Carefully turn the crankshaft clockwise until the web contacts the setting pin. No1 piston is now at TDC.

8   Remove the camshaft cover and offer the camshaft setting tool (No 21 - 105) to the tail of the camshaft. If the valve timing is correct, the

tool will enter the groove in the tail and will be a snug fit when the tool is packed up equally on each side (Fig. 1.16).

9   If the tool will not enter the groove, or if the groove is obviously not parallel with the head top face, adjust as follows.

10 Counterhold the camshaft sprocket and slacken the sprocket bolt. Tap the sprocket with a wooden or plastic mallet if necessary to break the taper, so that the camshaft can turn independently of the sprocket.

11 Turn the camshaft until the setting tool is a snug fit in the tail. Restrain the camshaft sprocket and tighten the sprocket bolt to the specified torque.

12 Remove the special tools and refit the disturbed components.

Using home-made tools
13 The camshaft setting tool is easily improvised from a piece of angle iron. The piece seen here has dimensions 25 x 25 x 100 mm approx, and is 5 mm thick. It fits very well, with no need for packing up and no perceptible play in the camshaft groove (photos).

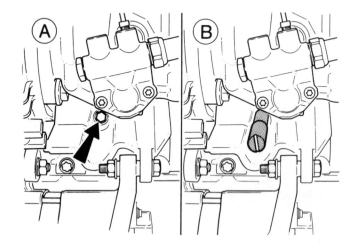

Fig. 1.15 TDC setting hole plug (arrowed, A) and setting pin fitted (B) (Sec 9)

9.6 Removing the TDC setting hole plug

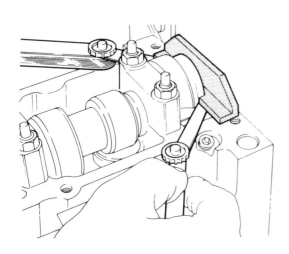

Fig. 1.16 Making the camshaft setting tool fit by packing it up with feeler blades (Sec 9)

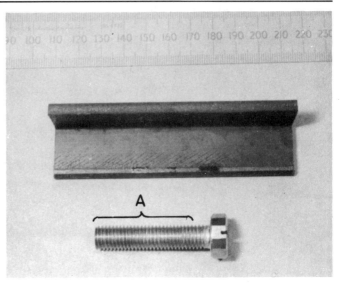

9.13A Home-made tools for setting the valve timing

A   Highlighted portion of bolt may need grinding, to work (see text)

9.13B Camshaft setting bracket in use

9.14 TDC setting pin (arrowed) in position

14 The TDC setting pin can be replaced by an M10 bolt, ground to a length (from the underside of the bolt head to the tip) of 47.5 mm (1.870 in). However, an ordinary bolt cannot be inserted without first removing the alternator bracket because there is insufficient clearance for the bolt head – therefore the bolt head must be ground down and a screw slot cut in it (photo).

15 Once the tools have been made, proceed as described in paragraphs 5 to 12.
Note: *If difficulty is experienced in using the bolt, it may be necessary to grind down the first 36 mm (1.42 in) of the threaded end of the bolt (see photo 9.13A) to a diameter of 6 mm (0.236 in).*

10 Cylinder head – removal and refitting

1   Disconnect the battery earth (negative) lead.

2   Remove the air cleaner as described in Chapter 3, Section 3.

3   Drain the cooling system as described in Chapter 2, Section 4. Save the coolant if it is fit for re-use.

4   Disconnect the radiator top hose from the thermostat housing.

5   Disconnect the coolant hoses from the cylinder head and thermostat housing (photos).

6   Disconnect the vacuum and oil return hoses from the vacuum pump (photo).

7   Disconnect the electrical leads from the temperature gauge sender, the fan thermoswitch, the oil pressure switch and the glow plug bus bar (photos).

8   Remove the fuel injection pipes as described in Chapter 3, Section 9. Also disconnect the fuel return pipe which runs from No 1 injector to the fuel pump.

9   Unbolt the dipstick tube bracket from the thermostat housing (photo). Unbolt and remove the thermostat housing itself. Also remove the bypass pipe which connects the housing to the water pump.

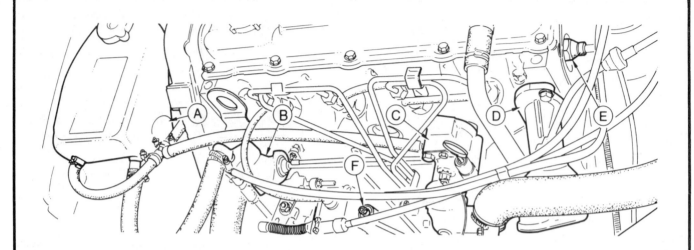

Fig. 1.17 Identification of components around the cylinder head. Escort/Orion shown, Fiesta similar (Sec 10)

A   Expansion tank   C   Thermostat housing   E   Oil pressure switch
B   Water pump inlet connector   D   Vacuum pump   F   Fuel shut-off solenoid

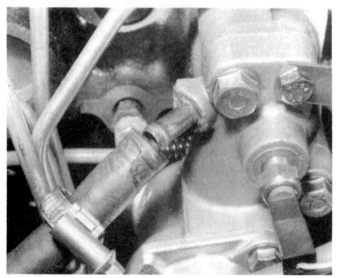

10.5A Disconnecting a coolant vent hose from the thermostat housing ...

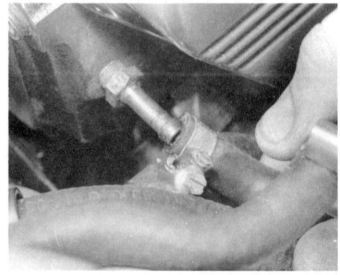

10.5B ... and from the cylinder head

10.5C Disconnecting a heater hose

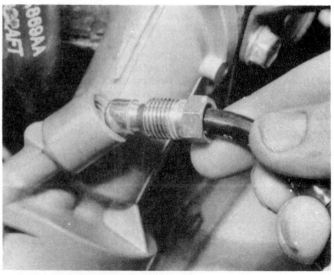

10.6 Disconnecting the vacuum hose from the pump

10 Unbolt the fuel filter bracket from the cylinder head. Move the bracket and filter aside, being careful not to strain the fuel lines.

11 Separate the exhaust downpipe from the manifold. Recover the gasket.

12 If wished, remove the glow plugs and/or fuel injectors – see Chapter 3, Sections 10 and 14. Alternatively they can be left in position for the time being.

13 Remove the camshaft drivebelt as described in Section 6, paragraphs 1 to 6 and 8 to 10.

14 Remove the camshaft sprocket bolt and washer, and the sprocket itself. Tap the sprocket with a mallet to break the taper.

15 Remove the drivebelt tensioner (one Torx bolt) and the drivebelt backplate (two hex head bolts).

16 Slacken the cylinder head bolts half a turn at a time at first, in the reverse of the tightening sequence (Fig. 1.19). Remove the bolts. Obtain new bolts for reassembly.

17 Check that nothing has been overlooked, then lift off the cylinder head (photo). It is very heavy. Recover the gasket.

18 Do not dispose of the old gasket until a new one has been obtained. Five thicknesses of gasket are available. The correct thickness is determined after measuring the protrusion of the pistons at TDC – see Specifications and Section 29. Gasket thickness is indicated by one to five teeth (standard bores) or holes (oversize bores) in the position shown in Fig. 1.18. If the pistons have not been disturbed and there is no evidence of piston/valve contact, it is probably satisfactory to fit a new gasket of the same thickness as that removed.

19 Commence refitting by turning the crankshaft to align the timing mark on the injection pump sprocket with the pip on the timing cover.

20 Set the camshaft in the correct position by means of the camshaft setting tool – see Section 9.

21 Make sure that the gasket mating surfaces on the block and head are clean and dry.

22 Fit the new gasket over the locating dowels on the block, making sure that it is the right way up. It will only fit one way (photo).

23 Lower the cylinder head onto the block and insert the new head bolts.

10.7A Fan thermoswitch connector on thermostat housing

10.7B Oil pressure switch on cylinder head

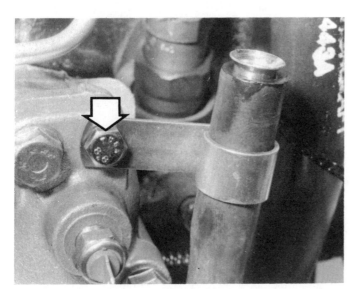

10.9 Bolt (arrowed) securing dipstick tube bracket

10.17 Removing the cylinder head

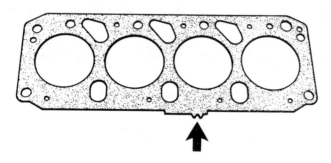

Fig. 1.18 Cylinder head gasket – thickness is indicated by
number of teeth (arrowed) (Sec 10)

10.22A Head gasket fitted to block

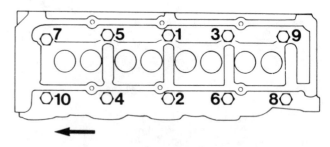

Fig. 1.19 Cylinder head bolts tightening sequence. Arrow
points to pulley end of engine (Sec 10)

10.22B Head gasket top marking

24 Tighten the bolts progressively to the Stage 1 specified torque,
following the sequence shown in Fig. 1.19 (photo).

25 In the same sequence, tighten the bolts to the Stage 2 specified
torque.

26 Wait at least two minutes, then tighten the bolts through the angle
specified for Stage 3, following the same sequence. No further
tightening is required.

27 Fit the drivebelt backplate and secure it with the two bolts; use a
little sealant on the bolt threads.

28 Fit and secure the drivebelt tensioner. Do not tighten the bolt fully
yet.

29 Fit the camshaft sprocket. Insert its bolt but only tighten it by hand,
so that the sprocket can still move on the taper.

30 Turn the crankshaft clockwise to TDC, No 1 firing. Refer to Section
9 if necessary.

31 Fit and tension the camshaft drivebelt as described in Section 6,
paragraphs 13 to 17.

10.24 Tightening a cylinder head bolt

32 Check the valve clearances as described in Section 7.

33 If they were removed, refit the glow plugs as described in Chapter 3, Section 14.

34 Similarly refit the injectors, if necessary, as described in Chapter 3, Section 10.

35 Refit and secure the camshaft cover, using a new gasket. Secure the breather hoses.

36 Reattach the exhaust downpipe to the manifold. Use a new gasket, and apply anti-seize compound to the stud threads.

37 Refit and secure the fuel filter and its bracket.

38 Refit the coolant bypass pipe and the thermostat housing, using new seals on the pipe and a new gasket on the housing. See Chapter 2, Sections 12 and 13. Secure the dipstick tube bracket to the thermostat housing.

39 Refit the fuel injection pipes as described in Chapter 3, Section 9.

40 Reconnect the fuel return pipe between the pump and No 1 injector (photo).

10.40 Connecting the fuel return pipe to No 1 injector

41 Reconnect the oil return and vacuum hoses to the vacuum pump.

42 Reconnect the electrical leads to the temperature gauge sender, the fan thermoswitch, the oil pressure switch and the glow plug bus bar.

43 Reconnect and secure all the coolant hoses, then refill the cooling system as described in Chapter 2, Section 6.

44 Refit the air cleaner as described in Chapter 3.

45 Reconnect the battery.

11 Cylinder head – dismantling, overhaul and reassembly

1 With the head removed as described in the previous Section, remove the injectors and glow plugs (if not already done). Clean the accessible parts of the head and mop out oil and coolant. Take care not to damage the protruding valves.

2 Unbolt and remove the inlet and exhaust manifolds. Recover the gaskets.

3 Unbolt the vacuum pump. Slacken its bolts evenly until any tension is released. Recover the O-ring seal.

4 Remove camshaft bearing caps and shells Nos 2 and 4.

5 Slacken the nuts securing camshaft bearing caps Nos 1, 3 and 5 one turn at a time, working from end to end so that the camshaft is released gradually. Remove the caps and shells. Keep all the shells with their respective caps if they are to be re-used.

6 Lift out the camshaft with its oil seal. Recover the lower half bearing shells, keeping them in order too if they are to be reused. Remove and discard the oil seal.

7 Remove the valve tappets and shims. Keep them in order in a segmented box or some similar arrangement.

8 Remove the vacuum pump operating plunger (photo).

9 Unbolt and remove the lifting eyes.

10 Unscrew and remove the oil pressure switch and the coolant connector (photo).

11 Using a valve spring compressor, depress one valve spring retainer to gain access to the collets. The valves are deeply recessed, so the end of the compressor may need to be extended with a tube or box section with a 'window' for access. Remove the collets and release the compressor. Recover the valve, spring and retainer (photos).

12 Repeat the procedure to remove the other seven valves. Keep the valve components in order if they are to be re-used.

13 Remove the valve stem oil seals from the valve guides, using long-nosed pliers.

14 Dismantling of the cylinder head is now complete. Refer to Section 12 for decarbonisation procedures.

15 Clean all components and examine them for wear. Oil seals, O-rings and gaskets should be renewed as a matter of course. Inspect the head for cracks or other damage.

16 Check the head gasket face for distortion using a straight-edge and feeler blades. Distortion in excess of the maximum specified means that the head must be renewed. No refinishing is permitted. Do not be deceived by the (permitted) projection of the swirl chambers (photo).

17 Inspect the valve seats and swirl chambers for burning or cracks. Both can be renewed, and valve seats can sometimes be recut, but again this is specialist work. Note that oversize seats and/or swirl chambers may have been fitted in production – see Specifications and Figs. 1.23 and 1.24.

18 Check each valve for straightness, freedom from burning or cracks, and for an acceptable fit in its guide. Excessive play in the guide may be caused by wear in either component; measure the valve stem with a micrometer, or try the fit of a new valve if available, to establish whether it is the valve or the guide which is worn.

19 Valve guides as such are not renewable. The guide bores must be reamed accurately to a specific oversize and valves with the appropriate oversize stems fitted. Consult a Ford dealer or other reputable specialist.

20 Slight marking of the sealing area on the valve head may be removed by grinding. Any more severe damage means that the valve must be refaced, if possible, or renewed. The amount of grinding needed to remove large burn marks, besides being tedious, may cause the valve to sit unacceptably deeply in its seat.

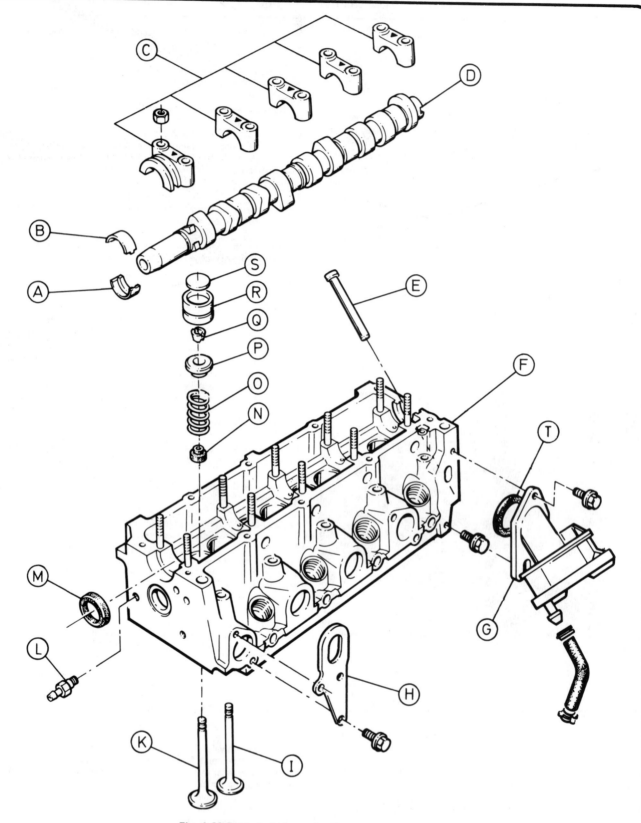

Fig. 1.20 Exploded view of cylinder head (Sec 11)

A	Camshaft bearing shell (lower)	E	Vacuum pump plunger
B	Camshaft bearing shell (upper)	F	Head
C	Camshaft bearing caps	G	Vacuum pump
D	Camshaft	H	Lifting eye
		I	Exhaust valve

A Camshaft bearing shell (lower)
B Camshaft bearing shell (upper)
C Camshaft bearing caps
D Camshaft

E Vacuum pump plunger
F Head
G Vacuum pump
H Lifting eye
I Exhaust valve

K Inlet valve
L Coolant connector
M Camshaft oil seal
N Valve stem oil seal
O Valve spring

P Spring retainer
Q Collets
R Tappet
S Shim
T O-ring

11.8 Removing the vacuum pump operating plunger

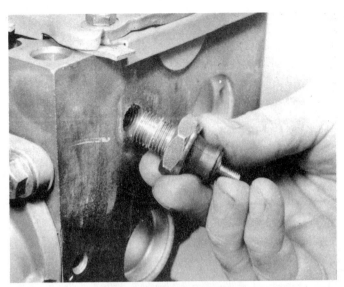

11.10 Removing the oil pressure switch

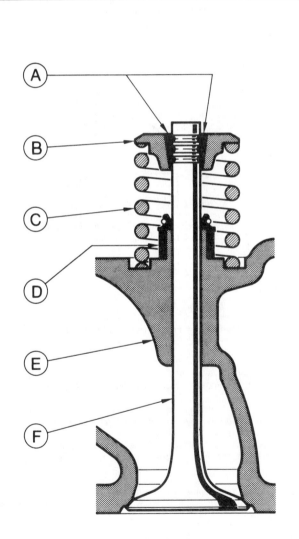

Fig. 1.21 Sectional view of a valve and associated components (Sec 11)

A Collets
B Spring retainer
C Valve spring
D Valve stem oil seal
E Cylinder head
F Valve

11.11A Valve spring compressor in use – note extension tube (arrowed)

Fig. 1.22 Ford valve spring compressor in use (Sec 11)

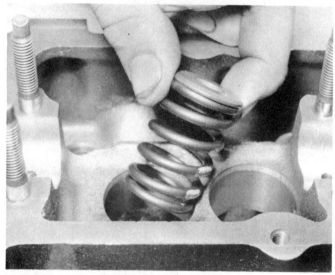

11.11B Removing a valve spring and retainer

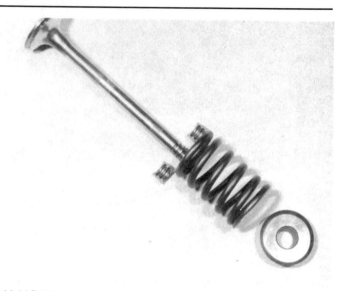

11.11C Valve, spring, retainer and collets

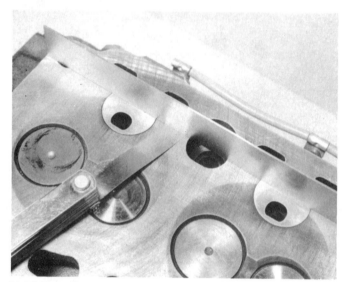

11.16 Measuring swirl chamber projection

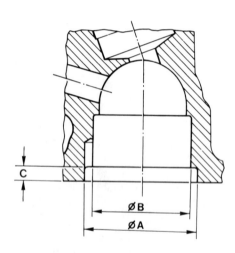

Fig. 1.23 Swirl chamber seat dimensions. For A, B and C see Specifications (Sec 11)

21 New or refaced valves and seats should be ground together as follows. (The coarse paste may be omitted if the fit is already good.)

22 Invert the head and support it securely. Smear a little coarse grinding paste round the sealing area of the valve head. Insert the valve in its guide and grind it to the seat with a to-and-fro motion. The customary tool for this operation is a stick with a rubber sucker on the end (photo). Lift the valve occasionally to redistribute the grinding paste.

23 When an unbroken ring of grinding paste is present on the valve head and seat, wipe them clean, then repeat the operation with fine grinding paste.

24 When all the valves have been ground in, clean away all traces of grinding paste, first with a paraffin-soaked rag then with clean dry rags, finally with compressed air if available. Do not overlook the valve guides. It will be obvious that even a small quantity of grinding paste remaining in the engine could cause extremely rapid wear.

25 Examine the valve springs for distortion or signs of fatigue. Measure their free length and compare it with that given in the Specifications. It is worth renewing the springs as a precautionary

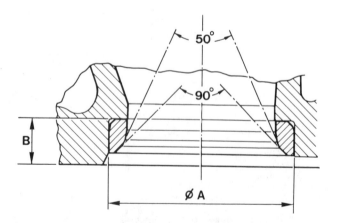

Fig. 1.24 Valve seat dimensions. For A and B see Specifications (Sec 11)

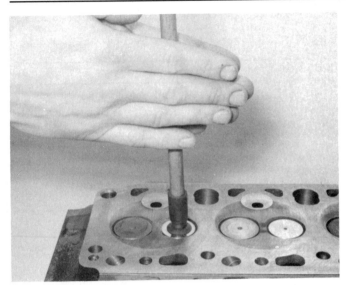

11.22 Grinding in a valve

measure if the old ones have seen much service, even if they appear to be in good condition.

26 Examine the tappets and their bores for scoring or other damage. Oversize tappets may already have been fitted in production. If purchasing new tappets, measure the old ones or take them along for comparison to be sure of obtaining the right size.

27 Renew the camshaft bearing shells unless they are obviously in perfect condition. Two sizes of shell are fitted, one for standard bearing bores and the other for oversize bores. Oversize shells are identified by a green mark. Either size may have been fitted in production.

28 Examine the camshaft bearing journals and the cam lobes for scoring or other deterioration. If a micrometer is available, check the journal diameters. Bearing clearance can be measured using Plastigage – see Section 27. Renew the camshaft if it is badly worn or if the journals are out of round. Once wear has begun on the lobes it usually progresses rapidly as the surface hardening is penetrated.

29 Inspect the manifold and camshaft bearing cap studs. Renew any which are in poor condition, or transfer them to the new head if one is being fitted. To remove a stud either use a proprietary stud extractor, or lock two nuts together on the exposed thread and use them to unscrew it. Studs which have come out by mistake should be cleaned up and refitted using thread locking compound.

30 Overhaul of the cylinder head is now complete. If the core plugs need attention, refer to Section 27.

31 Begin reassembly by oiling a valve stem and inserting it into its guide. Fit the new valve stem oil seal. It is advisable to protect the seal by covering the grooves in the valve stem with a plastic sleeve (which may be provided with the new seals) or with plastic film (photo). Lubricate the seal and press it into position with a tube or a small box spanner. Remove the protective sleeve or film.

32 Fit the valve spring (either way up) and the spring retainer. Apply the valve spring compressor and depress the spring retainer far enough to give access to fit the collets. A smear of grease on the collets will hold them in position on the grooves. When the collets are properly located, carefully release the valve spring compressor. Tap the spring retainer smartly with a mallet and tube to settle the collets.

33 Repeat the operations on the remaining seven valves and associated components.

34 Refit the oil pressure switch and the coolant connector. Use a little sealant on their threads.

35 Oil and refit the vacuum pump plunger.

36 Refit and secure the lifting eyes.

37 Oil and insert the tappets and shims, observing their previously fitted sequence when applicable (photos). Make a note of the shim thickness fitted at each position, if not already done, for reference when checking the valve clearances. Remember to fit the shims with the size markings downwards.

38 Fit the camshaft and its bearings as described in Section 8, paragraphs 8 to 13.

39 Fit a new camshaft oil seal as described in Section 13.

40 Refit the inlet and exhaust manifolds, using new gaskets. Tighten the securing nuts and bolts progressively to the specified torque. For the exhaust manifold tightening sequence see Chapter 3, Section 17.

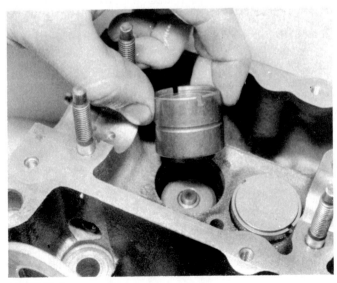

11.31 Fitting a valve stem oil seal. The end of the stem is covered with plastic film

11.37A Fitting a tappet ...

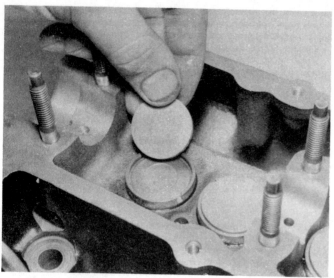

11.37B ... and its shim

41 Turn the camshaft so that the vacuum pump cam lobe is pointing away from the pump. Insert the vacuum pump lower bolt and screw it in a few turns. Fit a new O-ring to the vacuum pump and slide its slotted fixing hole onto the lower bolt. Fit the upper bolt, make sure that the O-ring is still correctly located, then tighten both bolts evenly.

42 The cylinder head is now ready for refitting as described in the previous Section.

12 Cylinder head and pistons – decarbonisation

1 With the cylinder head removed, as described in Section 10, the carbon deposits should be removed from the combustion spaces using a scraper and a wire brush fitted into an electric drill. Take care not to damage the valve heads, otherwise no special precautions need be taken as the cylinder head is of cast iron construction.

2 Where a more thorough job is to be carried out, the cylinder head should be dismantled as described in the preceding Section so that the valves may be ground in and the ports and combustion spaces cleaned, brushed and blown out after the manifolds have been removed.

3 Before grinding-in a valve, remove the carbon and deposits completely from its head and stem. With an inlet valve, this is usually quite easy, simply scraping off the soft carbon with a blunt knife and finishing with a wire brush. With an exhaust valve the deposits are very much harder and those on the valve head may need a rub on coarse emery cloth to remove them. An old woodworking chisel is a useful tool to remove the worst of the valve head deposits.

4 An important part of the decarbonising operation is to remove the carbon deposits from the piston crowns. To do this, turn the crankshaft so that two pistons are at the top of their stroke and press some grease between these pistons and the cylinder walls. This will prevent carbon particles falling down' into the piston ring grooves. Stuff rags into the other two bores.

5 Cover the oilways and coolant passages with masking tape and then using a blunt scraper remove all the carbon from the piston crowns. Take care not to score the soft alloy of the crown or the surface of the cylinder bore.

6 Rotate the crankshaft to bring the other two pistons to TDC and repeat the operations.

7 Wipe away the circle of grease and carbon from the cylinder bores.

8 Clean the top surface of the cylinder block by careful scraping.

13 Oil seals – renewal

1 The procedures described here are for renewal with the engine in the vehicle. With the engine removed, the steps taken to gain access may be ignored. Read through the procedures first to see what is involved – some are quite lengthy.

Camshaft

2 Remove the camshaft drivebelt as described in Section 6, paragraphs 1 to 11.

3 Unbolt and remove the camshaft sprocket. Tap the sprocket with a mallet if necessary to break the taper fit.

4 Unbolt and remove the drivebelt tensioner and the belt backplate.

5 Unbolt and remove No 1 camshaft bearing cap. Do not lose the shell.

6 Extract the old oil seal, preferably using fingers only. Take care not to scratch the bearing journal or the sealing surface if tools are used.

7 Clean old sealant from the bearing cap. Apply fresh sealant (to Ford spec SPM - 4G - 9112 - F/G) to the areas of the cap shown in Fig. 1.14.

8 Refit No 1 bearing shell and cap. Tighten the cap nuts to the specified torque.

9 Lubricate the new seal and make sure that its seat is clean. Also lubricate the taper on the camshaft nose.

10 Fit the new seal, lips inwards, and seat it with a piece of tube or a large socket (photos). The maker's tool uses a bolt and washers to draw the seal into position.

11 Refit the drivebelt backplate and the tensioner. Do not tighten the tensioner pivot bolt yet.

12 Refit the camshaft sprocket, making sure that the taper is clean and dry. Insert the sprocket bolt but do not tighten it.

13 Refit and tension the camshaft drivebelt as described in Section 6, paragraph 12 onwards.

13.10A Fit the new oil seal to the camshaft nose ...

13.10B ... and seat it with a tube or socket

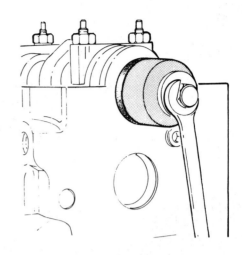

Fig. 1.25 Drawing in a camshaft oil seal (Sec 13)

Injection pump gear

14 Remove the camshaft drivebelt as described in Section 6, paragraphs 1 to 12.

15 Unbolt and remove the injection pump sprocket.

16 Remove the old seal using a suitable hooked tool. Alternatively, drill a small hole in the face of the seal, fit a self-tapping screw into the hole and lever or pull on the screw head to remove the seal. If all else fails, the timing cover will have to be removed (see Section 15).

17 Lubricate the new seal and make sure that its seat is clean.

18 Fit the new seal, lips inwards, and press it home. Ford tool 21 - 111 uses a couple of sprocket bolts to press the seal into position. An acceptable alternative is to use the old seal, a drilled metal bar and some bolts and spacers (photos). Care must be taken that the seal enters its seat squarely.

13.18A Fitting a new injection pump gear oil seal

13.18B Pressing the new seal into position using the old seal, a bar, bolts and spacers

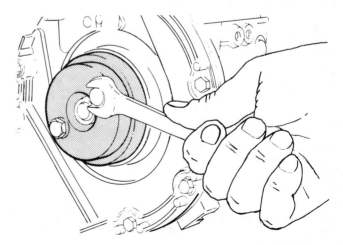

Fig. 1.26 Drawing in an injection pump gear oil seal (Sec 13)

19 Refit the injection pump sprocket, making sure that the locating dowel engages correctly. Fit the sprocket bolts and tighten them to the specified torque.

20 Refit and tension the camshaft drivebelt as described in Section 6, paragraph 13 onwards.

Crankshaft pulley – Fiesta
21 Disconnect the battery earth lead.

22 Drain the cooling system as described in Chapter 2, Section 4.

23 Separate the radiator top hose from the radiator, and the expansion tank hose from the water pump inlet.

24 Unclip and remove the camshaft drivebelt cover.

25 Disconnect the speedometer cable from the transmission.

26 Disconnect the clutch cable from the transmission.

27 Remove the starter motor as described in Chapter 7, Section 6.

28 Separate the front suspension lower arm balljoints on both sides.

29 Unbolt the front tie-bar brackets on both sides.

30 Unbolt the gearshift stabiliser from the transmission.

31 Support the engine/transmission assembly on a hoist.

32 Unbolt the engine/transmission mountings. Lower the unit until the crankshaft pulley is accessible from under the wheelarch.

33 Remove the alternator drivebelt.

34 Remove the crankshaft pulley bolt. This bolt is extremely tight. The makers call up two special tools (Nos 21 - 108 and 21 - 109), one of which locks the pulley bolt while the other turns the crankshaft by meshing with the ring gear through the starter motor aperture. On the bench a 32 mm socket can be used on the bolt, and suitable arrangements made to jam the crankshaft; with the engine suspended from a hoist it will be difficult to undo the bolt with normal hand tools.

Make quite sure that the engine is securely supported before trying to undo the bolt. Obtain a new bolt for reassembly.

35 Remove the crankshaft pulley. Note the locating pin (photo).

36 Remove the oil seal as described in paragraph 16.

37 Lubricate the new seal and clean its seat.

38 Fit the seal, lips inwards, and push it home as far as possible by hand. Seat the seal fully with the aid of a suitable tube or the old seal. It is possible to use the crankshaft pulley bolt and the pulley to apply pressure to the tube or seal.

39 Refit the crankshaft pulley. Oil the threads and the head contact face of the new bolt and insert it finger tight.

40 Tighten the crankshaft pulley bolt to the specified torque. If using the Ford special tools or equivalent, angular rotation for the second stage of tightening can be measured by attaching a graduated disc to the injection pump sprocket. Remember that the pump sprocket turns at half engine speed, so (for instance) 150° crankshaft movement will be read as 75° at the pump sprocket.

41 Refit and tension the alternator drivebelt – see Chapter 2, Section 11.

42 Raise the engine/transmission assembly and reattach its mountings. Remove the lifting tackle.

43 Refit the gearshift stabiliser.

44 Refit the front tie-bar brackets.

45 Refit the front suspension lower arm balljoints.

46 Refit the starter motor – see Chapter 7, Section 6.

47 Reconnect the clutch and speedometer cables.

48 Reconnect the coolant hoses to the radiator and the water pump inlet.

49 Check the injection pump timing (Chapter 3, Section 7) and adjust if necessary.

Fig. 1.27 Special tools for dealing with the crankshaft pulley bolt (Sec 13)

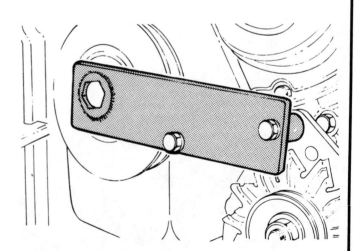

Fig. 1.28 Pulley bolt locking tool fitted (Sec 13)

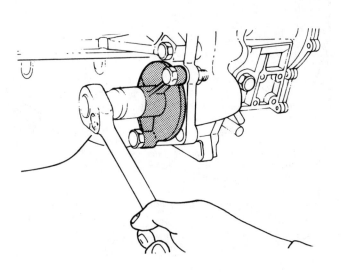

Fig. 1.29 Crankshaft turning tool in use (Sec 13)

13.35 Removing the crankshaft pulley. Note locating pin and hole (arrowed)

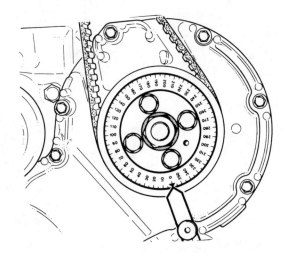

Fig. 1.30 A graduated disc attached to the injection pump sprocket (Sec 13)

50 Refill the cooling system as described in Chapter 2, Section 6.

51 Check the engine oil level and top up if necessary.

52 Reconnect the battery.

Crankshaft pulley – Escort/Orion

53 Disconnect the battery earth lead.

54 Unclip and remove the camshaft drivebelt cover.

55 Remove the starter motor as described in Chapter 7, Section 6.

56 Unbolt the alternator drivebelt splash shield (when fitted).

57 Support the engine/transmission with lifting tackle or a suitably padded jack.

58 Unbolt both anti-roll bar brackets from the body.

59 Remove the three bolts which attach the transmission rear mounting bracket to the body.

60 Remove the nut and bolt which secure the engine mounting to the right-hand inner wing.

61 Unbolt the gearshift stabiliser from the transmission.

62 Lower the engine/transmission until the crankshaft pulley is accessible.

63 Renew the seal as described in paragraphs 33 to 41.

64 Raise the engine/transmission, making sure that the right-hand mounting engages correctly. Fit its nut and bolt, but do not tighten them fully yet.

65 Reattach the transmission rear bracket and the anti-roll bar brackets.

66 Tighten the engine/transmission mountings and the anti-roll bar bracket fastening, then remove the lifting tackle or jack.

67 Reattach the gearshift stabiliser to the transmission.

68 Check the injection pump timing as described in Chapter 3, Section 7, and adjust if necessary.

69 Refit the alternator drivebelt splash shield, the starter motor and the camshaft drivebelt cover.

70 Check the engine oil level and top up if necessary.

71 Reconnect the battery earth lead.

Crankshaft rear

72 Remove the flywheel as described in Section 19.

73 Extract the oil seal as described in paragraph 16, or by using Ford tool No 21 - 010. Take great care not to damage the oil seal housing.

74 Lubricate the new seal and clean its seat.

75 Fit the new seal, lips inwards, and seat it. The Ford tool for installing the seal is in the form of a cup which is drawn in with a couple of flywheel bolts. A suitably drilled plate or bar could be used instead (photo).

76 Refit the flywheel, using new bolts, as described in Section 19.

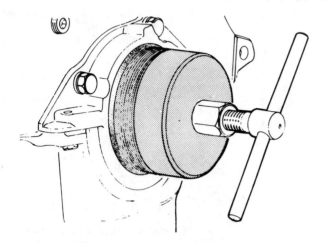

Fig. 1.31 Maker's tool for extracting the crankshaft rear oil seal (Sec 13)

14 Sump – removal and refitting

1   Disconnect the battery earth (negative) lead.

2   Remove the starter motor as described in Chapter 7, Section 6.

3   Raise and securely support the front of the vehicle.

4   Drain the engine oil by removing the sump drain plug. Refit the plug when draining is complete to avoid losing it.

5   Remove the flywheel cover plate, which is secured by two nuts (photos).

6   Remove the 16 bolts which secure the sump. Access to the two bolts nearest the flywheel is tight; a socket spanner, extension and universal joint will be required.

7   Pull the sump off the engine block. If it is stuck, strike its sides with a wooden or plastic mallet. Avoid levering between the mating faces if possible, as distortion or other damage may result.

8   Remove the old gasket from the sump or block.

9   Clean the sump both inside and out. Dress the sealing surface if it is distorted.

10 Clean the block mating face then apply non-setting jointing compound to the areas shown in Fig. 1.32.

11 Position a new gasket on the sump, using a smear of grease to retain it in position.

12 Offer the sump to the block. Insert the four corner bolts and tighten them finger tight.

13 Insert the remaining 12 bolts and tighten them to the specified torque.

14 Tighten the four corner bolts to the specified torque.

15 Refit the flywheel cover plate and the starter motor.

16 Make sure that the drain plug is fitted and tightened, then refill the engine with the specified quantity and grade of oil.

17 Reconnect the battery and lower the vehicle.

18 Check for leaks around the drain plug and sump gasket when the engine is next run.

13.75 Using a face puller to seat the oil seal

14.5A Removing a cover plate nut

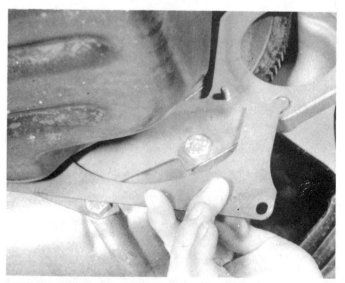

14.5B Removing the flywheel cover plate

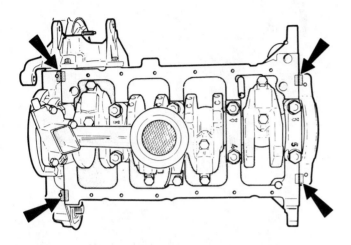

Fig. 1.32 Apply jointing compound to the critical sealing areas (arrowed) of the sump mating face (Sec 14)

15 Timing cover and gears – removal and refitting

1 Disconnect the battery earth (negative) lead.

2 Remove the camshaft drivebelt as described in Section 6.

3 Remove the alternator drivebelt as described in Chapter 2, Section 11.

4 Remove the crankshaft pulley. Refer to Section 13 for the procedures necessary to gain access to and to remove the pulley.

5 Unbolt and remove the injection pump sprocket. Slacken, but do not remove completely, the injection pump shaft nut.

6 Remove the 15 bolts which secure the timing cover. Note the location of the three longer bolts (photo).

7 Remove the timing cover and recover the gasket. Be prepared for some oil spillage. If the water pump pulley blocks removal of the cover, unbolt and remove it.

8 With the timing cover removed, the gears can be withdrawn. A pulley will be needed to draw off the injection pump gear, and this must be capable of being used in the space available. Refer to Section 25, paragraphs 30 and 33, for further details.

9 Refit the timing gears as described in Section 29, paragraphs 34 to 36.

10 The timing cover oil seals should be renewed as a matter of course. Drive the old seals out of the cover, but do not fit the new ones yet.

11 Refit the timing cover using a new gasket – a smear of grease will hold the gasket in position.

12 Secure the timing cover with the 15 bolts. The three longer bolts go at the top. Tighten the bolts evenly to the specified torque.

13 Fit new crankshaft pulley and injection pump sprocket oil seals. Refer to Section 13 if necessary.

14 Refit the water pump pulley if it was removed.

15 Refit the injection pump sprocket and tighten its bolts to the specified torque (photos).

16 Refit the crankshaft pulley. Secure the pulley with a new bolt, oiled on the threads and head contact face. Tighten the bolt to the specified torque – refer to Section 13, paragraph 40.

17 Reverse the steps taken to gain access to the crankshaft pulley.

18 Refit and tension the alternator drivebelt as described in Chapter 2, Section 11.

19 Refit and tension the camshaft drivebelt as described in Section 6.

15.6 Timing cover ready for removal. The three longer bolts are arrowed

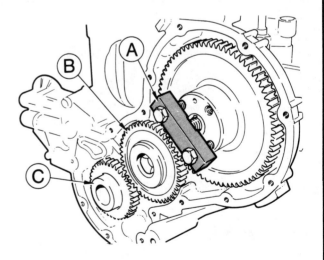

Fig. 1.33 Removing the injection pump gear (Sec 15)

A Puller
B Idler gear
C Crankshaft gear

15.15A Fitting the injection pump sprocket. Note locating pin and hole (arrowed)

15.15B Tightening a sprocket bolt

20 Check the injection pump timing as described in Chapter 3, Section 7.

21 Check the engine oil level and top up if necessary.

22 Reconnect the battery.

23 Check for leaks from the timing cover gasket and oil seals when the engine is next run.

16 Timing case – removal and refitting

1 Remove the sump as described in Section 14. Also remove the oil filter element.

2 Remove the timing cover and gears as described in Section 15.

3 Remove the oil pump pick-up pipe and strainer by unbolting the assembly, complete with bracket, from the block and the timing case. Recover the gasket.

4 Remove the three nuts which secure the fuel injection pump to the timing case.

5 Remove the seven bolts which secure the timing case to the block. Four of these are Torx bolts.

6 Pull the timing case clear of the crankshaft and injection pump and remove it. Recover the gasket.

7 Commence refitting by placing a new gasket on the cylinder block.

8 Offer the timing case to the block, observing the following points:

   (a) The flats on the oil pump must engage with those on the crankshaft

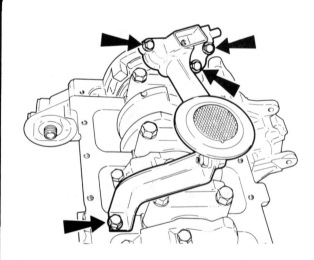

Fig. 1.34 Oil pump pick-up pipe and bracket retaining screws (arrowed) (Sec 16)

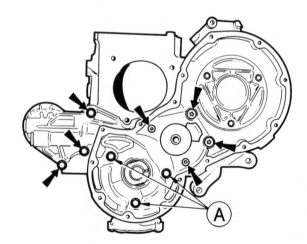

Fig. 1.35 Timing case securing bolts (arrowed) (Sec 16)

A   Oil pump bolts

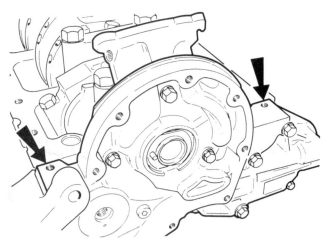

Fig. 1.36 Timing case and block sump mating faces
(arrowed) must be aligned (Sec 16)

(b) The centring spigot on the oil pump must enter the main
bearing bore
(c) The sump mating faces on the timing case must align with
those on the block to within 0.1 mm (0.004 in)

9   Insert the timing case-to-block bolts and tighten them to the
specified torque. Trim off any excess gasket at the sump face.

10 Refit the injection pump-to-timing case nuts and tighten them to
the specified torque.

11 Refit the oil pump pick-up pipe, bracket and strainer, using a new
gasket. Tighten the bolts to the specified torque.

12 Refit the timing gears and cover as described in Section 15.

13 Fit a new oil filter element as described in Section 4.

14 Refit the sump as described in Section 14.

17 Oil pump – removal, inspection and refitting

1   Remove the timing case as described in the previous Section.

2   Remove the three bolts which secure the oil pump to the timing
case (photo).

3   Remove the oil pump from the timing case. Extract the gears from
the pump housing, noting any identification marks to show which way
round they are fitted.

4   Clean all parts and inspect them for wear or damage. No wear limits
were published at the time of writing. Pump components are not
available individually. It is wise to renew the pump on a precautionary
basis at time of major overhaul, especially if there is evidence of oil
starvation elsewhere.

5   Clean the pick-up pipe and strainer in solvent and blow them dry.
Note that the pressure relief valve is built into the pick-up pipe and
cannot be dismantled, or renewed separately.

6   When refitting, lubricate the pump gears liberally, then fit them into
the pump housing (photos).

7   Fit the assembled pump to the timing case (photo) and secure with
the three bolts. Tighten the bolts to the specified torque.

8   Refit the timing case as described in the previous Section.

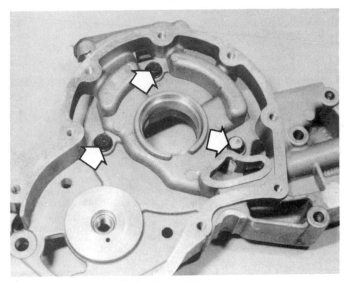

17.2 Oil pump securing bolts (arrowed)

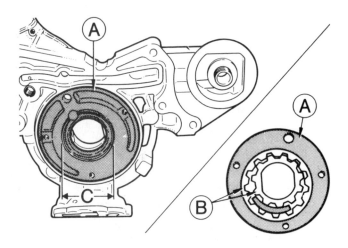

Fig. 1.37 Oil pump and timing case (Sec 17)

A   Pump housing   C   Centering spigot
B   Pump gears

17.6A Oil pump housing with gears removed

17.6B Outer gear fitted to oil pump housing. Face mark on gear (arrowed) shows which way round it is fitted

17.6C Oil pump with inner and outer gears fitted

17.7 Oil pump fitted to timing case

18 Pistons and connecting rods – removal and refitting

1   Remove the cylinder head as described in Section 10.

2   Remove the sump as described in Section 14.

3   To improve access, it is preferable to remove the oil pump pick-up pipe, bracket and strainer.

4   If there is a pronounced wear ridge at the top of any bore, it may be necessary to remove it with a scraper or ridge reamer to avoid piston damage during removal. Such a ridge may indicate that reboring is necessary, which will entail new pistons in any case.

5   Turn the crankshaft to bring two pistons to BDC. Check that the connecting rods and their caps are numbered on one side – make paint or punch identifying marks if necessary.

6   Remove the bolts from the two accessible connecting rod caps. Take off the caps and recover the bottom half bearing shells. Keep the shells with their caps if they are to be re-used.

7   Push the two pistons up through the bores. Gentle persuasion (eg with a hammer handle) may be needed to make the piston rings clear the wear ridge – see paragraph 4.

8   Remove the pistons complete with rings and connecting rods. Keep the upper half bearing shells with their pistons and rods if they are to be re-used.

9   Turn the crankshaft 180° to bring the other two pistons to BDC. Repeat the removal process.

10 Examination and renovation of pistons is considered in Section 27.

11 If new piston rings are to be fitted to old bores, the bores must be deglazed to allow the new rings to bed-in properly. Protect the big-end journals by wrapping them in masking tape, then use a piece of coarse emery paper to produce a cross-hatch pattern in each bore. A flap wheel in an electric drill may also be used, but beware of spreading abrasive dust. When deglazing is complete, unwrap the big-end journals and wash away all abrasive particles.

12 Commence refitting by laying out the assembled pistons and rods in order, with the bearing shells, connecting rod caps and new bolts. Stagger the ring gaps evenly.

13 Wipe any protective grease off the new bearing shells (if used). Make sure that the shell seats are clean, then press the shells into the rods and caps so that the locating tangs engage in the grooves (photos).

18.13A Fitting a bearing shell to the connecting rod ...

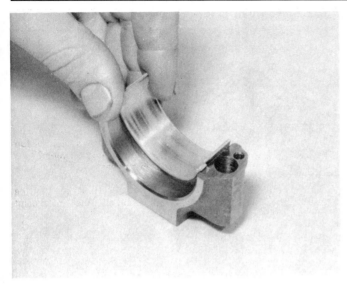

18.13B ... and to the connecting rod cap

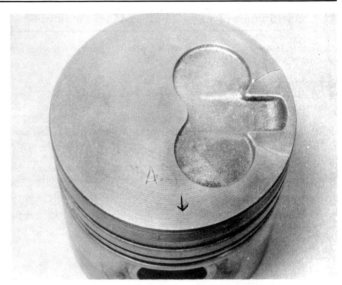

18.14 Arrow on piston crown points to oil pump end of engine

14 Lubricate the bores, pistons, crankpins and shells. Fit a piston ring compressor to the first piston to be fitted. Offer the piston to its bore, making sure that it is the correct bore, and that the arrow on the piston crown and the F mark on the connecting rod are both facing the oil pump end of the engine (photo).

15 Tap the piston through the ring compressor and into the bore, using a hammer handle or similar 'soft' tool. Release the ring compressor as the piston enters the bore.

16 Guide the connecting rod onto the crankpin, taking care not to scratch the bearing surface. Check also that the bearing shell is not displaced. Fit the connecting rod cap with shell, making sure it is the right way round.

17 Oil the threads of two new connecting rod cap bolts. Fit the bolts and tighten them in stages to the specified torque.

18 Repeat these operations to fit the other three pistons. Turn the crankshaft as necessary to bring the crankpins into positions convenient for fitting.

19 If new components have been fitted, check the piston protrusion as described in Section 29, paragraphs 45 to 49.

20 Refit the oil pump pick-up pipe, bracket and strainer, if removed, using a new gasket. Tighten the bolts to the specified torque.

21 Refit the sump as described in Section 14.

22 Refit the cylinder head as described in Section 10.

19 Flywheel – removal and refitting

1 Either remove the engine and transmission and separate them (Sections 22 and 23), or remove the transmission alone as described in the appropriate manual for petrol-engined vehicles.

2 Make alignment marks, then slacken the clutch pressure plate bolts evenly. Remove the bolts, the pressure plate and the driven plate.

3 Make alignment marks between the flywheel and the crankshaft

tail, then unbolt and remove the flywheel. Do not drop it, it is heavy. Obtain new bolts for reassembly.

4 Examination and overhaul of the flywheel is considered in Section 27.

5 Commence refitting by placing the flywheel on the end of the crankshaft. Observe the alignment marks if refitting the original components.

6 Insert the new securing bolts. Tighten them in stages to the specified torque (photo).

7 Refit and secure the clutch driven and pressure plates. Take the opportunity to renew any worn clutch components. Make sure that the driven plate is centred.

8 Refit the transmission, or mate and refit the engine/transmission assembly, as appropriate.

19.6 Tightening a flywheel bolt

20 Engine/transmission mountings – removal and refitting

1   Before removing any mounting, support the engine/transmission unit with a hoist or a suitably padded jack.

All models – right-hand
2   Remove the mounting bolt from under the right-hand wheel arch (photo).

3   Remove the nut and washer adjacent to the right-hand suspension turret.

4   Working from below, remove the three bolts which secure the mounting bracket to the rear of the block. Note the location of the long bolt.

5   Remove the mounting. It may be dismantled for renewal of the rubber component (photos).

Fiesta – left-hand
6   Unscrew the nuts (one front, one rear) securing the left-hand mountings to the transmission bearer (photos).

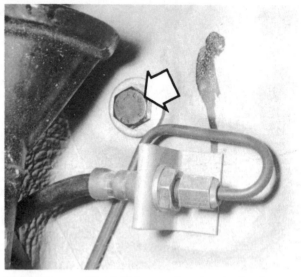

20.2 Engine mounting bolt (arrowed) under wheel arch

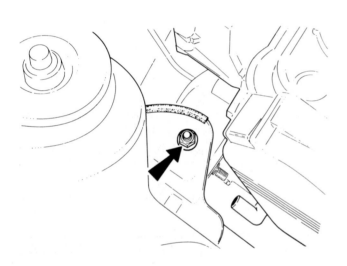

Fig. 1.38 Nut (arrowed) securing right-hand mounting (Sec 20)

20.5A Remove the bolt (arrowed) ...

20.5B ... to extract the engine mounting rubber

20.6A Transmission mounting nut (A) and bearer bolts (B) – front

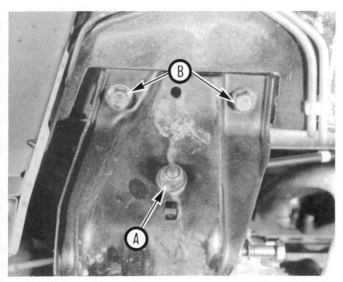

20.6B Transmission mounting nut (A) and bearer bolts (B) – rear

7   Support the bearer, remove its four securing bolts (two front, two rear) and remove it.

8   The rubber mountings can now be disconnected from the transmission support brackets.

Escort/Orion – rear
9   Unbolt the mounting from the body and from the transmission and remove it.

10 With the mounting removed, the flexible component can be detached for renewal.

Escort/Orion – front
11 The front mounting is attached to the anti-roll bar left-hand bracket. Remove the nut and washer which secure the flexible component to that bracket.

12 Raise the engine/transmission slightly. Unbolt the bracket from the transmission (four bolts) and remove the mounting complete.

13 Again, the flexible component can now be detached for renewal.

All mountings
14 Refit in the reverse order to removal, observing the original fitted sequence of washers, plates etc. As the nuts and bolts are tightened, check that the rubbers do not twist.

15 When the hoist or jack is lowered, check again that the mountings are not under excessive tension, causing twisting or deformation of the rubbers. Slacken and retighten the fastenings if necessary.

21 Engine – methods of removal

1   The engine and transmission are removed together from under the vehicle and then separated. Arrangements must therefore be made for lifting the vehicle at the end of the removal process so that the power unit can be extracted. Alternatively a pit can be used.

2   It is possible to remove the transmission alone, after which it would in theory be possible to remove the engine from above. This method is untested, however, and involves extra work.

22 Engine and transmission – removal

1   Disconnect the battery earth (negative) lead.

2   Remove the air cleaner as described in Chapter 3, Section 3.

3   Drain the cooling system as described in Chapter 2, Section 4. Remove the radiator top and bottom hoses. It is not essential, but access will be improved and the risk of damage reduced if the radiator and fan are removed – see Chapter 2, Section 9.

4   Drain the transmission oil as described in Chapter 4, Section 2.

5   Disconnect the coolant hoses from the cylinder head, water pump and thermostat housing.

6   Remove the bonnet. Again, this is not essential but it will improve access.

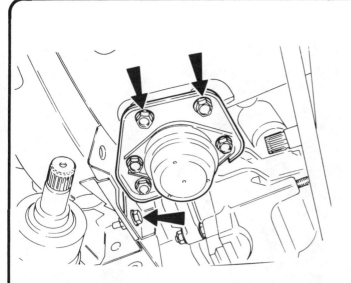

Fig. 1.39 Transmission rear mounting (Escort/Orion). Mounting-to-body bolts arrowed (Sec 20)

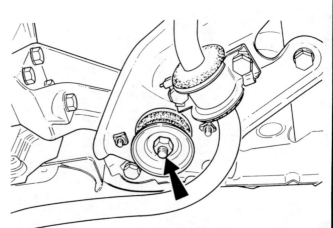

Fig. 1.40 Transmission front mounting (Escort/Orion). Nut (arrowed) secures flexible component to bracket (Sec 20)

7   Disconnect the throttle cable from the fuel injection pump. Refer to Chapter 3, Section 15.

8   Disconnect the following electrical leads:

   (a)   Alternator
   (b)   Temperature gauge sender
   (c)   Oil pressure switch
   (d)   Fan thermoswitch
   (e)   Glow plug feed
   (f)   Injection pump fuel shut-off solenoid and cold start device
   (g)   Oil level sensor (when fitted)
   (h)   Reversing light switch (photo)

9   Disconnect the transmission earth strap (photo).

10   Disconnect the fuel feed and return pipes, either at the filter and pump banjo unions or at the bulkhead (photos). The bulkhead connectors carry coloured stripes – white for feed, red for return. Arrows on the pipes do not necessarily indicate the direction of flow. Plug or cap open unions and tie loose pipes out of the way.

11   Disconnect the vacuum pipe from the vacuum pump.

12   Disconnect the clutch and speedometer cables from the transmission (photo).

13   Raise and support the front of the vehicle with the front wheels free. Remove the exhaust downpipe.

14   Select reverse gear. Make alignment marks, then disconnect the gearshift rod by undoing its clamp bolt and pulling it off the selector shaft (photo).

15   Unbolt the gearshift stabiliser from the transmission (photo). Recover the washer.

16   Remove the pinch-bolt and nuts and separate the track control arm balljoint on the left-hand side.

17   Remove the pivot bolt from the left-hand track control arm.

18   On Fiesta models only, unbolt the tie-bar bracket and remove the track control arm, tie-bar and bracket as an assembly (photo).

19   On all models, free the left-hand driveshaft from the differential by

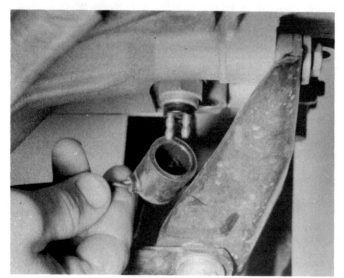

22.8 Disconnecting the reversing light switch

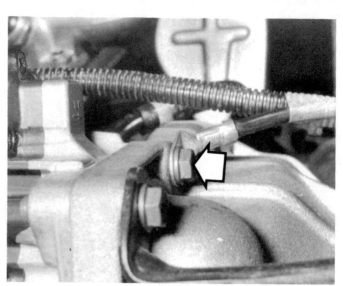

22.9 Transmission earth strap bolt (arrowed)

22.10A Fuel feed banjo union at filter

22.10B Fuel feed and return pipes at bulkhead. Note coloured identification stripe (arrowed)

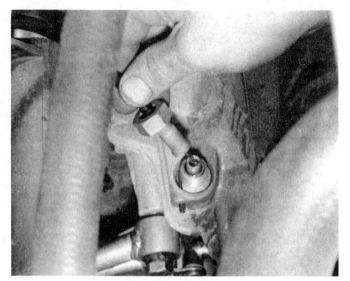

22.12 Disconnecting the speedometer cable

22.14 Undoing the gearshift rod clamp bolt

22.15 Gearshift stabiliser bolted to transmission

22.18 Left-hand tie-bar bracket (Fiesta)

levering between the CV joint and the differential housing, whilst an assistant pulls the left-hand front roadwheel outwards. Hammer on the lever if necessary to free the driveshaft.

20 Tie the driveshaft out of the way. Do not bend the inner joint at more than 20°, or the outer at 45°.

21 Insert a wooden or plastic plug into the driveshaft hole in the differential so that the side gears will not be dislodged. A piece of broom handle is ideal.

22 Remove the pinch-bolt and nut and separate the track control arm balljoint on the right-hand side (photos).

23 Remove the right-hand track control arm pivot bolt. On Fiesta models only, unbolt the tie-bar bracket and remove the track control arm, tie-bar and bracket (photos).

24 Withdraw and support the right-hand driveshaft, and plug the hole, in the same way as the left-hand one (photos).

25 Disconnect the starter motor cables. Free the cables from their clips and brackets.

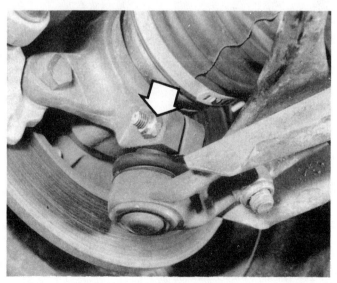

22.22A Track control arm balljoint pinch-bolt and nut (arrowed)

22.22B Track control arm balljoint separated

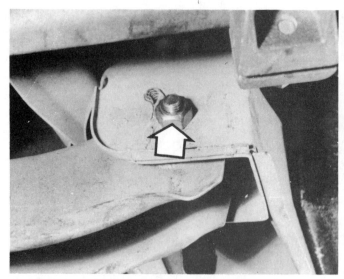

22.23A Remove the pivot nut and bolt (arrowed) ...

22.23B ... free the track control arm ...

22.23C ... and unbolt the tie-bar bracket (Fiesta only)

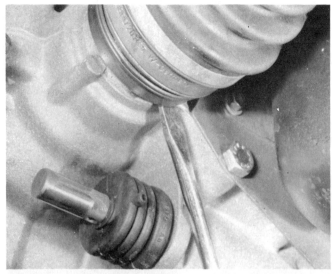

22.24A Freeing the right-hand driveshaft

22.24B Driveshaft hole plugged with a piece of broom handle

26 Attach lifting tackle to the engine, using the lifting eyes provided. Take the weight of the engine/transmission unit.

27 Detach the right-hand mounting from the body. It is secured by one bolt (accessible through the wheel arch) and one nut (next to the right-hand suspension turret).

28 On Fiesta models, remove the four bolts which secure the transmission bearer to the body.

29 On Escort/Orion models, unbolt the transmission rear mounting from the body and the front mounting from the rubber insulator. Also unbolt the anti-roll bar mounting brackets from the body and remove the anti-roll bar, brackets and track control arms together.

30 On all models, remove any splash shields, under-trays etc which may impede removal. Check that the gearshift linkage and stabiliser are clear – they can be unbolted from the floor and swivelled round if necessary.

31 Check that nothing has been overlooked, then lower the engine/transmission unit to the ground.

32 Raise the vehicle further if necessary and withdraw the unit from underneath. It will be found easier to move the engine/transmission if it is lowered onto a strong wooden or metal pallet fitted with ball type castors. A trolley jack is **not** suitable.

33 If the vehicle must be moved whilst the engine is out, temporarily refit the front suspension components, and support the driveshafts so that they can rotate without damage (photo).

23 Engine and transmission – separation

1 Unbolt and remove the starter motor.

2 Remove the flywheel cover plate, which is secured by two nuts.

3 Remove the remaining engine-to-transmission bolts (photo).

4 Withdraw the transmission from the engine. Once it is clear of the locating dowels, do not allow the transmission to hang on the input shaft.

5 Recover the split backplate from behind the flywheel.

6 Store the transmission as nearly as possible in its fitted position. Be prepared for oil to seep out of the driveshaft apertures in storage.

24 Engine dismantling – general

1 Clean the engine thoroughly using a water-soluble grease solvent or similar product. Keep dirt and water out of vulnerable components such as the fuel injection pump and the alternator.

2 Although there is no reason why only partial dismantling should not be carried out to renew some specific component, if the engine has seen much service it is probably worth dismantling it completely to assess the degree of wear in all areas.

3 When possible the engine should be dismantled on a workbench or stout table. If an engine dismantling stand is available, so much the better. Avoid working directly on a concrete floor, as grit presents a serious problem. If there is no alternative to working on the floor, cover it with an old piece of lino or carpet.

4 As well as the usual selection of tools, have available some wooden blocks for propping up the engine. A notebook and pencil will be needed, as will a couple of segmented boxes or a good supply of plastic bags and labels.

5 A waterproof marker pen is useful for making alignment marks without recourse to punches or chisels. Take care that the marks are not erased during cleaning, however.

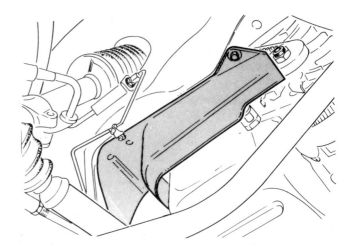

Fig. 1.41 Crankshaft pulley splash shield – Escort/Orion (Sec 22)

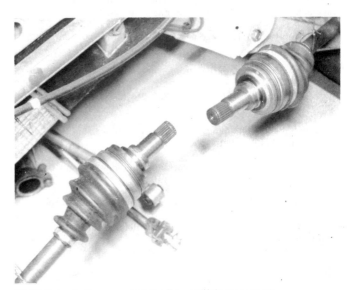

22.33 Driveshafts supported to allow vehicle movement

23.3 Removing an engine-to-transmission bolt

6 Whenever possible, refit nuts, washers etc to the components from which they were removed. This makes reassembly much simpler. Do not rely on memory.

7 Spills of oil, fuel and coolant are bound to occur during dismantling. Have rags and newspapers handy to mop up the mess.

8 Do not throw away old gaskets immediately, but save them for comparison with new ones or for use as patterns if new gaskets have to be constructed.

25 Engine – complete dismantling

1 If not already done, drain the engine oil.

2 Unbolt and remove the exhaust manifold.

3 Remove the alternator drivebelt.

4 Jam the flywheel ring gear and slacken the crankshaft pulley bolt. This bolt is extremely tight: make sure that the engine is well supported. If the appropriate tools are available, lock the bolt and turn the crankshaft by means of the ring gear – see Section 13.

5 Remove the oil filter and dipstick. When fitted, remove the oil level sensor.

6 Remove the alternator and its adjusting strap.

7 Disconnect the fuel supply line from the fuel injection pump. Be prepared for spillage.

8 Unbolt the fuel filter bracket from the cylinder head and remove the filter and bracket complete (photo).

9 Disconnect the fuel return hoses from the injectors and from the pump.

10 Remove the injection pipe as described in Chapter 3, Section 9.

11 Unscrew and remove the fuel injectors. Refer to Chapter 3, Section 10 if necessary. Recover the heat shields.

12 Disconnect the glow plug bus bar, then unscrew and remove the glow plugs.

13 Unbolt the dipstick tube bracket from the thermostat housing. Pull the dipstick tube off its spigot.

14 Unbolt and remove the thermostat housing and its connecting pipe.

15 Slacken the vacuum pump retaining bolts evenly, a turn at a time, until the spring pressure is released. Remove the vacuum pump and the oil return hose.

16 Unclip and remove the camshaft drivebelt cover.

17 Remove the breather hoses, then unbolt and remove the camshaft cover. Recover the gasket, sealing strip and plug.

18 Turn the crankshaft until the groove in the tail of the camshaft is parallel with the top of the cylinder head, and the larger semi-circular segment is uppermost.

19 Slacken the camshaft sprocket bolt, counterholding the sprocket to avoid straining the drivebelt.

20 Unscrew the drivebelt tensioner pivot bolt. Remove the tensioner.

21 Mark the camshaft drivebelt running direction if it is to be re-used, then remove it. Do not turn the crankshaft or camshafts with the belt removed, or piston-valve contact may occur.

22 Remove the camshaft sprocket bolt and the sprocket itself. Tap the sprocket with a wooden or plastic mallet if necessary to break the taper.

23 Unbolt and remove the drivebelt backplate.

24 Slacken the cylinder head bolts, half a turn at a time at first, in the reverse of the tightening sequence (Fig. 1.19). Remove the bolts, lift off the head and recover the gasket.

25 For cylinder head dismantling, see Section 11.

26 Remove the crankshaft pulley bolt and pulley.

27 Unbolt and remove the injection pump sprocket.

28 Unbolt the water pump and remove it with its inlet connector (photo).

29 Unscrew the injection pump shaft nut to the end of the shaft. Remove the three nuts which secure the fuel injection pump to the timing case. Slacken, but do not remove, the bolts which secure the pump bracket to the block.

30 Break the taper fit between the pump shaft and the gear with the aid of a suitable puller. A stout metal bar, suitably drilled, can be used with two bolts and (if necessary) some spacers (photo). The bolts must be long enough to engage in a good portion of the threaded holes in the gear, but not so long as to pass right through.

31 Remove the puller and the shaft nut. Remove the fuel pump bracket bolts and withdraw the pump.

32 Unbolt and remove the timing cover; be prepared for oil spillage. Recover the gasket.

33 Remove the pump gear, unbolt and remove the idler gear, and pull the crankshaft gear off the crankshaft. Recover the drive pin if it is loose (photos).

34 Slacken the clutch pressure plate bolts a turn at a time. Make alignment marks, then remove the clutch pressure plate and driven plate.

35 Make alignment marks betwen the crankshaft and flywheel, then unbolt and remove the flywheel.

36 Unbolt and remove the sump. If possible, raise the engine to do this rather then inverting it, so that any sludge stays in the sump. Recover the sump gasket.

25.8 Two of the fuel filter bracket bolts (arrowed). There is a third bolt on the other side

25.28 Removing a water pump bolt. Other two bolts are arrowed

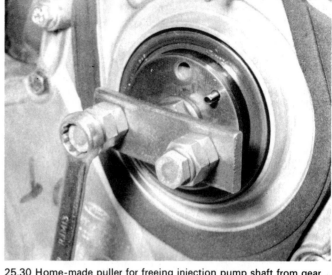

25.30 Home-made puller for freeing injection pump shaft from gear

25.33A Idler gear bolt (arrowed)

25.33B Removing the crankshaft gear – note drive pin and hole (arrowed)

37 Position the engine on its side so that both top and bottom faces are accessible.

38 Unbolt and remove the oil pump pick-up pipe, bracket and strainer. Recover the gasket.

39 Unbolt and remove the timing case complete with oil pump. Recover the case-to-block gasket and (if it did not come away with the injection pump) the case-to-pump gasket.

40 Unbolt and remove the crankshaft rear oil seal housing. Press out and discard the oil seal. Recover the gasket.

41 Inspect the connecting rod caps and the rods for identification marks or numbers. Make paint or punch marks if necessary so that the caps can be refitted to the same rods and the same way round.

42 Unbolt and remove the connecting rod caps, turning the crankshaft as necessary to gain access. Recover the bearing shells, keeping them with their caps if they are to be re-used (photo).

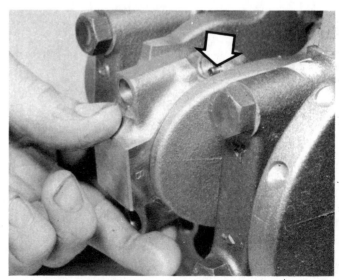

25.42 Removing a connecting rod cap. Note locating dowel (arrowed)

43 Push out the pistons and connecting rods through the top of the block. Refer to Section 18, paragraph 4. Keep the top half bearing shells with their rods if they are to be re-used.

44 Check that the main bearing caps are marked – they should each carry a number (1 to 5) and an arrow or triangle pointing towards the oil pump end of the engine. Make paint or punch marks if necessary.

45 Unbolt and remove the main bearing caps. Recover the lower half bearing shells, keeping them with their caps if they are to be re-used.

46 Lift out the crankshaft (photo). Do not drop it, it is heavy.

47 Recover the top half bearing shells, keeping them in order if they are to be re-used, and the two half thrust washers from No 3 main bearing.

48 If it is wished to remove the alternator bracket, a female Torx socket will be needed to deal with the special bolts which secure it. If some damage to the bolt heads can be accepted, a self-locking wrench can be used instead.

49 Dismantling of the engine is now complete.

25.46 Lifting out the crankshaft

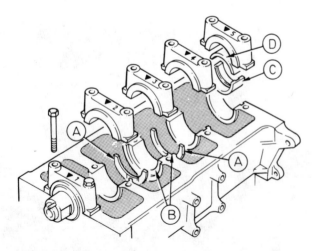

Fig. 1.42 Main bearing components (Sec 25)

A *Thrust washers*	C *Upper half shell (with*
B *Thrust washer seats*	*groove)*
	D *Lower half shell (plain)*

26 Examination and renovation – general

1 With the engine completely dismantled, all components should be cleaned and examined as detailed in the appropriate Sections of this Chapter.

2 Most components can be cleaned with rags, a soft brush (eg an old toothbrush) and paraffin or some other solvent. Do not immerse parts with oilways in solvent, since it can be very difficult to remove and if left may contaminate the oil. Probe oilways with a pipe cleaner or similar item, and blow through with compressed air if available.

3 When faced with a borderline decision as to whether to renew a particular part, take into consideration the expected future life of the engine and the degree of trouble or expense which will be caused if the part fails before the next overhaul.

4 If extensive overhauling is required, estimate the likely cost and compare it with the cost of a complete reconditioned engine. The difference may not be great, and the reconditioned engine will have a guarantee.

27 Engine components – examination and renovation

Cylinder block and bores
1 Clean out the nooks and crannies inside the block.

2 Remove plugs and covers, and clean their seats and threads. Expansion type plugs should be renewed whenever they are disturbed, so it is in order to remove them by destructive means – eg by drilling a hole in the middle of the plug, inserting a self-tapping screw and using the screw to pull out the plug.

3 Oil gallery plugs should be removed and the galleries blown through with compressed air. Coat the plug threads with sealant (to Ford spec SM 4G 4644 AA/AB) when refitting.

4 Smear sealant on expansion plug seating areas when fitting them. Tap the plug into position with the flat face of a hammer, then spread it by striking the centre a couple of times with a ball face hammer.

5 If cracks in the block are suspected, it may be necessary to have it crack tested professionally. There are various ways of doing this, some involving special dyes and chemicals, some using ultrasonic or electromagnetic radiation.

6 Bore wear is indicated by a wear ridge at the top, as previously mentioned. For accurate assessment a bore micrometer is required. A rougher measurement can be made by inserting feeler gauges between a piston (without rings) and the bore wall. Compare the clearance at the bottom of the bore, which should be unworn, with that just below the wear ridge. No wear limits are specified, but out-of-round or taper in excess of 0.1 mm (0.004 in) would normally be considered grounds for a rebore. Scuffs, scores and scratches should also be attended to.

7 If reboring is undertaken, it is normal practice for the machine shop to obtain the oversize pistons and rings at the same time.

8 Where the degree of wear does not justify a rebore, the fitting of proprietary oil control rings may be considered. Any improvement brought about by such rings may not last long, however.

Crankshaft and bearings
9 The crankshaft is another item which may need to be crack tested. Normally an uncracked crankshaft will 'ring' clearly if suspended from a cord and struck, while a cracked shaft will sound dull. This test is not infallible.

10 Examine the bearing shells for wear and scratches on the working surfaces. New shells should be fitted in any case, unless the old ones are obviously in perfect condition and are known to have covered only a nominal mileage. Refitting used shells is false economy.

11 Examine the bearing journals on the crankshaft for scoring or other damage, which if present will probably mean that regrinding or renewal is necessary. If a micrometer is available, measure the journals in several places to check for out-of-round and taper. No limits are specified, but typically 0.025 mm (0.001 in) is the maximum acceptable.

12 Note that the crankshaft may already have been reground, and that the makers only specify one stage of regrinding. Factory-reground crankshafts are indicated by green paint marks on No 1 crank web: a green line shows that the main bearing journals have been reground, a green spot shows the same for the big-end journals. The corresponding undersize bearing shells also carry a green mark.

13 Bearing running clearances can be measured by using Plastigage, which is a calibrated plastic filament. If several measurements are taken, out-of-round and taper can also be determined as an alternative to using a micrometer. Proceed as follows.

14 Fit the top half main bearing shells, clean and dry, to their seats in the block. Place the crankshaft on the shells. Put a thread of Plastigage along the journal to be measured. Fit the main bearing cap with its shell, again clean and dry, and secure it with the (old) bolts. Do not turn the crankshaft.

15 Tighten the main bearing cap bolts to the specified torque, then remove them. Carefully lift off the cap and bearing shell. The Plastigage will have been squashed more or less flat: by reading the width of the squashed strip against a calibrated scale, the clearance can be known (photo).

16 Scrape off the remains of the Plastigage and repeat the process on the other main bearings. Only one bearing cap should be fitted at a time when performing this check.

17 Big-end bearing clearances can be measured in the same way. They should be measured at the TDC position for the piston concerned, as this is where the most wear occurs.

18 As with the bearing shells, the thrust washers should normally be renewed as a matter of course. A crankshaft which has been factory machined to accept oversize thrust washers carries yellow lines on the centre webs. Oversize thrust washers also carry a yellow mark.

Pistons, piston rings and connecting rods

19 Remove the piston rings from a piston with the aid of some old feeler blades or similar thin metal strips (photo). Carefully spread the top ring just far enough to slide the blades in between the ring and the piston, then remove the ring and blades together. Be careful not to scratch the piston with the ends of the ring.

20 Repeat the process to remove the second and third rings, using the blades to stop the rings falling into the empty grooves. Always remove rings from the top of the piston. Keep each set of rings with its piston if the old rings are to be re-used.

21 Measure the end gaps of the rings by fitting them, one at a time, to their bores. Push the ring to the bottom (unworn) section of the bore with a piston to keep it square. Measure the end gap with feeler blades (photo) and compare it with that given in the Specifications. If the gap is too big, the ring is worn and should be renewed.

22 If renewing the rings, note that two sizes of 'standard' rings are available. The first size fits pistons of classes A and B, the second classes C and D (see Specifications and below). Refer to Section 18, paragraph 11, and deglaze the bores if new rings are fitted. Check the end gaps of the new rings before fitting, in case they are too tight. Careful filing or grinding of the ends of the ring will correct this.

23 Clean the pistons and inspect them for damage. Look for holes or dents in the crown, and for scores or other signs of picking-up on the sides. Scorch marks on the skirt show that blow-by has been occurring.

24 If the pistons pass this preliminary inspection, clean all the carbon out of the ring grooves using a piece of old piston ring. Protect your

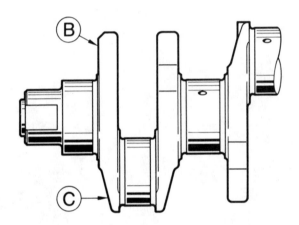

Fig. 1.43 Crankshaft undersize markings (Sec 27)

B   Main bearing undersize mark (line)
C   Big-end bearing undersize mark (spot)

27.15 Reading the width of a squashed Plastigage strip

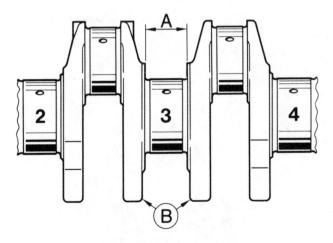

Fig. 1.44 Thrust washer oversize marking on crankshaft (Sec 27)

A   Centre main bearing width   B   Oversize marks (yellow lines)

27.19 Using a feeler blade for piston ring removal

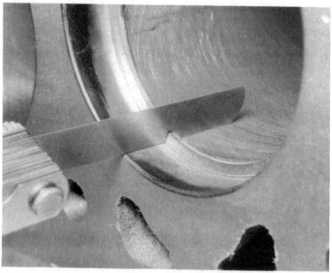

27.21 Measuring a piston ring end gap

fingers – piston rings are sharp. Do not remove any metal from the ring grooves or lands.

25 Roll each ring around its groove to check for tight spots, and check the vertical clearance of the rings in their grooves (photo). Excessive clearance which is not due to worn rings must be due to piston wear. Unless the pistons can be machined to accept special rings, renewal is required.

26 If renewing the pistons without reboring, ensure that pistons of the correct production class are obtained. The piston grade mark is stamped into the piston crown and a corresponding code mark on the cylinder block denotes the bore class (photos).

27 To separate a piston from its connecting rod, prise out the circlips and push out the gudgeon pin (photo). Hand pressure should be sufficient to remove the pin. Identify the piston so that it can be refitted to the correct rod.

28 Wear between the gudgeon pin and the connecting rod small-end bush can be cured by renewing both pin and bush. Bush renewal is a specialist job, however, because press facilities are required and because the new bush must be reamed accurately to fit the pin.

27.25 Checking the vertical clearance of a piston ring

27.26A Letter on crown denotes piston class ...

27.26B ... corresponding with bore class letters on block (at flywheel end)

27.27 Removing a gudgeon pin circlip

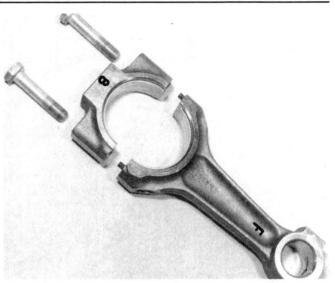

27.31 Connecting rod 'front' mark (F) and length class letter (B)

29 New gudgeon pins and circlips are supplied when purchasing new pistons of Ford manufacture. It is wise to renew the circlips in any case. If renewing the gudgeon pins separately from the pistons, note that they are graded by weight. Punch marks on the front of the pin denote the weight class, one mark being the lightest and six the heaviest. Only the lightest three grades are available as spares, and they must be fitted with the appropriate pistons as follows:

Piston Class	Gudgeon pin marks
A and B	3
C and D	2
E and F	1

30 The connecting rods themselves should not be in need of renewal unless seizure or some other major mechanical failure has occurred. Damage to the cap and bearing shell seats is possible if bearing failure was allowed to proceed to an advanced stage.

31 Four different lengths of connecting rod are supplied in production in order to equalise piston protrusion between the four cylinders. The length class is denoted by a letter stamped on the front (oil pump side) of the connecting rod cap (photo). The letter A denotes the shortest rod, D the longest. Unless there are good reasons for selecting a different length, and a supply of different length rods for experimentation, new rods should be of the same length class as those they replace.

32 Reassemble the pistons and rods. Make sure that the pistons are fitted the right way round – the arrow on the piston crown and the F (front) mark on the connecting rod must be on the same side. Oil and insert the gudgeon pins and secure with new circlips. The circlip gaps should be upwards. When assembled, the piston should pivot freely on the rod.

33 Fit the piston rings using the same technique as for removal. If the oil control ring was dismantled, reassembly it by inserting the wire into the spring; cover the spring join with the outer segment (photos). Observe the TOP markings on the two compression rings. Stagger the ring gaps evenly.

Oil pump
34 Refer to Section 17.

Timing case and gears
35 Inspect the timing case and cover for cracks and damage to the gasket mating faces.

36 Inspect the timing gears for damaged teeth. Check the fit of the crankshaft and injection pump gears on their shaft. Renew the gears if they are damaged.

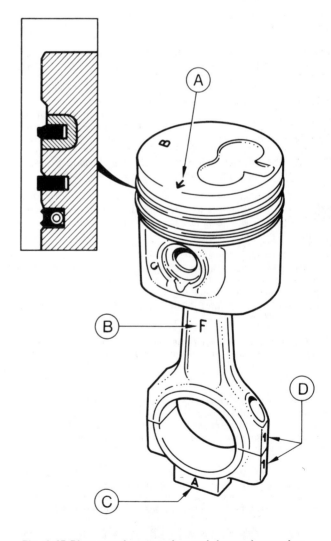

Fig. 1.45 Piston and connecting rod. Inset shows ring profiles (Sec 27)

A Arrow	C Length class mark
B Front mark	D Cylinder number

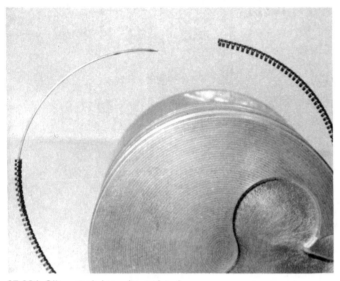

27.33A Oil control ring wire and spring

27.33B Fitting the oil control ring outer segment

37 Spin the idler gear on its bearing and check for roughness. The bearing can be renewed separately from the idler gear if necessary (photo).

Camshaft drivebelt and sprockets

38 Inspect the drivebelt for cracks, fraying, broken teeth (especially at the roots) and contamination. It is as well to renew the belt in any case at time of major overhaul.

39 Spin the drivebelt tensioner wheel on its bearing to check for roughness. Renew the tensioner complete if the bearing is in poor condition.

40 Inspect the sprockets for any signs of damage, paying particular attention to the teeth. Clean off any oil or other contamination. Renew damaged sprockets.

Cylinder head and camshaft

41 Refer to Section 11 for examination and renovation procedures.

42 If it is wished to remove the oil gallery plugs, of which there are many, refer to paragraph 3 of this Section. For expansion plugs see paragraphs 2 and 4.

43 Check that the lubrication jet for the vacuum pump plunger and cam is clear. Remove the plug and blow through the jet if necessary (photo).

Flywheel

44 Examine the clutch mating surface of the flywheel for scoring or cracks. Light grooving or scoring may be ignored. Surface cracks or deep groving can sometimes be removed by specialist machining, provided not too much metal is taken off; otherwise the flywheel must be renewed.

45 Inspect the starter ring gear for damaged or missing teeth. A damaged ring gear can be renewed separately. The average DIY mechanic may prefer to leave the job to a Ford dealer or other competent workshop; for the enthusiast the procedure is as follows.

46 Drill two adjacent holes, 7 or 8 mm (say 0.3 in) in diameter, through the ring gear as shown (Fig. 1.46). Take care not to drill into the flywheel.

47 Knock the ring gear off the flywheel with a hammer. Use light blows, evenly spaced around the ring.

27.37 Idler gear and bearing

27.43 Lubrication jet (arrowed) for vacuum pump plunger and cam

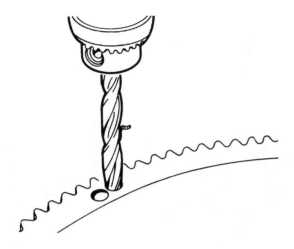

Fig. 1.46 Drilling holes in the ring gear (Sec 27)

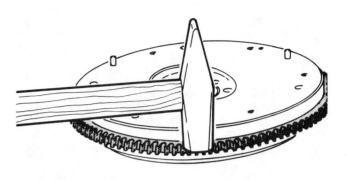

Fig. 1.47 Driving the ring gear off the flywheel (Sec 27)

48 Heat the new ring gear evenly to between 260° and 280°C (500° and 536°F). This is just about within the capacity of most domestic ovens. Take care not to overheat the ring gear or its temper will be lost.

49 Using tongs or asbestos gloves, place the ring gear on the flywheel and tap it into place. Allow it to cool naturally.

50 If renewing the flywheel, transfer the clutch locating dowels.

Miscellaneous
51 The makers recommend that the following bolts be renewed whenever they have been slackened:

    (a) *Flywheel securing*
    (b) *Main bearing cap*
    (c) *Connecting rod cap*
    (d) *Crankshaft pulley*
    (e) *Cylinder head*

52 Renew the driveshaft circlips.

29 Engine – complete reassembly

1 Position the block for access to the bottom end. Wipe clean the main bearing shell seats in the block.

2 Wipe any protective coating off new bearing shells. Fit the top half main bearing shells (with the oil groove) to their seats. All the shells are the same except for No 1, which is narrower. Make sure that the tangs on the shells engage in the recesses in the seats (photo).

3 Fit the thrust washers on both sides of No 3 main bearing, grooved side outwards. Use a smear of grease to hold them in position (photo).

4 Lubricate the top half shells and lower the crankshaft into position. Inject oil into the crankshaft oilways.

5 Fit the bottom half main bearing shells to their caps. These shells are all plain, except for No 1 which is grooved. Make sure that the locating tangs and recesses align. Oil the shells.

6 Fit the main bearing caps and shells over the crankshaft. Make sure that each cap is fitted in its correct position and the right way round (arrow or triangle pointing to the oil pump end).

28 Engine reassembly – general

1 Before commencing reassembly, make sure that all parts are clean and that the new components required have been obtained. A full set of oil seals and gaskets must be purchased. (For selection of the correct head gasket, refer to the next Section).

2 Besides the critical area bolts listed in the previous Section, renew any nuts, bolts or studs with damaged threads.

3 A full set of hand tools will be needed, including a dial test indicator and stand. A squirt type oil can, filled with clean engine oil, should be used to lubricate working parts.

4 Small quantities of grease, thread locking compound, anti-seize compound and various types of sealant will be called for.

5 Have available a good quantity of clean lint-free rags for wiping excess oil off hands and engine parts.

6 If not already done, obtain or construct the tools needed for setting the valve timing – see Section 9.

29.2 Fitting a main bearing shell to the block

29.3 Thrust washer fitted to No 3 bearing – grooves (arrowed) face outwards

29.7 Tightening a main bearing cap bolt using a torque wrench

7   Insert new bolts, with threads oiled, to secure the main bearing caps. Tighten the bolts to the Stage 1 specified torque (photo) making sure that the front of No 1 bearing cap is aligned with the front of the block (Fig. 1.48).

8   Check that the crankshaft rotates freely. Some stiffness is to be expected with new shells, but there must be no tight spots or binding.

9   Check the crankshaft endfloat, levering it back and forth and measuring the movement with a dial test indicator or feeler blades (photo).

10 When satisfied that the crankshaft fitting is correct, tighten the main bearing cap bolts through the angle specified for Stage 2 tightening. Use a protractor or marked card if necessary to indicate the angle (photo). Once the bolts have been tightened like this, they must be renewed if they are slackened again.

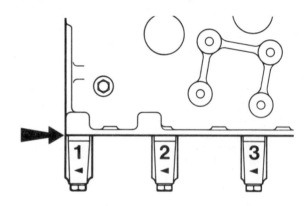

Fig. 1.48 Bearing cap must be flush with block at point arrowed (Sec 29)

29.9 Checking crankshaft endfloat

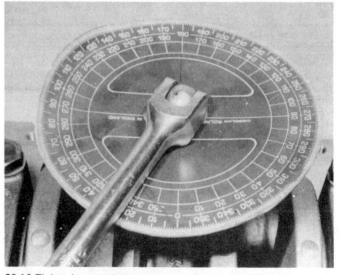

29.10 Tightening a main bearing cap bolt through a given angle

11 Check again that the crankshaft is free to rotate, then position the block to receive the pistons.

12 Lay out the assembled pistons and rods with their bearing shells and new cap bolts. Stagger the piston ring gaps equally.

13 Wipe any protective grease off the new bearing shells, then fit them to the rods and caps so that the locating tangs engage in the grooves.

14 Lubricate the bores, pistons, crankpins and shells. Fit a piston ring compressor to one piston. Offer the piston to its bore, making sure that it is the right way round (arrow on piston crown, and F mark on connecting rod, both facing the oil pump end of the engine).

15 Tap the piston through the ring compressor and into the bore using a hammer handle or similar item. Release the ring compressor as the piston enters the bore (photo).

16 Guide the connecting rod onto the crankpin, taking care not to scratch the bearing surface. Check also that the bearing shell is not displaced. Fit the connecting rod cap with its shell, making sure that it is the right way round.

17 Oil the threads of two new connecting rod cap bolts. Insert the bolts and tighten them to the Stage 1 specified torque.

18 Check that the crankshaft is still free to rotate, then tighten the bolts through the angles specified for Stages 2 and 3. Once the bolts have been tightened like this, they must be renewed if they are slackened again.

19 Repeat the operations to fit the other pistons, then stand the engine on the head mating face. Use a couple of blocks to keep the weight off the dowels.

20 Fit the crankshaft rear oil seal housing, using a new gasket. Insert the three retaining bolts, smearing their threads with sealant to Ford spec SM 4G 4644 AA/AB. Wipe off surplus sealant (photo).

21 Align the seal housing with the sump mating face (photo), then tighten the housing retaining bolts to the specified torque. Lubricate a new oil seal and fit it, lips inwards, to the seal housing – see Section 13 for details.

22 If the alternator bracket was removed, refit it now, otherwise there will be a problem with access to one of its retaining bolts (photo).

29.15 Tapping a piston through the ring compressor and into the bore

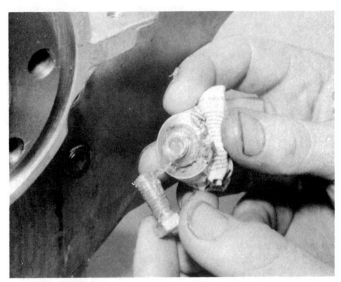

29.20 Applying sealant to a rear oil seal housing bolt

29.21 Checking the alignment of the seal housing and block sump mating faces

29.22 Refitting a stud to the timing case – it had to be removed for access to the alternator bracket bolt (arrowed)

23 Fit the timing case with oil pump, using a new gasket (photo). Turn the oil pump flats to engage with those on the crankshaft. The centring spigot on the oil pump must enter the main bearing bore.

24 Fit the seven bolts which secure the timing case to the block. Align the sump mating faces on the timing case with those on the block to within 0.1 mm (0.004 in), then tighten the bolts to the specified torque.

25 Fit the oil pump pick-up pipe, bracket and strainer, using a new gasket. Fit the securing bolts and tighten them to the specified torque (photos).

26 Trim off any excess gasket, then apply non-setting jointing compound to the areas shown in Fig. 1.32 (photos).

27 Position a new sump gasket on the block. Fit the sump and secure it with the four corner bolts, but only tighten them finger tight (photo).

28 Insert the remaining 12 bolts and tighten them to the specified torque (photo), then tighten the four corner bolts to the specified torque.

29.23A Timing case gasket fitted to block

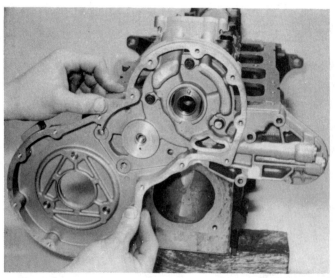

29.23B Fitting the timing case

29.25A New gasket fitted to oil pump pick-up flange

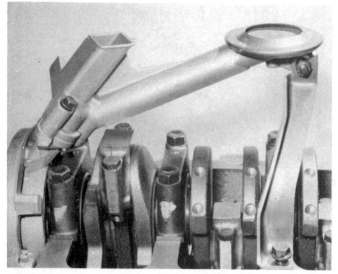

29.25B Oil pump pick-up pipe, bracket and strainer in position

29.26A Trimming off excess gasket

29.26B Applying jointing compound to one of the critical sealing areas

29.27 Fitting the sump

29.28 Tightening a sump bolt

29 Stand the engine on the sump and chock it securely.

30 Fit the flywheel and secure it with new bolts. Tighten the bolts in three stages as specified.

31 Fit the clutch driven plate, making sure that it is the right way round (photo), and secure it by fitting the pressure plate over it. Tighten the pressure plate bolts finger tight.

32 Centre the driven plate (photo) and tighten the pressure plate bolts progressively to the specified torque. Refer to Chapter 4 Specifications.

33 Fit the fuel injection pump and bracket, using a new gasket. Only tighten its nuts and bolts finger tight.

34 Refit the crankshaft gear drive pin (if removed) and the gear. Turn the crankshaft to bring Nos 1 and 4 pistons to TDC.

29.31 Clutch driven plate marking

29.32 Using a proprietary alignment tool to centre the clutch driven plate

29.35A Crankshaft and idler gears fitted with dots adjacent

29.35B Tightening the idler gear bolt

35 Lubricate the idler gear bearing. Fit the gear and bearing, with the narrower segment of the gear inwards and the dots on the gears adjacent (the dot on the idler gear is the one between two teeth) (photo). If a washer was fitted under the idler gear bolt head, discard it.

Fit the bolt, with dry threads, and tighten it to the specified torque.
36 Fit the Woodruff key to the pump shaft. Turn the shaft as necessary and fit the pump gear so that its dot aligns with the other dot on the idler gear. Prise the idler gear segments into line using a screwdriver,

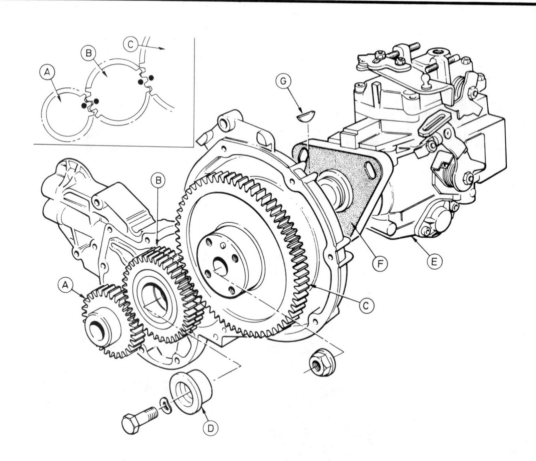

Fig. 1.49 Timing gears and associated components. Inset shows correct alignment of dots (Sec 29)

| A   Crankshaft gear | C   Pump gear | E   Fuel injection pump | G   Woodruff key |
| B   Idler gear | D   Bush | F   Gasket | H   Washer (discard if fitted) |

29.36 Prising the idler gear teeth into alignment to allow meshing of the pump gear. Again, dots are adjacent

29.37 Tightening the pump shaft nut

and slide the pump gear into mesh with the narrower segment (photo). Do not use force.

37 Apply sealant to the injection pump shaft threads. Before it sets, fit the pump shaft nut. Jam the flywheel and tighten the pump shaft nut to the specified torque (photo).

38 Refit the timing cover, using a new gasket (photo). Secure it with the 15 bolts, tightened to the specified torque. The three longer bolts go at the top.

39 Lubricate the lips of a new oil seal and fit it, lips inwards, over the nose of the crankshaft gear. Seat the seal with a tube or large socket.

40 Similarly fit a new oil seal to the front of the injection pump gear. If available, use Ford tool No 21 – 111 to seat the seal; otherwise use a tube or socket. Refer also to Section 13.

41 Refit the water pump and inlet connector, using new gaskets. Refer to Chapter 2, Section 12.

42 Refit the injection pump sprocket, making sure that the locating pin engages correctly. Fit the bolts and tighten them to the specified torque.

43 Fit the crankshaft pulley. Oil the threads and contact face of a new pulley bolt. Fit the bolt, jam the flywheel and tighten the bolt to the Stage 1 specified torque.

44 The piston protrusion must now be checked in order to determine the required thickness of head gasket. Proceed as follows.

45 Turn the crankshaft to bring two pistons to TDC. Position a dial test indicator on the block and zero the indicator on the gasket mating face (photo).

46 Transfer the indicator plunger to the crown of one of the pistons, at a point approximately 5 mm (0.2 in) from the edge of the piston and on the gudgeon pin axis. Slowly turn the crankshaft back and forth past TDC, noting the highest reading on the indicator. Record this reading (photo).

47 Repeat this measurement procedure, first on the opposite edge of the same piston, then taking two measurements on each of the other pistons. Record all the readings.

29.38 Timing cover gasket in position

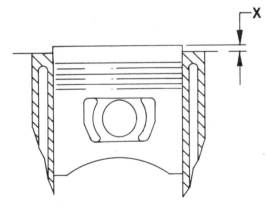

Fig. 1.50 Piston protrusion (X) must be measured to determine head gasket thickness (Sec 29)

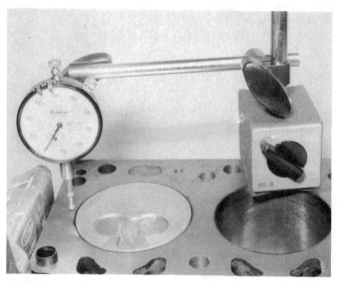

29.45 Zero the dial test indicator on the block

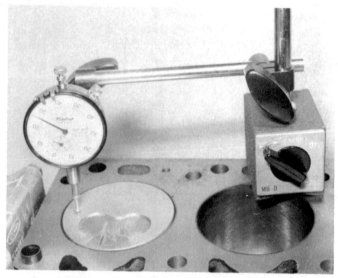

29.46 Measuring piston protrusion with the dial test indicator

48 The largest of the eight readings should be used to determine the required thickness of head gasket. See Specifications for details.

49 If a dial test indicator is not available, piston protrusion may be measured using a straight-edge and feeler blades (photo). This method is inevitably less accurate and cannot be recommended.

50 Turn the crankshaft to align the timing mark on the injection pump sprocket with the pip on the timing cover.

51 Make sure that the head gasket mating faces are clean and dry. Fit the selected gasket, the right way up, over the dowels on the cylinder block.

52 Lower the assembled cylinder head onto the block.

53 Insert the new head bolts and tighten them progressively to the Stage 1 specified torque, following the sequence in Fig. 1.19.

54 In the same sequence, tighten the bolts to the Stage 2 specified torque.

55 Wait at least two minutes, then tighten the bolts through the angle specified for Stage 3, following the same sequence. No further tightening is required. (If preferred, this final tightening can be left until after refitting the engine, since it is difficult to restrain the engine on the bench. In this case, do not refit the camshaft cover until the bolts have been tightened).

56 Fit the belt backplate and secure it with the two bolts; use a little sealant on the bolt threads.

57 Fit the drivebelt tensioner, but do not tighten its pivot bolt yet.

58 Fit the camshaft sprocket. Insert the securing bolt and washer, but only tighten it finger tight at this stage. The sprocket must still be able to move on its taper.

59 Position the camshaft by means of the setting tool – see Section 9.

60 Turn the crankshaft clockwise to TDC, No 1 firing. Refer to Section 9 again if necessary.

61 Fit the camshaft drivebelt and tension it as described in Section 6, paragraphs 13 to 17.

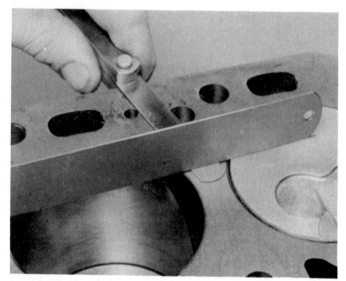

29.49 Measuring piston protrusion using a straight-edge and feeler blades

62 Check the valve clearances (if not already done) as described in Section 7. Adjust if necessary.

63 Turn the crankshaft so that the vacuum pump cam lobe is pointing away from the pump. Insert the vacuum pump lower bolt and screw it in a few turns. Fit a new O-ring to the vacuum pump and slide its slotted fixing hole onto the lower bolt. Fit the upper bolt, make sure that the O-ring is still correctly located, then tighten both bolts evenly.

64 Fit the vacuum pump oil return hose.

65 Refit the camshaft cover, using a new gasket, sealing strip and plug. Locate the washers and reinforcing strips correctly and tighten the bolts to the specified torque.

66 Refit the crankcase ventilation hoses and the dipstick tube.

67 Fit the thermostat housing and connecting pipe, using a new gasket and new pipe seals. Make sure that the gasket is the right way round – see Chapter 2, Section 13. Secure the dipstick tube bracket to the thermostat housing.

68 Refit the glow plugs and their bus bar – see Chapter 3, Section 14.

69 Refit the fuel injectors, using new heat shields. See Chapter 3, Section 10.

70 Refit the injection pipe as described in Chapter 3, Section 9.

71 Fit the fuel return hoses to the injectors and to the pump. Make sure that a blanking cap is fitted to the spare return connector on No 4 injector.

72 Refit the fuel filter and its bracket. Tighten the bracket bolts to the specified torque.

73 Reconnect the fuel supply line to the fuel injection pump.

74 Grease the sealing ring of a new oil filter. Fit the filter and tighten it by hand only – see Section 4. Refit the dipstick.

75 Refit the oil level sensor, when applicable.

76 Refit the alternator and its drivebelt. Tension the drivebelt as described in Chapter 2, Section 11.

77 Slacken the crankshaft pulley bolt, then jam the flywheel and retighten the bolt to the Stage 1 specified torque (photo).

78 Check the security of the flywheel jamming arrangement. Have an assistant restrain the engine, then tighten the pulley bolt through the angle specified for Stage 2 (photo). A long extension bar, and a strong assistant, will be needed. See also Section 13, paragraphs 34 and 40.

79 Check the fuel injection pump timing as described in Chapter 3, Section 7.

80 Refit the camshaft drivebelt cover.

81 Fit the exhaust manifold, using a new gasket. Use a little anti-seize compound on the nuts and bolts. Tighten the nuts and bolts as described in Chapter 3, Section 17.

82 Rebuilding of the engine is now complete.

30 Engine – refitting to transmission

1 Make sure that the clutch driven plate is accurately centred, otherwise the transmission input shaft will not enter. Put a smear of grease on the input shaft splines.

2 Fit the split backplate behind the flywheel and engage it on the dowels.

3 Offer the transmission to the engine, rocking it slightly if necessary until the input shaft enters the clutch. Push the transmission home until it is engaged on the dowels – do not allow it to hang on the input shaft.

4 Insert the engine-to-transmission bolts and nip them up.

5 Fit the starter motor and tighten its mounting bolts.

6 Fit the flywheel cover plate and secure it with the two nuts.

7 Tighten the remaining engine-to-transmission bolts.

31 Engine and transmission – refitting

1 Position the engine/transmission unit under the engine bay. Attach the lifting tackle and carefully raise the unit into position.

2 Reattach the engine/transmission mountings to the body. On Escort/Orion models, also refit the anti-roll bar brackets, with anti-roll bar and track control arms attached.

29.77 Jamming the flywheel using a bolt and a piece of scrap metal in the ring gear

29.78 Tightening the crankshaft pulley bolt

3 Tighten the engine/transmission mounting nuts and and bolts, and the anti-roll bar bracket bolts when applicable, then remove the lifting tackle.

4 Reconnect the starter motor main cable and command lead.

5 Fit new circlips to the driveshafts (photo).

6 Remove the plugs securing the differential gears. Carefully insert the right-hand driveshaft into the transmission. Push it in by applying pressure to the right-hand front roadwheel until the circlip engages (photo).

7 Refit the right-hand track control arm (and on Fiesta models, the tie-bar and bracket). Secure the balljoint.

8 Similarly refit the left-hand driveshaft, track control arm and associated components.

9 If the gearshift linkage and stabiliser were unbolted from the floor, move them back into position. Refit the nuts but do not tighten them yet.

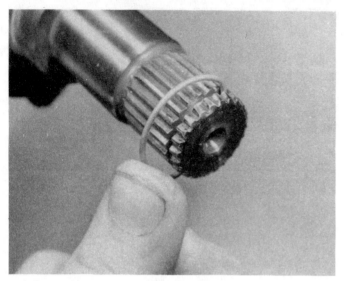

31.5 Fitting a new circlip to the driveshaft

31.6 Fitting a driveshaft to the transmission

10 Bolt the gearshift stabiliser to the transmission. Remember to fit the washer between them.

11 Tighten the nuts which secure the gearshift linkage to the floor, if applicable.

12 Attach the gearshift rod to the transmission selector shaft. Observe the alignment marks made when dismantling, or adjust from scratch as follows.

13 Have an assistant hold the gear lever in the reverse gear position. Lock the lever in this position by passing Ford tool 16 – 032, or an equivalent pin or bar, through the hole in the gear lever under-casing (photo). Use another pin to turn the selector shaft clockwise (viewed from front of vehicle) as far as the stop, push the shaft into the transmission, then tighten the shift rod clamp bolt. Remove the drift and locking tool.

14 Refit the front part of the exhaust system, using a new gasket at the manifold flange. Apply a little anti-seize compound to the nuts and bolts.

15 Reconnect the clutch and speedometer cables to the transmission.

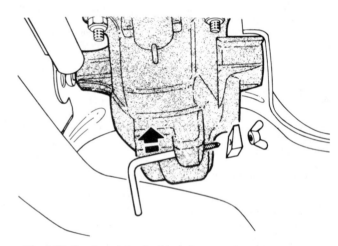

Fig. 1.51 Ford tool for locking the gear lever in reverse
(Sec 31)

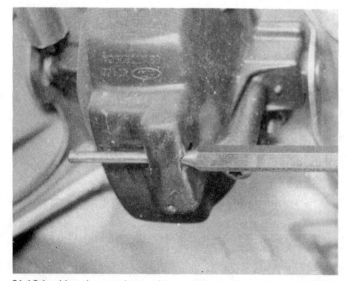

31.13 Locking the gear lever with a suitable rod – in this case a pin punch

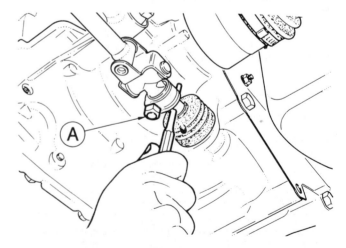

Fig. 1.52 Using a pin punch to turn the selector shaft
(Sec 31)

A   Clamp bolt

16 Reconnect the engine electrical services as follows:

   (a) Reversing light switch
   (b) Oil level sensor (when fitted)
   (c) Injection pump fuel shut-off solenoid and cold start device
   (d) Glow plug feed
   (e) Fan thermoswitch
   (f) Oil pressure switch
   (g) Temperature gauge sender
   (h) Alternator

17 If it was not done on the bench, tighten the cylinder head bolts through the final stage and refit the camshaft cover.

18 Reconnect the transmission earth strap.

19 Reconnect the vacuum pipe to the vacuum pump.

20 Reconnect the fuel feed and return pipes at the filter and pump or at the bulkhead, as appropriate.

21 Reconnect the throttle cable to the injection pump. See Chapter 3, Section 15.

22 Refit the radiator and cooling fan, if they were removed.

23 Refit the coolant hoses to the radiator, thermostat housing, water pump and cylinder head.

24 Refill the cooling system as described in Chapter 2, Section 6.

25 Refill the transmission with the specified quantity and grade of oil.

26 Refill the engine with the specified quantity and grade of oil.

27 Fit a new air cleaner element as described in Chapter 3, Section 3.

28 Refit any drivebelt splash shields, transmissions shields etc.

29 Refit the bonnet if it was removed.

30 Check that nothing has been overlooked, then reconnect the battery earth lead.

31 Refer to Section 32 before starting the engine.

32 Engine – initial start-up after overhaul

1 Check that oil, fuel and coolant have all been replenished and that the battery is well charged.

2 If a new injection pump has been fitted, prime it as described in Chapter 3, Section 8.

3 Start the engine in the usual way. Considerable cranking may be necessary to bleed the fuel system before the engine starts. See also Chapter 3, Section 9.

4 Once the engine starts, keep it running at a fast tickover. Check that the oil pressure light goes out, then check for leaks of oil, fuel and coolant.

5 If all is well, continue to run the engine until operating temperature is reached, denoted by the cooling fan cutting in.

6 Adjust the idle speed as described in Chapter 3, Section 5.

7 Stop the engine and check again for leaks of vital fluids.

8 Tighten the exhaust system connection if necessary, being careful to avoid burns if the system is very hot.

9 Check oil and coolant levels and top up if necessary.

10 If many new parts have been fitted, the engine should be treated as new and run in at reduced speeds and loads for the first 600 miles (1000 km) or so. After this mileage it is beneficial to change the engine oil and oil filter.

11 There is no need to tighten the cylinder head bolts further after the running-in period, but the valve clearances should be checked as described in Section 7.

33 Compression test – description and interpretation

1 A compression test involves measuring the pressure developed in each cylinder when the engine is being cranked by the starter motor. It can be a valuable aid in fault diagnosis. A special compression tester will be needed, with an adaptor to connect it to a glow plug hole. Rather than buy such a tester it may be cheaper to let a Ford dealer or other specialist do the test.

2 The engine must be at normal operating temperature, the battery well charged and the valve clearances correct.

3 Disconnect the glow plug relay, then remove the glow plug bus bar and the glow plugs themselves. Refer to Chapter 3, Section 14 if necessary.

4 Disconnect the fuel injection pump fuel shut-off solenoid.

5 Screw the compression tester adaptor into one of the glow plug holes. Crank the engine on the starter and record the maximum pressure indicated on the tester.

6 Repeat the operations on the other three cylinders and record the pressures developed.

7 Compare the pressures with those given in the Specifications. Absolute values are not so significant as variation between cylinders.

8 A low reading in one cylinder may be due to burnt or poorly seating valves, to piston/bore wear, to a blown head gasket or a cracked head. With petrol engines it is normal to introduce a teaspoon of oil into a low-reading cylinder: if this improves the compression temporarily, worn pistons or bores are indicated. Be wary of using this diagnostic aid on a Diesel engine, since there is much less combustion chamber space at TDC and a hydraulic lock may be caused.

9 A low reading obtained for two adjacent cylinders suggests strongly that the head gasket has blown between them.

10 Further tests (eg leakdown and cooling system pressure tests) may be needed to determine the likely causes of poor compression.

11 When the tests are complete, refit and reconnect the glow plugs, glow plug relay and fuel shut-off solenoid.

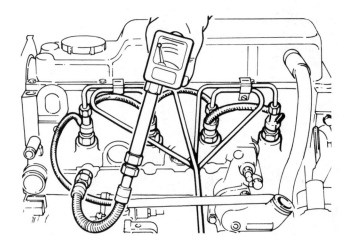

Fig. 1.53 Compression tester screwed into a glow plug hole (Sec 33)

34 Fault diagnosis – engine

Faults in the fuel injection system can produce noises suggesting imminent bearing failure. To locate such a fault, slacken each injector union in turn with the engine running. The noise will disappear when the union on the faulty injector is slackened. Air or other contaminants in the fuel can also cause knocking noises.

Symptom	Reason(s)
Engine fails to turn when starter operated	Battery discharged or defective Battery terminals corroded or connections loose Starter solenoid connections loose Engine/transmission earth strap loose or broken Starter solenoid or switch defective Starter motor defective Major mechanical failure (seizure)
Engine turns normally but will not start	Fuel tank empty Incorrect starting procedure Pump fuel shut-off solenoid disconnected or defective Wax in fuel (in cold conditions only) Camshaft drivebelt broken Valve timing incorrect Injection pump timing incorrect Poor compression (see below) Other fuel system fault (see Chapter 3) Exhaust system blocked
Engine idles unevenly	Fuel system fault (see Chapter 3) Valve clearances incorrect Valve timing incorrect Valve(s) sticking or burnt Valve spring(s) broken Blown head gasket
Poor compression	Valve clearances incorrect (too small) Valve(s) sticking or burnt Valve spring(s) broken Head gasket blown Piston/bores worn or damaged Head or block cracked
Lack of power	Poor compression (see above) Injection timing incorrect Other fuel system fault (see Chapter 3) Valve timing incorrect Serious overheating (see Chapter 2) Exhaust system restricted Air cleaner clogged Brakes binding
Oil consumption excessive	Incorrect oil level or grade Crankcase ventilation hoses blocked or perished Valve stem-to-guide clearance excessive, or seals damaged Pistons/bores worn or damaged External leakage
Unusual noises	Valve clearances incorrect Worn valvegear Peripheral component fault (eg water pump or alternator) Worn or damaged alternator/water pump drivebelt Worn or damaged camshaft drivebelt Piston ring(s) broken Piston slap (worst when cold) Big-end bearings worn (worst when off load) Main bearings worn (worst when on load) Fuel injection fault (see Chapter 3)
Excessive smoke in exhaust	Oil being burnt (blue smoke) Fuel system fault (white or black smoke) – see Chapter 3

Chapter 2 Cooling system

For modifications, and information applicable to later models, see Supplement at end of manual

Contents

Specifications

General
System type .... Water-based coolant. Sealed, pressurized system, pump circulation
Blow-off pressure .... 1.0 bar (14.5 lbf/in²)
Test pressure .... 1.4 bar (20.3 lbf/in²) for 10 sec

Coolant
Type/specification .... Soft water, and antifreeze to Ford spec SSM 97B 9103 A (Duckhams Universal Antifreeze and Summer Coolant)

Capacity:
    Fiesta .... 8.5 litres (15.0 pints) approx
    Escort and Orion .... 9.3 litres (16.4 pints) approx
Recommended concentration of antifreeze .... 45% by volume
Protection at recommended concentration:
    Slush point .... −31°C (−24°F)
    Solidifying point .... −38°C (−36°F)
Specific gravity at recommended concentration (without other additives) 1.065

Thermostat
Type .... Wax
Opening commences .... 86° to 90° (187° to 194°F)
Fully open temperature .... 100°C (212°F)
Tolerance on above temperature for used thermostat .... ± 3°C (5°F)

Radiator fan
Type .... Electric, controlled by thermoswitch
Thermoswitch location .... Thermostat elbow

Water pump
Type .... Centrifugal
Drive .... V-belt from crankshaft pulley
Drivebelt tension (using tension gauge):
    New .... 350 to 450 N (79 to 101 lbf)
    Used .... 250 to 350 N (56 to 79 lbf)

Torque wrench settings

	Nm	lbf ft
Water pump to block	20 to 25	15 to 18
Water pump pulley	7 to 10	5 to 7
Thermostat housing to head	18 to 22	13 to 16
Water pump hose connector	10	7
Cylinder head hose connectors:		
Exhaust side	10	7
Pulley side	20	15
Drain plug (in block)	19 to 25	14 to 18
Radiator mountings	7 to 10	5 to 7
Fan motor to shroud	8 to 10	6 to 7
Shroud to radiator	7 to 10	5 to 7

1 General description

The cooling system is sealed and pressurized, as is now general practice. Water-based coolant is circulated round the block and cylinder head by a belt-driven pump. When the temperature of the coolant reaches a certain value, a thermostat opens to allow circulation through the radiator, where heat is lost to the air. Coolant also flows through the heater matrix to provide a source of heat for the driver and passengers.

Essential to the operation of the system is the expansion or header tank. This tank provides a reservoir to allow for expansion and contraction of the coolant with changes in temperature. It also incorporates a filler/pressure relief valve cap. Air or gas bubbles which form in the coolant escape via the expansion tank, having been conducted there by vent hoses.

The radiator is of the crossflow type, with plastic side tanks. Normally, sufficient cooling is provided by airflow resulting from the vehicle's forward motion. If the coolant temperature exceeds a certain

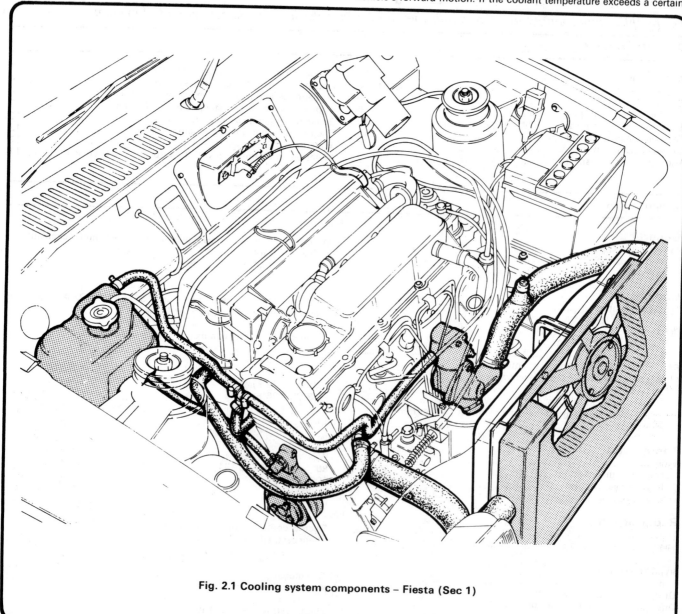

Fig. 2.1 Cooling system components – Fiesta (Sec 1)

Fig. 2.2 Cooling system components – Escort/Orion (Sec 1)

value, a thermoswitch brings an electric fan into operation to increase radiator cooling.

2 Maintenance and inspection

1   Weekly, every 250 miles (400 km) or before a long journey, check the coolant level by inspecting the expansion tank. The tank is translucent, so the level can be verified without removing the cap. The level should be between the MAX and MIN marks; if it is below the MIN mark, proceed as follows.

2   **Take great care to avoid scalding if the system is hot.** Place a thick cloth over the expansion tank cap and turn the cap anti-clockwise as far as the first stop. Wait for any steam to be released, then depress the cap, turn it further anti-clockwise and remove it completely.

3   Top up to the MAX mark using antifreeze mixture of the correct type and concentration – see Section 14. In an emergency plain water may be used, but this will dilute the antifreeze remaining in the system. Do not add cold water to an overheated engine, or damage may result.

Fig. 2.3 Expansion tank MAX mark (arrowed) – Fiesta (Sec 2)

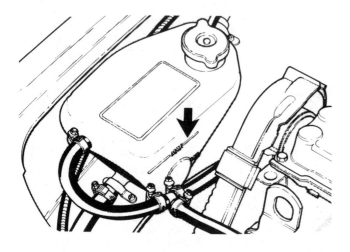

Fig. 2.4 Expansion tank MAX mark (arrowed) – Escort/Orion (Sec 2)

4   Refit the expansion tank cap when the level is correct. Check for leaks if frequent topping-up is required. Normally loss from this type of system is minimal.

5   At every major service interval, inspect all coolant hoses and hose clips for security and good condition. Renew damaged or defective hoses without delay.

6   At alternate major service intervals, check the condition and tension of the water pump/alternator drivebelt. Refer to Section 11 for details.

7   Every two years or 36 000 miles (60 000 km), drain the cooling system, flush it if necessary and refill with new coolant. Refer to Sections 4, 5, 6 and 14. At the same time consider renewing the

coolant hoses and the water pump/alternator drivebelt on a preventive basis.

8   It is prudent to check the antifreeze concentration at the beginning of winter if the coolant is not due for renewal. Checking is done using a special hydrometer which is possessed by most garages.

3   Pressure test – description and interpretation

1   In cases where leakage is difficult to trace, or some other malfunction of the cooling system is suspected, a pressure test can prove helpful. The test involves pressurising the system by means of a hand pump and an adaptor which is fitted to the expansion tank in place of the filler cap. The resourceful home mechanic may be able to improvise something from (eg) a spare filler cap and tyre inflation equipment; alternatively, the test can be performed by a Ford dealer or most other garages.

2   Bring the engine to normal operating temperature, then switch it off.

3   Place a thick cloth over the expansion tank cap. Turn the cap anti-clockwise to the first stop and wait for any pressure to be released. Depress the cap and turn it further anti-clockwise to remove it. Take care to avoid scalding.

4   Connect the pressure test equipment to the expansion tank filler hole. Apply the specified test pressure and check that it is held for at least ten seconds. If the pressure drops within ten seconds, check for leaks. Release the pressure and disconnect the equipment.

5   Besides leaks from hoses, pressure can also be lost through leaks in the radiator and heater matrix. A blown head gasket, or a cracked head or block, can give rise to 'invisible' leakage. Usually there are other clues to this condition, such as coolant contamination of the oil or combustion gases entering the coolant.

6   The condition of the filler/pressure relief valve cap must not be overlooked. Normally it is tested with similar equipment to that used for the pressure test. The blow-off pressure is given in the Specifications, and is also usually stamped on the cap. Renew the cap if it will not hold the specified pressure, or if its condition is otherwise doubtful.

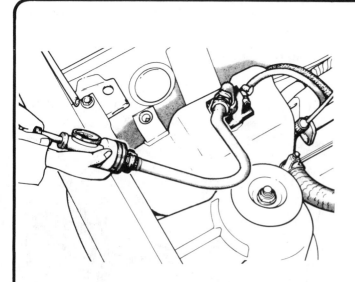

Fig. 2.5 Pressure testing the cooling system (Sec 3)

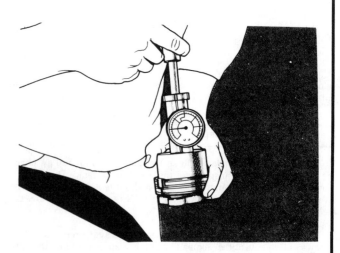

Fig. 2.6 Testing the blow-off pressure of the expansion tank cap (Sec 3)

4 Cooling system – draining

1 Disconnect the battery earth lead.

2 Place a thick cloth over the expansion tank cap. Turn the cap anti-clockwise as far as the first stop and wait for any pressure to be released, then depress it and turn it further anti-clockwise to remove it. Take care to avoid scalding.

3 Position a drain tray beneath the radiator. (Use a clean tray if the coolant is to be salvaged.) Slacken the radiator drain plug, located at the bottom left-hand corner, until coolant flows out (photo). Do not remove the drain plug. Take care to avoid scalding if the coolant is hot.

4 When draining from the radiator is complete, move the tray under the engine and remove the block drain plug, located near the dipstick tube (photo). Allow the coolant to drain from the block.

5 Close or refit the drain plugs now so that they are not lost or forgotten.

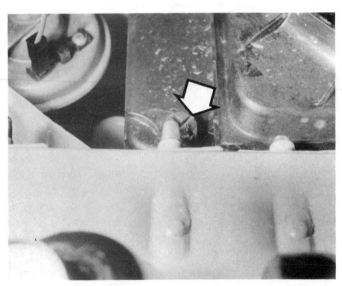

4.3 Radiator drain plug (arrowed)

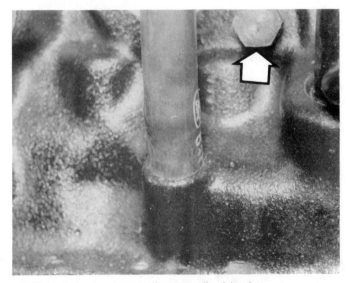

4.4 Block drain plug (arrowed) next to dipstick tube

5 Cooling system – flushing

1 Flushing should not be necessary if the specified coolant has been used and renewed at the correct intervals. When coolant renewal has been neglected, however, or if much running has been done using plain water or inferior coolant mixtures, rust and scale may clog the system and cause overheating. Flushing may then be beneficial and should be carried out as follows.

2 Drain the system as described in the previous Section.

3 Remove the thermostat as described in Section 13.

4 Disconnect the bottom hose from the radiator. Insert a garden hose into the thermostat housing and run water through the engine in the reverse direction to normal flow, so that it goes in via the thermostat housing and out at the bottom hose. Continue until the water emerges clean.

5 Run the water through the radiator in the normal direction of flow, ie top to bottom. In severe cases of obstruction, reverse flushing may be helpful, but the radiator should be removed and inverted for this.

6 Chemical descalers or flushing agents should be used only as a last resort. Use such materials in accordance with their maker's instructions.

7 When flushing is complete, refit the thermostat and reconnect the disturbed hoses.

8 Refill the system as described in the next Section.

6 Cooling system – filling

1 Make sure that the drain plugs are secure, and that all hoses are in good condition and their clips tight.

2 When a bleed screw is fitted in the radiator top hose, slacken it.

3 Fill with coolant via the expansion tank filler hole (photo). If new antifreeze is being introduced, pour in the specified quantity of antifreeze first, followed by clean soft water.

4 Fill the system slowly, massaging the large coolant hoses to disperse airlocks.

5 When a bleed screw is fitted, close it when coolant begins to emerge (photo).

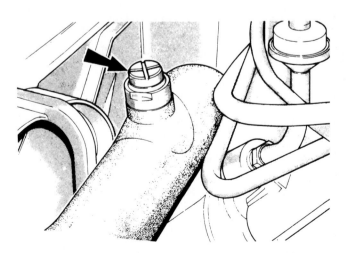

Fig. 2.7 Bleed screw (arrowed) may be found in radiator top hose. A different type can be seen in the photos (Sec 6)

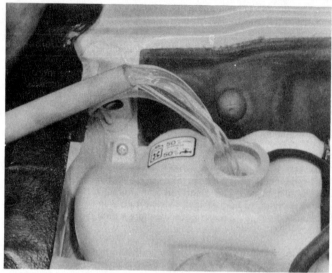

6.3 Filling the cooling system

6.5 Close the bleed screw as coolant emerges

6   Fill the system up to the MAX mark on the expansion tank, then refit the cap.

7   Reconnect the battery. Start the engine and run it up to operating temperature (indicated by the fan cutting in). Check for leaks.

8   Stop the engine and allow it to cool. Check the level in the expansion tank and top up again to the MAX mark if necessary.

9   Recheck the level after the vehicle is next run.

7   Radiator fan switch – testing, removal and refitting

1   The radiator fan switch is located on the thermostat elbow. If it fails, the fan may run all the time (switch short-circuit) or not at all (open-circuit).

2   A short-circuit failure will be self-evident. To check for open-circuit failure, unplug the switch electrical connector and bridge the connector terminals with a screwdriver blade. With the ignition on, the fan should run – if not, the fan itself, or its wiring, must be at fault. If the fan runs now but did not when controlled by the switch, and overheating was occurring, the switch is almost certainly at fault.

3   To remove the switch, first drain the cooling system as described in Section 4.

4   Unplug the switch electrical connector. Unscrew the switch and remove it. Recover the fibre washer (photos).

5   The switch may be tested off the vehicle in a similar fashion to the thermostat (Section 13), using a low voltage test lamp across the switch contacts. The precise operating temperature of the switch was not known at the time of writing. A deflective switch must be renewed.

6   Refit the switch using a new fibre washer and a little sealant on the threads. Plug in the electrical connector.

7   Refill the cooling system as described in Section 6.

8   Radiator fan and motor – removal and refitting

1   Disconnect the battery earth lead.

7.4A Radiator fan switch and connector

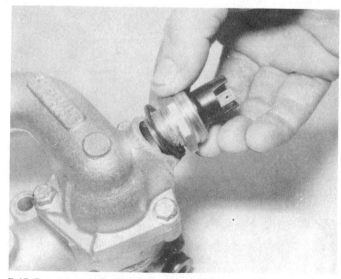

7.4B Removing the radiator fan switch (thermostat housing removed)

2   Unplug the wiring connector from the fan. Free the wiring harness from the clip which secures it to the fan shroud (photo).

3   Remove the four bolts which secure the shroud to the radiator. Carefully remove the fan, motor and shroud together (photos).

4   Undo the three nuts and remove the fan and motor from the shroud (photo).

5   Make alignment marks between the fan hub and the motor shaft, then prise off the retaining clip and washer and remove the fan (photo).

6   Although the motor cover can be removed (photo), no spares are available for it. A competent auto electrician might be able to renew the brushes or make other simple repairs; otherwise, a defective motor must be renewed.

7   Renew the fan if it is damaged. An out-of-balance fan will quickly damage the motor bearings.

8   Commence refitting by securing the motor to the shroud. Make sure that the drain hole will be at the bottom when the assembly is in the vehicle. Tighten the nuts to the specified torque.

8.2 Radiator fan wiring connector

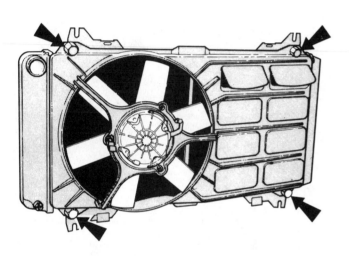

Fig. 2.8 Radiator fan shroud securing bolts (arrowed) –
Escort/Orion (Sec 8)

8.3A One of the fan shroud securing bolts (Fiesta)

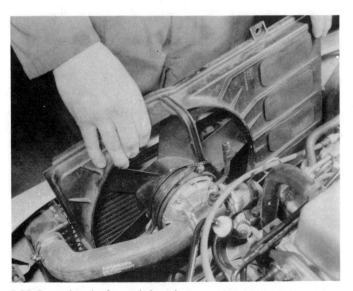

8.3B Removing the fan and shroud

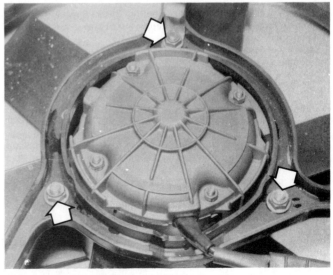

8.4 Fan motor-to-shroud nuts (arrowed)

8.5 Removing the fan retaining clip

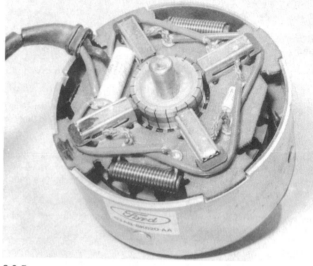

8.6 Fan motor with cover removed

9   Refit the fan to the motor shaft, observing the alignment marks and engaging the drive pin in the recess of the fan (photo). Secure with the washer and a new retaining clip.

10 Refit the shroud, fan and motor assembly to the radiator. Secure it with the four bolts tightened to the specified torque.

11 Reconnect the wiring connector and secure the harness to the shroud.

12 Reconnect the battery. Run the engine to operating temperature and check that the fan operates correctly.

9   Radiator – removal, repair and refitting

1   Remove the fan motor, fan and shroud as described in the previous Section. (Alternatively, the radiator/fan assembly can be removed together and separated subsequently.)

2   Drain the cooling system as described in Section 4.

3   Disconnect the radiator top and bottom hoses. Beware of exerting too much force on the connecting stubs, as the plastic side tanks may be damaged (photo).

4   Remove the two retaining bolts from the top of the radiator (photo).

5   Free the radiator from its lower mountings and carefully remove it (photo).

6   Radiator repairs should be left to a Ford dealer or other competent specialist. Techniques which were used to repair older type radiators may damage or destroy modern ones such as these. In an emergency, 'cold' repairs using epoxy resin or similar products may be attempted, but may prejudice future permanent repairs.

7   Commence refitting by carefully lowering the radiator into position so that the lower mountings are engaged (photo).

8   Insert the two retaining bolts and tighten them to the specified torque.

9   Reconnect the radiator hoses and tighten the hose clips. Use a little liquid detergent as a lubricant on the stubs if necessary.

8.9 Fan motor shaft, showing drive pin (arrowed)

9.3 Radiator bottom hose connection

9.4 Removing one of the radiator securing bolts

9.5 Removing the radiator with top hose still attached

9.7 One of the radiator lower mountings on the front crossmember

10 Refill the cooling system as described in Section 6.

11 Refit the fan, motor and shroud as described in the previous Section.

10 Expansion tank – removal and refitting

1   Partially drain the cooling system, referring if necessary to Section 4, until the expansion tank is empty.

2   Disconnect the coolant and vent hoses from the expansion tank.

3   On models so equipped, disconnect the coolant level warning switch.

4   Remove the securing screws and lift out the tank.

5   Commence refitting by placing the tank in position and securing it with the screws.

Fig. 2.9 Expansion tank securing screws (arrowed) – Fiesta (Sec 10)

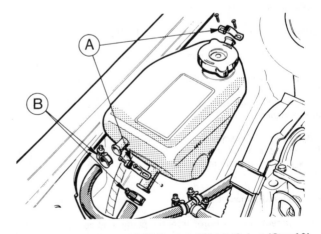

Fig. 2.10 Expansion tank fittings – Escort/Orion (Sec 10)

A   Securing clips   *B   Hose clips*

6 Reconnect the coolant and vent hoses, and (when applicable) the level warning switch.

7 Refill the cooling system as described in Section 6.

11 Water pump/alternator drivebelt – inspection and renewal

1 The drivebelt is somewhat inaccessible. If adjustment is necessary it will have to be done from below, so start by driving the front of the car up onto ramps or over an inspection pit.

2 Disconnect the battery earth (negative) lead.

3 Inspect the drivebelt for cracks, fraying or other damage. Ideally the engine should be turned by hand so that the whole length of the belt can be inspected.

4 If the belt is in good condition, check the tension and adjust if necessary as described in paragraph 8 onwards To renew the belt, proceed as follows.

5 Renew the alternator splash shield, when fitted.

6 Slacken the alternator pivot and adjusting strap nuts and bolts. Push the alternator towards the engine and slip the belt off the pulleys.

7 Fit the new belt over the pulleys. Move the alternator away from the engine until the belt tension seems roughly correct, then nip up the alternator fastenings.

8 Tension is correct when the belt can be deflected 4.0 mm (0.16 in) by firm fingertip pressure in the middle of the longest run. If a belt tension gauge is available, this should be used to give a more accurate reading. Desired values are given in the Specifications.

9 If adjustment is necessary, slacken the alternator fastenings and move the alternator relative to the engine to alter the belt tension. A belt which is too slack will slip and wear rapidly; a belt which is too tight will cause rapid wear of the alternator and water pump bearings. Tighten the alternator fastenings when adjustment is correct.

10 Reconnect the battery earth lead and refit the splash shield, when applicable.

11 Recheck the tension of a new belt after a few hundred miles.

12 Water pump – removal and refitting

1 Disconnect the battery earth lead.

2 Drain the cooling system as described in Section 4.

3 Unclip and remove the camshaft drivebelt cover.

4 Slacken the three bolts which secure the water pump pulley.

5 Remove the water pump/alternator drivebelt as described in the previous Section.

6 Remove the two bolts which secure the thermostat housing to the cylinder head. Pull the housing away from the head and disconnect the bypass pipe from it. Remove the bypass pipe and seals completely (photos).

7 Unbolt and remove the water pump pulley.

8 Disconnect the two hoses from the pump inlet connector, and the heater hose from the connector on the pump (photos).

9 Remove the air cleaner element as described in Chapter 3, Section 3.

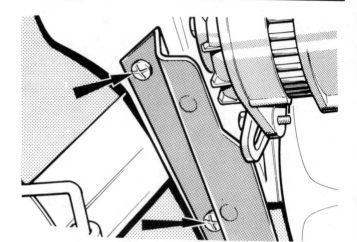

Fig. 2.11 Alternator splash shield securing screws (arrowed). Shield is not fitted to all models (Sec 11)

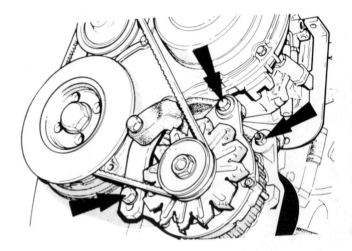

Fig. 2.12 Alternator pivot and strap fastenings (arrowed) (Sec 11)

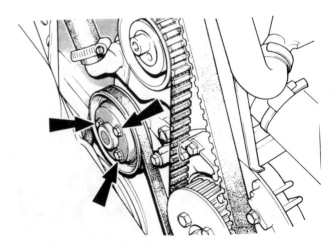

Fig. 2.13 Water pump pulley retaining bolts (arrowed) (Sec 12)

12.6A Removing the bypass pipe from the thermostat housing

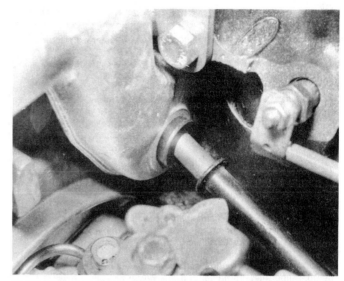

12.6B Removing the bypass pipe from the water pump inlet connector

12.6C Water pump bypass pipe seal (arrowed)

12.8A Disconnecting the radiator bottom hose from the water pump inlet connector

12.8B Disconnecting the expansion tank hose from the water pump inlet connector

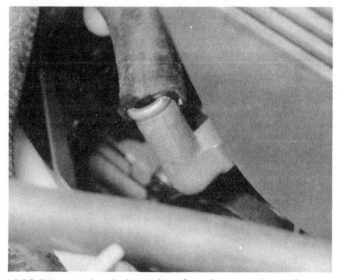

12.8C Disconnecting the heater hose from the connector on the pump itself

10 Unscrew and remove the heater hose connector from the pump.

11 Remove the two retaining bolts and take off the pump inlet connector. Recover the gasket.

12 On Escort and Orion models only, remove the oil filter element.

13 Attach lifting tackle to the engine. Take the weight of the engine and remove the right-hand mounting. Refer to Chapter 1, Section 20, if necessary.

14 Raise the engine far enough to give clearance to remove the water pump. Remove the three securing bolts and withdraw the pump. Recover the gasket (photo).

15 Although the bearing and shaft are available separately, press tools will be needed to fit them. Renewal of the pump is the most practical course if it is worn or damaged.

16 Clean all gasket mating surfaces and obtain new gaskets for the pump, pump inlet connector and thermostat housing.

17 Fit a new gasket to the water pump, with the incomplete bolt hole positioned correctly. Slide the pump into position, fit the three retaining bolts and tighten them evenly to the specified torque.

18 Refit the pump inlet connector, using a new gasket. If the gasket has a coloured tab, position it as shown in Fig. 2.14. Insert and tighten the two retaining bolts.

19 Refit and secure the water pump pulley and the heater hose connector. Do not attempt to tighten the pulley bolt yet.

20 Lower the engine and refit its mounting. Remove the lifting tackle.

21 On Escort and Orion models, fit a new oil filter element.

22 Refit the bypass pipe, using new seals.

23 Refit the thermostat housing to the cylinder head. Use a new gasket with the coloured tab (when present) positioned as shown in Fig. 2.15. Tighten the securing bolts (photos).

24 Reconnect the heater hose to the pump connector, and the inlet hoses to the inlet connector.

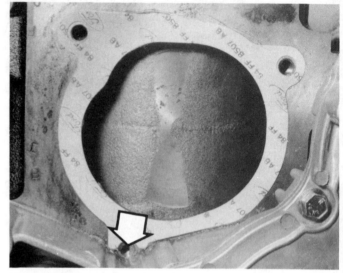

12.14 Water pump gasket on the block. Incomplete bolt hole (arrowed) is shared with timing case

25 Refit and tension the water pump/alternator drivebelt as described in the previous Section.

26 Tighten the water pump pulley bolts to the specified torque.

27 Refit the camshaft drivebelt cover.

28 Refill the cooling system as described in Section 6.

29 Refit the air cleaner element as described in Chapter 3, Section 3.

30 Reconnect the battery. Run the engine to normal operating temperature, then switch it off and allow it to cool down. Inspect the engine for leaks of coolant, and (if it was disturbed) the oil filter for oil leaks. Rectify if necessary.

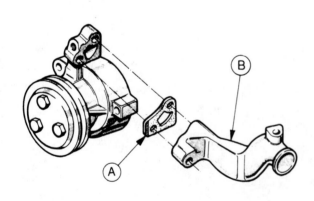

Fig. 2.14 Water pump and inlet connector. If gasket has a coloured tab, position it as shown (Sec 12)

A　Coloured tab　　　　　B　Inlet connector

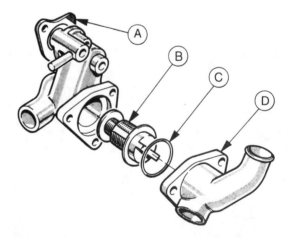

Fig. 2.15 Thermostat housing and associated components (Secs 12 and 13)

A　Coloured tab on gasket　　C　O-ring
B　Thermostat　　　　　　　　D　Thermostat elbow

12.23A Thermostat housing gasket in position. This one had no coloured tab

12.23B Refitting the thermostat housing

31 Check the coolant level and top up if necessary.

32 If the oil filter was disturbed, check the engine oil level and top up if necessary.

13 Thermostat – removal, testing and refitting

1 Disconnect the battery earth lead.

2 Drain the cooling system as described in Section 4.

3 Disconnect the radiator hose from the thermostat elbow (photo).

4 Disconnect the electrical leads from the radiator fan switch and the temperature gauge sender.

5 Unbolt and remove the thermostat elbow. Extract the thermostat and recover the O-ring.

6 If the thermostat is stuck open, badly scaled, corroded or distorted, renew it without question. An apparently serviceable thermostat can be tested as follows.

7 Place the thermostat in a saucepan of cold water and check that it is closed. Heat the water: the thermostat should commence to open as boiling point is approached, and be completely open when the water is boiling. (Actual temperatures are given in the Specifications.) Allow the water to cool and check that the thermostat closes again. Discard it if it does not behave as described.

8 Commence refitting by cleaning the thermostat housing and elbow mating faces.

9 Fit the thermostat, making sure it is the right way round, and a new O-ring (photos). Refit the elbow and secure it with the three bolts.

10 Reconnect the electrical leads to the temperature gauge sender and the radiator fan switch.

11 Reconnect the radiator hose to the thermostat elbow.

12 Refill the cooling system as described in Section 6.

13 Reconnect the battery and run the engine up to operating temperature. Check for leaks around the disturbed components. Stop the engine, allow it to cool and top up the coolant level if necessary.

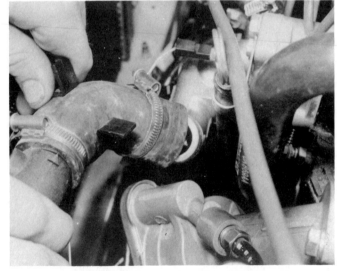

13.3 Disconnecting the radiator top hose from the thermostat housing

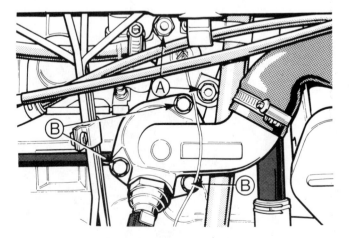

Fig. 2.16 Thermostat housing-to-block bolts (A) and elbow retaining bolts (B) (Sec 13)

Fig. 2.17 Testing a thermostat (Sec 13)

14 Antifreeze mixture – general

1   Do not operate the vehicle with plain water in the system, except in an emergency. Apart from the risk of freezing in winter weather, serious corrosion and rust and scale formation may occur.

2   In climates where frost protection is not required, a corrosion inhibitor must be used in accordance with its maker's instructions.

3   Only use ethylene glycol based antifreeze, to the maker's specification, and soft water – rainwater is ideal. Do not use antifreeze containing methanol, which is inflammable and may evaporate.

4   The recommended concentration of antifreeze for the UK climate is given in the Specifications. Do not use widely different concentrations without first seeking expert advice.

5   Antifreeze must be renewed at the specified intervals to maintain the anti-corrosion properties.

15 Temperature gauge sender – renewal

1   The temperature gauge sender is screwed into the thermostat housing. If it malfunctions it must be renewed.

2   Disconnect the battery earth lead.

3   Place a thick cloth over the expansion tank cap. Turn the cap anti-clockwise to the first stop, allow any pressure to escape, then remove and refit the cap. This will depressurize the system and minimise coolant loss.

4   Disconnect the wire from the temperature gauge sender (photo).

5   Apply a little sealant to the threads of the new sender unit and have it ready for installation. Unscrew and remove the old sender and screw in and tighten the new one.

6   Connect the wire to the new sender unit.

7   Reconnect the battery earth lead.

8   Run the engine to operating temperature and check the gauge for correct operation.

9   Stop the engine and allow it to cool. Check the coolant level and top up if necessary.

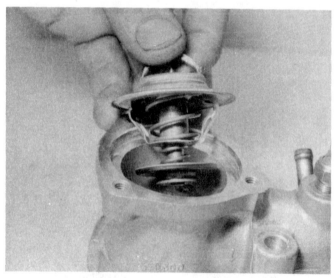

13.9A Fitting the thermostat to the housing (housing removed)

13.9B Thermostat O-ring

15.4 Temperature gauge sender and connector

16 Fault diagnosis – cooling system

Symptom	Reason(s)
Overheating	Insufficient coolant in system
	Pump drivebelt slipping or broken
	Thermostat jammed shut
	Radiator cooling fan inoperative
	Radiator blocked (internally or externally)
	Blockage in major coolant hose
	Engine oil level low or incorrect grade
	Exhaust system restricted
	New engine not yet run in
	Brakes binding
	Cylinder head gasket blown
	Cylinder head or block cracked
Overcooling	Thermostat jammed open, missing, or incorrect rating
Coolant loss	External leakage (hoses, clips, radiator or heater matrix, water pump gland etc)
	Internal leakage (head gasket, cracked head or block)
	Pressure cap defective or incorrect rating
	Overheating
Temperature gauge reading erratic	Sender unit defective
	Wiring defective
	Gauge defective
	Instrument voltage stabiliser defective (will affect fuel gauge also)

Chapter 3 Fuel and exhaust systems

For modifications, and information applicable to later models, see Supplement at end of manual

Contents

Specifications

General

System type	Rear mounted fuel tank, combined lift and injection pump, indirect injection
Firing order	1 - 3 - 4 - 2 (No 1 at pulley end)
Glow plugs	Champion CH79
Air filter	Champion U515
Fuel filter:	
Early type Bosch (separate element)	N/A
Later-type Bosch ('spin-on' cartridge)	Champion L111
CAV RotoDiesel	Champion L131 or L137

Fuel

Fuel type	Commercial Diesel fuel for road vehicles (DERV)
Fuel capacity	34 to 50 litres (7.5 to 11.0 gallons) according to model

Injection pump

Make and type	Bosch VE or CAV Rotodiesel (see Supplement)
Rotation (viewed from crankshaft pulley end)	Clockwise
Drive	By gear from crankshaft

Injectors (Bosch)

Type	Pintle
Opening pressure	143 ± 7 bar (2074 ± 102 lbf/in²)
Back leakage time (from 125 to 100 bar/1813 to 1450 lbf/in²)	More than 5 seconds
Needle seat leakage	No visible droplets after 10 seconds at 10 bar (145 lbf/in²) below opening pressure

Injectors (CAV)

Type	Pintle
Opening pressure	120 ± 6 bar (1740 ± 87 lbf/in²)
Back leakage time (from 100 to 70 bar/1450 to 1015 lbf/in²)	More than 5 seconds
Needle seat leakage	Holds 100 bar (1450 lbf/in² for 10 seconds)

Adjustment data

Idle speed	880 ± 50 rpm
Maximum no load speed	5350 ± 50 rpm
Deceleration time (no load at idle)	5 seconds maximum
Injection pump timing:	
Bosch – see Chapter 3, Section 7	0.92 ± 0.01 mm (0.0362 ± 0.0004 in) at TDC
CAV RotoDiesel – see Chapter 8, Section 5	1.40 ± 0.07 mm (0.0551 ± 0.0028 in) at TDC

Torque wrench settings

	Nm	lbf ft
Fuel injection pump to timing case	18 to 22	13 to 16
Fuel injection pump bracket to block	18 to 22	13 to 16
Fuel injection pump shaft nut	40 to 50	30 to 37
Drivebelt sprocket to pump gear	18 to 22	13 to 16
Glow plugs to head	25 to 30	18 to 22
Injectors to head	60 to 80	44 to 59
Injection pipe unions	15 to 25	11 to 18
Fuel filter bracket to head	20 to 25	15 to 18
Manifolds to head:		
Nuts	10 to 16	7 to 12
Bolts	18 to 22	13 to 16
Exhaust downpipes to manifold flange	35 to 40	26 to 30
Exhaust downpipe-to-centre section joint through-bolts and nuts:		
Fiesta	38 to 45	28 to 33
Escort/Orion	48 to 64	35 to 47
Escort centre-to-rear section U-bolt nuts	35 to 40	26 to 30
Fuel pipe banjo union bolts	16 to 20	12 to 15

1 General description

The fuel system consists of a rear-mounted fuel tank, a fuel filter, fuel injection pump, injectors and associated components (photos). The exhaust system is similar to that used on petrol-engined vehicles.

Fuel is drawn from the tank by the transfer pump incorporated in the injection pump. En route it passes through the fuel filter, located in the engine bay, where foreign matter and water are removed. The injection pump is gear-driven from the crankshaft and supplies fuel under very high pressure to each injector in turn as it is needed. The amount of fuel delivered is determined by the pump governor, which reacts to throttle position and to engine speed. Injection timing is varied automatically to suit the prevailing speed and load.

Rigid pipes connect the pump and injectors. There are four injectors, situated where spark plugs would be found on a petrol engine. Each injector sprays fuel into a pre-combustion or 'swirl' chamber as its piston approaches TDC on the compression stroke. This system is known as indirect injection. The injectors only open under very high pressure. Lubrication is provided by allowing a small quantity of fuel to leak back past the injector internal components. The leaked-back fuel is returned to the pump and then to the fuel tank.

1.0A General view of injection components on engine

1.0B Side view of injection pump – cold start element arrowed

1.0C End view of injection pump — fuel shut-off solenoid arrowed

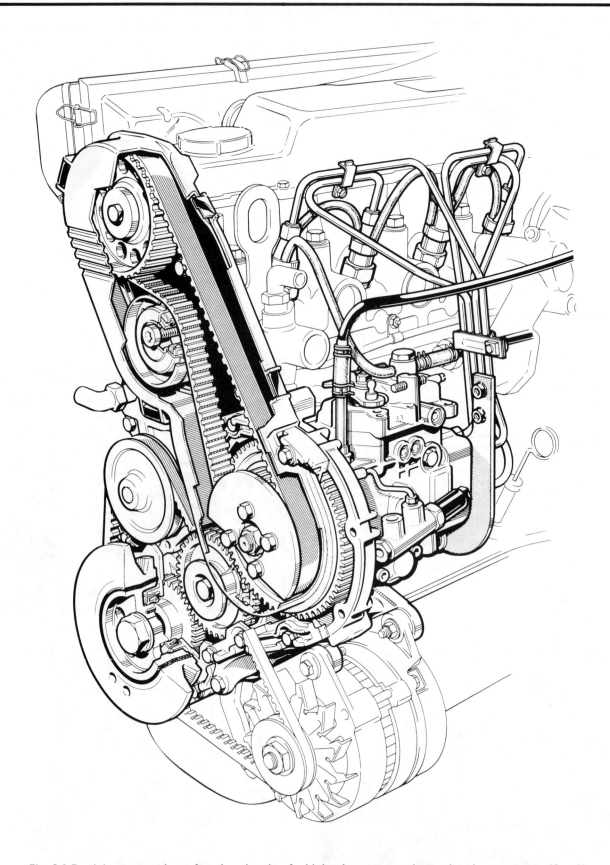

Fig. 3.1 Partial cutaway view of engine showing fuel injection pump and associated components (Sec 1)

Two systems, both automatic, assist cold starting. A cold start advance device on the injection pump alters the injection timing and causes fuel delivery to be increased during cold starts. It contains a

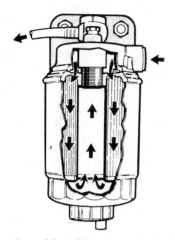

Fig. 3.2 Direction of fuel flow through the filter (Sec 1)

heating element which is energised when the engine is running. Preheater or 'glow' plugs are fitted to each swirl chamber: they are electrically heated before, during and immediately after a cold start. A warning light illuminates when the ignition is switched on, showing that the glow plugs are in operation. When the light goes out, preheating is complete and the engine can be started. The glow plugs are controlled by a special relay which incorporates a temperature sensor.

To stop the engine, a solenoid valve at the rear of the fuel pump is used. The valve is of the 'fail safe' type, so it must be energised to allow the engine to run. When power is removed from the valve, its plunger moves under spring pressure and interrupts fuel delivery.

The fuel system on Diesel engines is normally very reliable. Provided that clean fuel is used and the specified maintenance is conscientiously carried out, no problems should be experienced. The injection pump and injectors may require overhaul after high mileages have been covered, but this cannot be done on a DIY basis.

Warning: *It is necessary to take certain precautions when working on the fuel system components, particularly the fuel injectors. Before carrying out any operations on the fuel system, refer to the precautions given in 'Safety first! at the beginning of this manual, and to any additional warning notes at the start of the relevant Sections.*

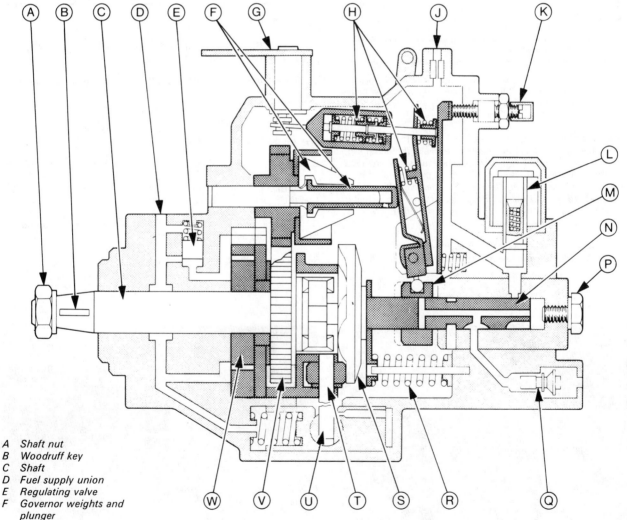

A   Shaft nut
B   Woodruff key
C   Shaft
D   Fuel supply union
E   Regulating valve
F   Governor weights and
    plunger
G   Throttle lever
H   Governor springs and
    linkage
J   Fuel return union
K   Maximum fuel adjustment
    (sealed)

Fig. 3.3 Sectional view of the fuel injection pump (Sec 1)

L   Fuel shut-off solenoid
M   Control sleeve
N   Pumping element
P   Plug

Q   Delivery valve (1 of 4)
R   Return spring
S   Cam plate
T   Cam roller

U   Advance unit
V   Governor drive wheel
W   Transfer pump

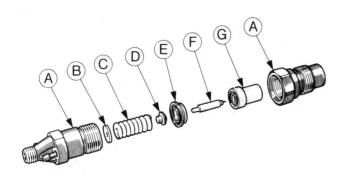

Fig. 3.4 Fuel injector components (Sec 1)

A Body sections
B Adjusting shim
C Spring
D Peg

E Adaptor plate
F Needle
G Nozzle

2 Maintenance and inspection

1   At every refuelling, take care not to introduce water or dirt into the fuel tank. Only use commercial Diesel fuel intended for road vehicles (DERV). Do not use marine, agricultural or aviation fuel, nor fuel from anonymous cans or bowsers.

2   In winter it may be necessary to use a fuel additive to prevent fuel waxing. Diesel fuel sold in the UK in winter is normally protected from waxing down to –9°C (+16°F). If lower temperatures are expected, add a proprietary anti-waxing additive to the fuel tank as directed by the maker of the additive. The additive is only effective when mixed with the fuel **before** waxing occurs. Note that summer grade fuel in the UK is liable to wax below 0°C (32°F), so it should not be used without anti-waxing additives in winter.

3   The use of petrol or paraffin (kerosene) as anti-waxing additives is not recommended. Petrol will lower the flashpoint of the fuel to potentially dangerous levels; paraffin cannot be used because it is not taxed as a vehicle fuel.

4   At every major service interval, or more frequently if dictated by local conditions, drain the water layer from the fuel filter as described in Section 4.

5   At the same interval, check the idle speed and adjust if necessary.

6   Every 24 000 miles (40 000 km) or two years, whichever comes first, renew the fuel filter element as described in Section 4.

7   At the same interval, renew the air cleaner element as described in Section 3. More frequent renewal may be necessary if the vehicle is driven in very dusty conditions – eg mostly on unmade roads.

8   Inspect the exhaust system at alternate major service intervals, or whenever excessive noise becomes evident. Refer to Section 18.

9   Apart from routine inspections for leaks and component security, which should form part of every major service, no other fuel system maintenance is specified.

3 Air cleaner – element renewal

1   Disconnect the battery earth lead.

2   Release the seven spring clips which secure the air cleaner cover. The two lowest clips are out of sight.

3   Release the throttle cable from the clips on the air cleaner cover.

4   Disconnect the air inlet hose from the cover.

5   Remove the cover and extract the air cleaner element, noting which way round it is fitted (photo).

6   Wipe clean inside the cover and the accessible part of the manifold.

7   Fit the new element, making sure that it is the right way round and that the sealing strip is engaged properly.

8   Refit the air cleaner cover and secure it with the spring slips. Reconnect the air inlet hose (photos).

9   Reconnect the battery earth lead.

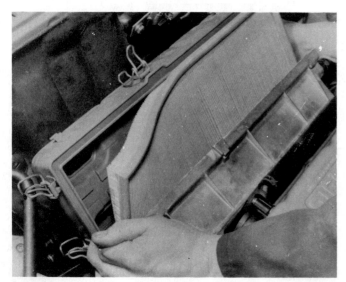

3.5 Removing the air cleaner element from the cover

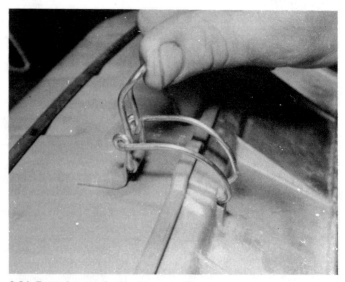

3.8A Fastening an air cleaner cover clip

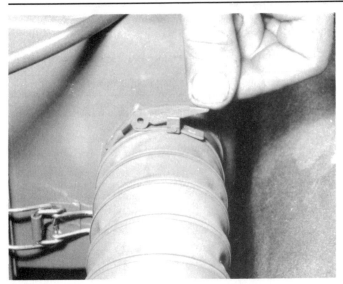

3.8B Air cleaner inlet hose

Fig. 3.5 Draining the fuel filter (Sec 4)

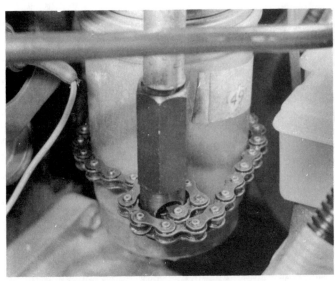

4.9 Using a chain wrench to unscrew the fuel filter

4 Fuel filter – draining and element renewal

Note: *The following procedures apply only to early type Bosch filters (with a separate element); for information on the later type Bosch ('spin-on' cartridge) filter and the CAV RotoDiesel filter, refer to Chapter 8, Section 5, Part A.*

1 During operations on the fuel filter, place rags or other material beneath the filter to prevent fuel entering the clutch housing.

Draining water
2 Disconnect the battery earth lead.

3 Attach a tube to the drain spigot on the base of the fuel filter. Place the other end of the tube in a clean jar or can.

4 Open the drain cock by unscrewing the knurled wheel.

5 Allow the filter to drain until clean fuel, free of dirt or water, emerges from the tube. Close the drain cock and remove the tube.

6 Dispose of the contaminated fuel safely.

7 Reconnect the battery earth lead.

Element renewal
8 Drain the filter as just described, but allow it to drain completely. Clean around the sealing area between the filter head and body.

9 Unscrew and remove the filter body. Use a chain or strap wrench if it is tight (photo). Remove and discard the element and seal.

10 Using a clean, non-fluffy rag, wipe clean the filter head and body. Fit the new element into the filter body and apply clean fuel to the new sealing ring. Screw the filter body into position, tightening it by hand only. Make sure that the drain cock is closed.

11 Reconnect the battery and start the engine. Considerable cranking may be necessary to purge the air from the system. (The filter can be filled with clean fuel via the vent plug on its head if wished, but it is extremely important that no dirt be introduced).

12 Check for leaks from the filter seal; tighten further if necessary. Stop the engine and remove the clutch housing protection material.

5 Idle speed – checking and adjustment

1 The usual type of tachometer (rev counter), which works from ignition system pulses, cannot be used on Diesel engines. If it is not felt

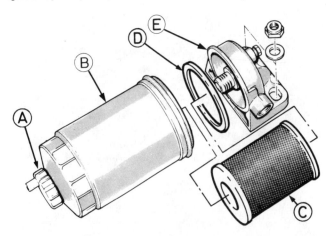

Fig. 3.6 Components of fuel filter assembly – early type Bosch unit with separate element shown (Sec 4)

A   Drain cock   D   Sealing ring
B   Filter body   E   Filter head
C   Filter element

that adjusting the idle speed 'by ear' is satisfactory, one of the following alternatives must be used:

(a) *Purchase or hire of an appropriate tachometer*
(b) *Delegation of the job to a Ford dealer or other specialist*
(c) *Timing light (strobe) operated by a petrol engine running at the desired speed. If the timing light is pointed at a chalk mark on the Diesel engine crankshaft pulley, the mark will appear stationary when the two engines are running at the same speed (or multiples of that speed)*
(d) *Calculating the mph/rpm relationship for a particular gear and running the engine, in that gear, with the front wheels free. The speedometer accuracy may not be adequate, especially at low speeds. Stringent safety precautions must be observed*

2 Before making adjustments, warm up the engine until it is at normal operating temperature.

3 Connect the tachometer, if used, or make the necessary alternative arrangements. Start the engine and allow it to idle. Compare the idle speed with that specified.

4 If adjustment is necessary, slacken the idle speed screw locknut on the fuel injection pump. Turn the idle speed screw clockwise to increase the speed, anti-clockwise to decrease it. When the speed is

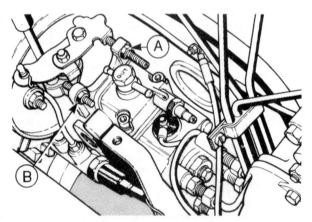

Fig. 3.7 Injection pump speed adjusting screws
(Secs 5 and 6)

A *Idle speed*   B *Maximum speed – do not alter*

correct, tighten the locknut without disturbing the position or the screw (photo).

5 Disconnect the tachometer or other instruments, as appropriate.

6 Maximum speed – checking and adjustment

1 The maximum no load speed may be checked if wished, using one of the methods described in the previous Section. Running the engine with the wheels free is **not** recommended, because of the risk of damage or injury if anything goes wrong.

2 The maximum speed adjusting screw is sealed in production. Adjustment should only be made by a Ford dealer or authorised fuel injection specialist. Unauthorised adjustment may invalidate the warranty.

3 When checking the maximum speed, do not hold the engine at this speed for more than five seconds. Keep well clear of the water pump/alternator drivebelt and pulleys.

4 The engine speed should drop from maximum to idle within the specified time when the throttle is released. If not, check that the throttle linkage is not binding or obstructed; if this is in order, seek specialist advice.

7 Fuel injection pump timing – checking and adjustment

1 This is not a routine operation. It should only be necessary if the pump has been disturbed; after fitting a new pump; or if the crankshaft pulley bolt has been disturbed in the course of other work such as renewal of the crankshaft front oil seal. Whenever the crankshaft pulley bolt is slackened, it is possible for the drive gear to move very slightly in relation to the crankshaft – hence the need to check the injection pump timing.

2 Two special tools will be needed: a TDC setting pin (see Chapter 1, Section 9) and a dial test indicator with a suitable mounting or stand.

3 Slacken the pump mountings so that it is just free to be twisted back and forth within the limits of its slotted fixing holes.

4 Remove the camshaft drivebelt cover. Turn the engine until the pump sprocket timing mark is aligned with the pointer on the timing cover (photo).

5 Remove the screw plug and insert the TDC setting pin. Carefully turn the engine in the normal direction of rotation until the crankshaft web contacts the setting pin, showing that No 1 piston is at TDC.

5.4 Adjusting the idle speed screw and locknut

7.4 Pump sprocket mark aligned with pointer on timing cover

6 Protect the alternator against fuel spillage, then unscrew and remove the central plug from the rear of the pump (photo).

7 Mount the dial test indicator so that its probe enters the plug hole and bears on the plunger inside. It is preferable, though not essential, that the indicator be mounted on the pump rather than on the block. Depending on the length of the indicator probe, it may be necessary to remove the injection pipes – see Section 9.

8 Turn the engine slowly anti-clockwise, observing the dial test indicator: the reading will decrease and then become steady. Stop turning when the reading is steady and zero the indicator (photo).

9 Turn the engine clockwise again until the setting pin is contacted. Read the dial test indicator: the value shown should correspond to that given for pump timing in the Specifications. If not, turn the pump one way or the other until it does.

10 Tighten the pump mountings. If the dial test indicator is mounted on the block, tightening the mountings may cause the reading to change. This does not matter provided that the indicator is reset to its new zero.

11 Repeat the operations from paragraph 8 onwards until the correct result is obtained with the pump mountings tightened.

12 Remove the dial test indicator and the TDC setting pin.

13 Refit the disturbed components, not forgetting the screw plug for the TDC pin hole.

14 Run the engine for a minute or two to bleed any air from the fuel lines.

8 Fuel injection pump – removal and refitting

1 Disconnect the battery earth lead.

2 Depressurise the cooling system by removing the expansion tank filler cap, taking precautions against scalding if the system is hot.

3 Disconnect the coolant vent hose from the thermostat housing and cylinder head. Be prepared for some coolant spillage. Move the vent hose out of the way.

4 It is not essential, but access will be greatly improved if the radiator and cooling fan are removed as described in Chapter 2, Section 9.

5 Remove the camshaft drivebelt cover.

6 Disconnect the throttle cable from the pump – see Section 15.

7 Clean around the unions, then disconnect the fuel supply and return hoses from the pump (photos). Be prepared for fuel spillage: protect the alternator against the entry of fuel. Plug or cap hoses and unions to keep fuel in and dirt out.

8 Disconnect the electrical leads from the fuel shut-off solenoid and the cold start device.

9 Remove the injection pipes as described in Section 9. Again, plug or cap open unions.

10 Release the nut which secures the pump driveshaft to its gear. Unscrew it as far as the end of the shaft.

11 Turn the engine until the timing marks on the pump sprocket and the timing cover are aligned.

12 Obtain or make a TDC setting pin – see Chapter 1, Section 9. Remove the screw plug and insert the pin, then turn the engine clockwise until the crankshaft web contacts the pin.

13 Make alignment marks between the pump flange and the timing case, then remove the three nuts and washers which secure the pump

7.6 Removing the central plug (arrowed) from the rear of the pump

7.8 Dial test indicator with probe in plug hole

8.7A Fuel supply banjo union (arrowed) at pump

8.7B Either remove the return banjo union, or disconnect the return hoses (arrowed) from it

8.13 One of the three flange nuts (A) and the bracket nut and bolt (B)

to the timing case. Slacken, but do not remove, the pump bracket nut and bolt (photo).

14 Remove two opposite bolts from the pump sprocket. Use two longer M8 bolts (not the sprocket bolts), a suitably drilled bar and some washers or spacers to release the pump shaft from its taper fit in the gear. The correct length of bolt will depend on the thickness of the bar: if too long or too short, damage to the gear or timing case may result. See also Chapter 1, Section 25, paragraph 30. Tighten the bolts evenly to break the taper.

15 Remove the bolts, bar etc and transfer them to a position suitable for restraining the pump sprocket from moving (Fig. 3.9). When the pump is removed, the sprocket and gear will not be positively located; if the gear comes out of mesh with the idler, it will be necessary to remove the timing cover to re-engage it.

16 Remove the pump driveshaft nut and the bracket nut and bolt. Withdraw the pump and bracket, being careful not to lose the Woodruff key. Recover the gasket.

17 Commence refitting by placing a new gasket on the timing case. Offer the pump to the case, with the Woodruff key positioned to enter the keyway in the gear. Take care not to push the gear out of mesh. Fit the securing nuts and washers, but only tighten them finger tight at this stage. Loosely fit the bracket nut and bolt.

18 Apply sealant to the screw thread on the pump shaft. Fit the shaft nut and carefully tighten it to draw the shaft taper into the gear. When satisfied that the shaft has entered the gear without jamming, tighten the nut to the specified torque.

19 Remove the gear puller/restrainer components. Refit and tighten the pump sprocket bolts.

20 Adjust the pump timing as described in the previous Section. The alignment marks made during removal will provide a starting point if the original pump is being refitted.

21 Refit the injection pipes as described in Section 9.

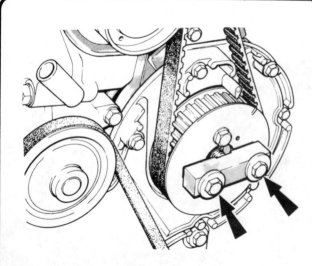

Fig. 3.8 Releasing the pump driveshaft. Tighten the bolts (arrowed) to break the taper (Sec 8)

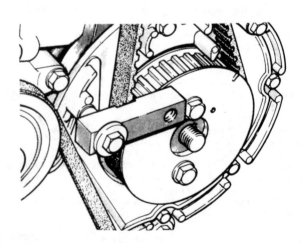

Fig. 3.9 Using the same tool to hold the sprocket in position (Sec 8)

22 Reconnect the fuel shut-off solenoid, the cold start device and the throttle cable.

23 Refit the camshaft drivebelt cover.

24 Refit the radiator and fan, if they were removed.

25 Reconnect the coolant vent hose. Refill or top up the cooling system as necessary – see Chapter 2.

26 Prime the pump by pouring or injecting clean fuel into the fuel inlet and outlet orifices. Take great care not to introduce dirt or foreign matter into the pump.

27 Reconnect the fuel supply and return hoses.

28 Reconnect the battery earth lead.

29 Start the engine. A good deal of cranking may be necessary: the self-bleeding process can be speeded up by slackening each injector pipe union in turn whilst an assistant cranks the engine on the starter motor. Tighten the unions when fuel emerges.

30 Run the engine for a minute or two to purge any remaining air from the injection system. Check the disturbed components for leaks of fuel, oil or coolant.

9 Injection pipes – removal and refitting

1 The injection pipes should be removed as a set. Individual pipes may then be renewed if necessary after slackening the anti-rattle clips.

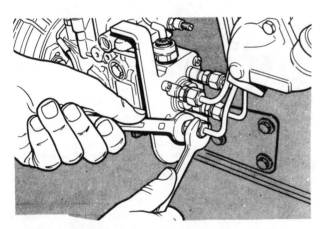

Fig. 3.10 Counterhold the pump adaptor when slackening or tightening a union nut (Sec 9)

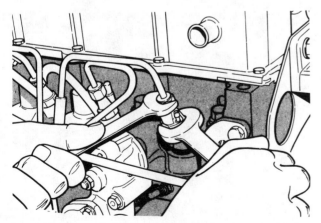

Fig. 3.11 Counterhold the injector body when slackening a union nut (Sec 9)

2 Disconnect the battery earth lead. Clean around the pipe unions at the injectors and at the pump.

3 Protect the alternator against fuel spillage. Counterhold the pump adaptors and unscrew the pipe union nuts.

4 Similarly unscrew the injector union nuts, counterholding the injector bodies as the nuts are slackened.

5 Remove the pipe assembly. Plug or cap open unions to keep fuel in and dirt out.

6 When refitting, make sure that all the anti-rattle clips are in place. Do not bend or strain the pipes. Blow through the pipes with compressed air (from an air line or a foot pump) to expel any debris.

7 Counterhold the pump adaptors and tighten the pump union nuts.

8 Reconnect the battery earth lead.

9 With the injector union nuts finger tight, have an assistant crank the engine on the starter in short bursts until fuel emerges from the unions. Tighten the injector unions – there is no need to counterhold the injectors.

10 Run the engine for a minute or two to purge any remaining air from the system. Check the disturbed unions for leaks.

10 Fuel injectors – removal, testing and refitting

Warning: *Exercise extreme caution when working on the fuel injectors. Never expose the hands or any part of the body to injector spray, as the high working pressure can cause the fuel to penetrate the skin, with possibly fatal results. You are strongly advised to have any work which involves testing the injectors under pressure carried out by a dealer or fuel injection specialist.*

1 Disconnect the battery earth lead. Clean around the injectors and the injection pipe unions.

2 Remove the fuel return hoses from the injectors (photo).

3 Remove the injection pipes as described in the previous Section.

4 Unscrew and remove the injectors. A box spanner or deep socket, 27 mm/1$\frac{1}{16}$ in AF will be required.

5 Retrieve the heat protection washers from the injector bores. Obtain new washers for reassembly.

6 Take care not to drop the injectors, nor allow the needles at their tips to become damaged.

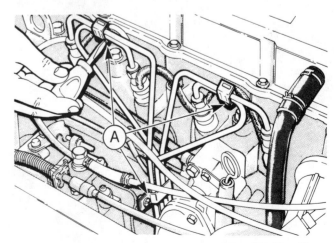

Fig. 3.12 Injection pipe anti-rattle clips (A) (Sec 9)

7 Testing of injectors is quite simple, but requires a special high pressure pump and gauge. Should such equipment be available, use it in accordance with its maker's instructions, referring to the Specifications for the desired values. **Do not** expose the skin to spray from the injectors – the pressure is high enough to penetrate the skin.

8 Defective injectors should be renewed or professionally repaired. DIY repair is not a practical proposition.

9 Commence refitting by inserting new heat protection washers, domed faces downwards, to the injector bores (photo).

10 Insert the injectors and screw them in by hand, then tighten them to the specified torque (photos). No outer sealing washer is used: the injectors are a taper fit in the head.

11 Reconnect the fuel return hoses. Make sure that a blanking cap is fitted to the unused connector on No 4 injector.

12 Refit the injection pipes as described in the previous Section.

13 Reconnect the battery and run the engine for a minute or two. Check for leaks around the disturbed components.

10.2 Disconnecting a fuel return hose from an injector

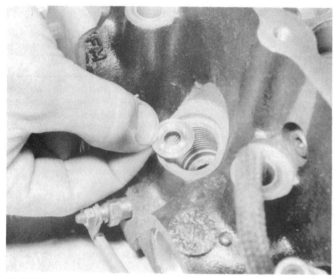

10.9 Fitting a new heat protection washer

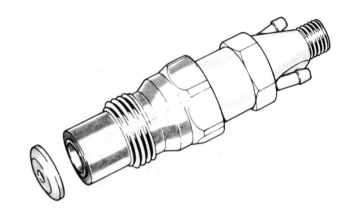

Fig. 3.13 Fuel injector and heat protection washers. Observe correct fitting direction of washers (domed side downwards) (Sec 10)

10.10A Refitting an injector

10.10B Tightening an injector, using a deep socket and a torque wrench

11 Fuel shut-off solenoid — removal and refitting

1   If the fuel shut-off solenoid is disconnected, the engine will not run. The same applies if the solenoid is defective. If the plunger jams in the raised position, the engine will not stop. A defective solenoid should be removed for inspection or renewal as follows.

2   Disconnect the battery earth lead.

3   Disconnect the electrical lead from the solenoid (photo).

4   Wipe clean around the solenoid, then unscrew it from the fuel injection pump using a deep socket or box spanner. **Caution:** *if the solenoid has recently been energised, it may be hot.* Recover the spring and plunger (photo).

5   A defective solenoid must be renewed. Renew the sealing O-ring in any case.

6   Refit the plunger, spring and solenoid to the pump. Tighten the solenoid body moderately.

7   Reconnect the solenoid lead and the battery earth lead. Run the engine to check for correct operation.

11.3 Fuel shut-off solenoid electrical connector

12 Cold start element – renewal

1   The electrically-operated cold start element is screwed into the advance device (photo). No test data are available, but if the element is suspect it can be renewed as follows.

2   Disconnect the battery earth lead.

3   Disconnect the electrical lead from the cold start element.

4   Wipe clean around the element, then unscrew and remove it. **Caution:** *if it has just been energised, the element may be hot.*

5   Fit the new element, using a new sealing washer, and tighten it moderately.

6   Reconnect the electrical lead and the battery earth lead.

7   Run the engine to check for correct operation.

11.4 Solenoid, spring and plunger – O-ring is arrowed

13 Preheater system – description and testing

1   Each swirl chamber has a preheater plug (commonly called a glow plug) screwed into it. The plugs are electrically operated before, during and immediately after starting the engine. The duration of the preheating and afterglow periods is determined by a special relay which incorporates a temperature sensor.

2   During the preheating phase, an instrument panel warning light is illuminated. No attempt should be made to start the engine until the light goes out.

3   If the system malfunctions, testing is ultimately by substitution of known good units, but some preliminary checks may be made as follows.

4   Connect a voltmeter (0 to 20 volt) or 12 volt test lamp between any glow plug terminal and earth. Have an assistant switch on the ignition: the test lamp or voltmeter should give a positive indication for several seconds, corresponding to the preheating period, then give a zero reading or go out. If not, the relay (or associated wiring) is at fault. Switch off the ignition.

5   If an ammeter of suitable range (0 to 50 amp approx) is available, connect it between the glow plug feed wire and the bus bar. During the preheating period the ammeter should show a current draw of

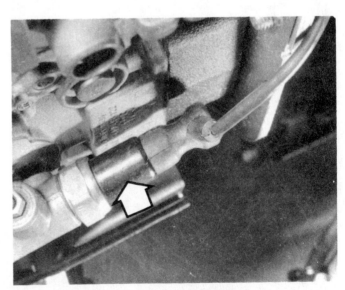

12.1 Cold start element (arrowed) on side of fuel pump

approximately 8 amps per working plug, ie 32 amps if all four plugs are working.

6   If one or more plugs appear not to be drawing current, remove the bus bar and check each plug separately with a continuity tester or self-powered test lamp. Before condemning a plug, make sure that the problem is not simply a loose or dirty connection.

7   The whole preheater system is protected by a fusible link which will melt in the event of a short-circuit. Refer to Chapter 7 for further details.

14 Glow plugs and relay – removal and refitting

Glow plugs
1   Disconnect the battery earth lead and glow plug relay

2   Disconnect the feed wire from the bus bar (photo).

3   Unscrew the terminal nut from each plug to be removed (photo). Remove the nuts, washers and bus bar.

4   Clean around the glow plug seats, then unscrew and remove them (photo).

5   When refitting, apply a little anti-seize compound to the glow plug threads. Screw the glow plugs into place and tighten them to the specified torque.

6   Refit the bus bar and washers and secure with the nuts. Make sure that the clamping areas are clean.

7   Reconnect the feed wire and the battery earth lead.

Glow plug relay
8   The relay is located on the left-hand side of the engine bay. It is secured by a single screw (photo).

9   Disconnect the battery earth lead, then remove the relay securing screw.

10 Peel back the rubber boot and unplug the electrical connector from the relay (photo).

11 Refit in the reverse order to removal.

14.2 Glow plug feed wire connection

14.3 Unscrewing a glow plug terminal nut

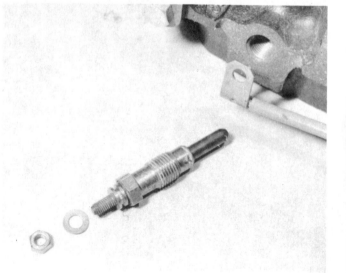

14.4 Glow plug removed from cylinder head

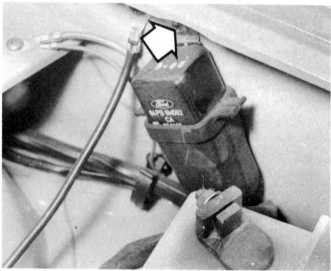

14.8 Glow plug relay – securing screw arrowed

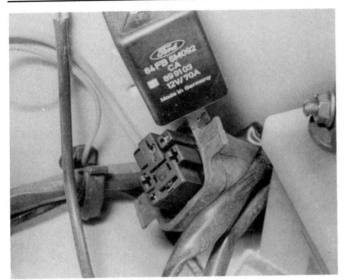

14.10 Electrical connector unplugged from the glow plug relay

15 Throttle cable – removal and refitting

1   Disconnect the battery earth lead.

2   Free the cable inner from the pump by prising off the retaining clip. If this is done carefully, the clip can be re-used; otherwise, obtain a new clip for reassembly.

3   Free the cable outer from the pump bracket by depressing the retaining tangs. If this proves difficult in situ, unbolt the bracket from the pump and remove it with the cable.

4   Unclip the cable from the air cleaner cover.

5   Working inside the vehicle, remove any under-dash trim blocking access to the throttle pedal.

6   Disconnect the cable inner from the pedal by prising off the retaining clip. Again, if handled carefully the clip can be re-used.

7   Free the cable outer retainer from the bulkhead.

8   Withdraw the cable from the engine bay.

9   Transfer any hardware to the new cable, if applicable.

10 Commence refitting by passing the pedal end inner through the bulkhead. Press home the bulkhead retainer and connect the inner to the pedal, securing it with the retaining clip.

11 Reconnect the cable to the pump, securing the inner with a retaining clip and the outer by pressing the retainer into the bracket until it snaps home (photos).

12 Adjust the cable if necessary, using the threaded adjuster at the pump end of the cable, so that with the pedal released there is a small amount of slack in the inner. Have an assistant operate the throttle pedal and check that the throttle lever on the pump moves through its full range of travel (as limited by the idle and maximum speed adjusting screws). Adjust further if necessary.

13 Clip the cable into place on the air cleaner cover.

14 Refit the under-dash trim, if applicable.

15 Reconnect the battery earth lead.

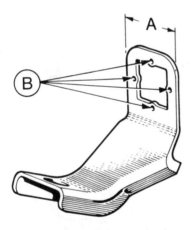

Fig. 3.14 A tool for releasing the throttle cable can be made from an old cable bracket modified as shown (Sec 15)

A = 25 mm (1 in) approx   B Punch holes

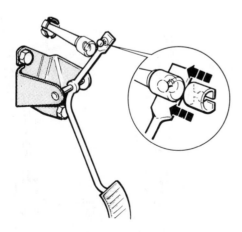

Fig. 3.15 Throttle cable-to-pedal attachment (Sec 15)

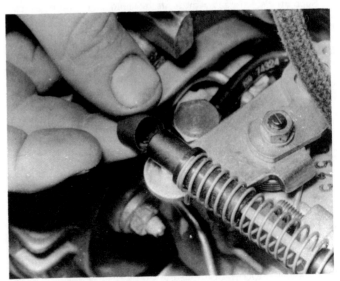

15.11A Fitting the throttle cable inner retaining clip

15.11B Throttle cable outer retainer partly engaged in bracket

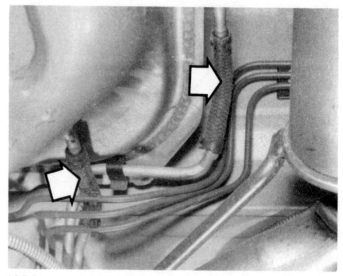

16.5 Disconnect the fuel pipe flexible links (arrowed)

16 Fuel tank – removal and refitting

1   Apart from being considerably safer, fuel tank removal is performed in the same way as on petrol-engined models.

2   Disconnect the battery earth lead.

3   Remove the fuel filler cap. Empty the tank as far as possible by syphoning fuel out of the filler neck. Store the evacuated fuel in clean, closed containers.

4   Raise and securely support the rear of the vehicle.

5   Identify and disconnect the fuel supply and return pipes (photo). Be prepared for fuel spillage. Plug the open pipe ends.

6   If it is accessible, disconnect the electrical lead from the fuel gauge sender unit. (If it is not accessible, disconnect it as the tank is lowered for removal).

7   Support the tank and remove its retaining bolts and/or straps. Carefully lower the tank to the ground, disengaging the filler neck from the seal in the tank.

8   Despite the relative safety of Diesel fuel, repairs to the tank which involve the use of heat should not be attempted.

9   Refit in the reverse order to removal, using new seals and pipes as necessary.

10   Refill the tank and check for leakage.

17 Manifolds – removal and refitting

Inlet

1   Disconnect the battery earth lead.

2   Remove the air cleaner as described in Section 3.

3   Disconnect the manifold-to-camshaft cover breather hose (photo).

4   Unbolt and remove the manifold. Recover the gasket.

5   Commence refitting by placing a new gasket over the studs.

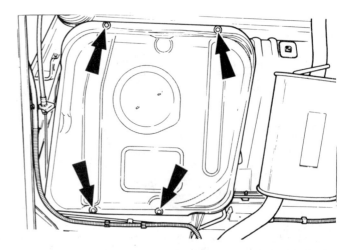

Fig. 3.16 Fuel tank securing bolts (arrowed) – Fiesta (Sec 16)

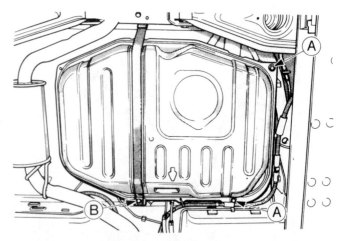

Fig. 3.17 Fuel tank securing bolts (A) and strap bolt (B) – Escort/Orion. Other arrangements may be found (Sec 16)

17.3 Releasing the hose clip from the camshaft cover breather hose

17.6 Refitting the inlet manifold

6   Place the manifold over the studs and secure it with the nuts and bolts (photo). Tighten them evenly to the specified torque.

7   Reconnect the breather hose, refit the air cleaner and reconnect the battery.

Exhaust
8   Remove the inlet manifold as just described.

9   Disconnect the exhaust downpipe from the manifold flange. Recover the gasket.

10 Unbolt the exhaust manifold from the cylinder head. Remove the manifold and recover the gasket.

11 Commence refitting by placing a new gasket over the studs.

12 Fit the manifold and secure it with the nuts and bolts (photo). Only tighten them finger tight at this stage. It is a good idea to use anti-seize compound on the threads.

13 Tighten the nuts and bolts to the specified torque, following the sequence shown in Fig. 3.18.

14 Refit and secure the exhaust downpipe, using a new gasket.

15 Refit the inlet manifold as just described.

18 Exhaust system – inspection, removal and refitting

1   The exhaust system is similar to that fitted to petrol-engined models. There are considerable differences between the Fiesta and the Escort/Orion systems.

2   Inspect the system periodically for leaks, corrosion and other damage, and check the security and condition of the mountings. Small leaks are more easily detected if an assistant partly obstructs the tailpipe with a wad of cloth whilst the engine is idling.

3   Proprietary pastes and bandages are available for the repair of holes and splits. They work well in the short term, but renewal of the section concerned will probably prove more satisfactory in the long run.

4   The rubber mountings will crack and split eventually, and should then be renewed. It is sound practice to renew the mountings when renewing other parts of the system.

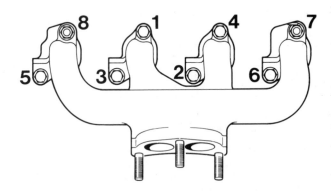

Fig. 3.18 Tightening sequence for exhaust manifold nuts and bolts (Sec 17)

17.12 Refitting the exhaust manifold

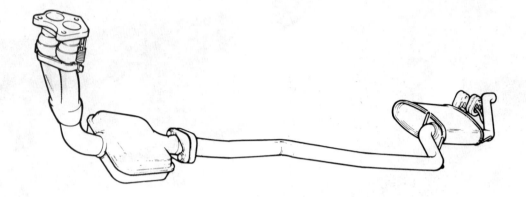

Fig. 3.19 Exhaust system – Fiesta (Sec 18)

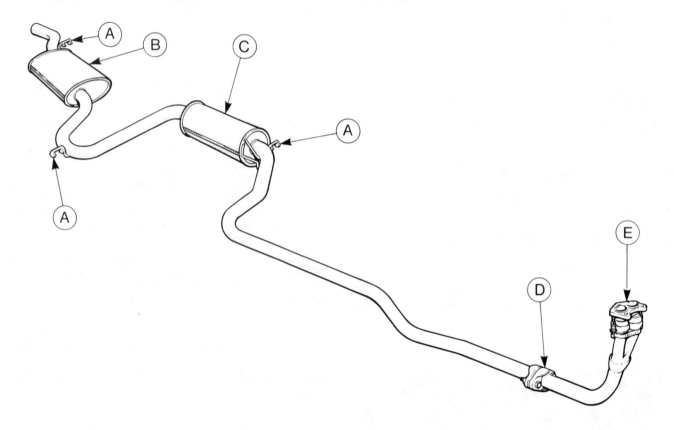

Fig. 3.20 Exhaust system – Escort/Orion (Sec 18)

A   Mountings   C   Front muffler   E   Manifold flange
B   Muffler (silencer) D   Connecting flange

5   It is generally best to remove the whole system, even if only part is to be renewed, as it is easier to separate the sections away from the vehicle.

6   To remove the system, separate the downpipe-to-manifold joint by undoing the three nuts. Unhook the exhaust system from its mountings and remove it. Recover the gasket (photo).

7   To remove the downpipe alone, separate the connecting flange joint as well as the manifold joint (photo).

8   Refit in the reverse order to removal, using a new gasket on the manifold joint. Apply anti-seize compound to all nuts and bolts.

9   Before tightening the connecting flange nuts and bolts, check that there is adequate clearance between the downpipe and surrounding components, and that the rubber mountings are not stressed. ('Adequate clearance' means at least 25 mm/1 in, except for the Fiesta in the areas shown in Fig. 3.21). Move the downpipe spring-loaded balljoints as necessary to achieve this, then tighten the nuts and bolts (photo).

18.6 Exhaust downpipe-to-manifold joint with gasket fitted

18.7 Exhaust connecting flange joint

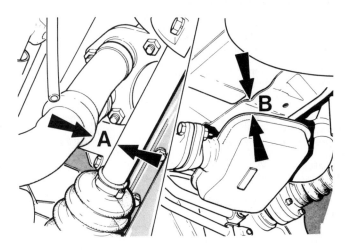

**Fig. 3.21 Exhaust downpipe and resonator clearances –
Fiesta (Sec 18)**

A = 30 mm (1.2 in)   *B = 8 mm (0.3 in)*

18.9 Exhaust spring-loaded balljoints – downpipe removed for
clarity

---

19 Fault diagnosis – fuel injection system

Symptom	Reason(s)
Engine turns normally but will not start	Fuel tank empty
	Incorrect starting procedure
	Fuel tank cap vent blocked
	Fuel filter blocked
	Wax in fuel (in very cold conditions)
	Fuel shut-off solenoid disconnected, defective or corroded
	Preheater system faulty
	Cold start device disconnected or defective
	Ignition timing incorrect
	Pump defective
	Poor compression (see Chapter 1)
	Early type glow plugs fitted (short glow duration)
Idling erratic when warm	Air in fuel lines
	Idle speed adjustment incorrect
	Injection timing incorrect
	Injector(s) defective

Symptom	Reason(s)
Engine 'hunts' when idling	Fuel tank cap vent blocked Fuel filter blocked
Misfiring under load	Injector(s) not seating properly, or otherwise defective Engine defect (eg head gasket, valve seating etc)
Lack of power	Fuel tank cap vent blocked Fuel filter blocked Wax in fuel (in very cold conditions) Air cleaner blocked Air or water in fuel Injection timing incorrect Injector(s) defective Other problem (eg brakes binding, poor engine compression, etc)
Fuel consumption excessive	External leakage Air cleaner blocked Injector(s) defective Injection timing incorrect Inappropriate driving style or conditions Other problem (eg brakes binding, poor engine compression, etc)
Engine will not stop	Fuel shut-off solenoid defective
Engine will not rev when cold	Fuel level too low Fuel tank cap vent blocked Fuel shut-off solenoid defective Fuel filter blocked Wax in fuel (in very cold conditions) Injection timing incorrect Engine mechanical problem
White smoke in exhaust	Injection timing incorrect Low compression Water entering cylinders
Black smoke in exhaust	Air cleaner blocked Injector(s) defective
Blue smoke in exhaust	Engine oil entering cylinders Injector(s) defective

Chapter 4 Clutch, transmission and driveshafts

For modifications, and information applicable to later models, see Supplement at end of manual

Contents

Specifications

Clutch

Type	Single dry plate, diaphragm spring, cable actuated
Driven plate diameter	190 mm (7.5 in) nominal
Adjustment	Automatic in use
Pedal stroke:	
Fiesta	145 mm (5.7 in) approx
Escort/Orion	155 mm (6.1 in) approx

Transmission

Type	Manual, five forward speeds and one reverse; synchro on all forward gears
Ratios:	
1st	3.58:1
2nd	1.91:1
3rd	1.28:1
4th	0.95:1
5th	0.76:1
Reverse	3.62:1
Final drive ratio:	
Fiesta	3.33:1
Escort/Orion	3.84:1
Lubricant type/specification	Hypoid gear oil, viscosity SAE 80EP, to Ford spec SQM 2C 9008 A (Duckhams Hypoid 80)
Lubricant capacity	3.1 litres (5.5 pints) approx

Driveshafts

Type	Open, tubular, CV joints, at each end

Torque wrench settings

	Nm	lbf ft
Transmission-to-engine bolts	35 to 45	26 to 33
Clutch housing cover plate	35 to 45	26 to 33
Mountings – Fiesta:		
Bearer to transmission	80 to 100	59 to 74
Bearer to body	52	38
Mountings – Escort/Orion:		
Front	41 to 51	30 to 38
Rear	52 to 64	38 to 47
Gearshift stabiliser to transmission case	50 to 60	37 to 44
Gearshift rod clamp bolt	14 to 17	10 to 13
Gearshift housing to floor pan	15 to 22	11 to 16
Oil filler/level plug	23 to 30	17 to 22
Clutch pressure plate to flywheel	16 to 20	12 to 15
Driveshaft nut	205 to 235	151 to 173

1 General description

The transmission and associated components are virtually identical to those used in petrol-engined models. Drive is taken from the engine to the transmission by means of a single plate clutch. The only transmission fitted at the time of writing is a five-speed manual one, with integral differential and final drive. From the final drive a pair of open driveshafts, of unequal length, drive the front wheels. The longer driveshaft carries one or two torsional damper weights.

Except as described in this Chapter, repair and overhaul operations are essentially the same as for petrol-engined vehicles.

2 Maintenance and inspection

Clutch

1 Clutch adjustment is automatic in use, by means of a ratchet device at the pedal. If pedal free play becomes excessive, this can be corrected by lifting the pedal as far as its stop and then releasing it.

2 No other routine maintenance is specified for the clutch. If the cable becomes stiff or jerky it should be renewed. Components such as the release bearing and the driven plate should be inspected if they become accessible during other operations, and renewed if necessary.

Transmission

3 At alternate major service intervals, or more frequently if oil leakage is known to be a problem, check the transmission oil level as follows.

4 With the vehicle parked on level ground, locate the oil filler/level plug (photo). If it is necessary to raise the vehicle for access to the plug, maintain its level attitude as far as possible. Wipe around the plug, then unscrew and remove it.

5 The oil level should be within 10 mm (0.4 in) of the bottom edge of the filler plug hole. Top up if necessary, using oil of the specified grade, until oil starts to drip out of the hole. Allow any surplus to drip out, then refit and tighten the filler/level plug.

6 Check for oil leaks if frequent topping-up is necessary. Renew leaking oil seals or repair other damage.

7 Oil changing is not considered necessary as a routine operation. Should it be wished to drain the lubricant, however, this can be done by removing the selector shaft locking components.

Driveshafts

8 Regularly inspect the driveshaft CV joint gaiters for cracks, splits or other damage. Prompt renewal may save the joint itself.

3 Transmission – removal and refitting

Transmission removal and refitting procedures are the same as for petrol-engined models, apart from the starter motor removal procedure (see Chapter 7) and the different positions of the transmission-to-engine bolts.

4 Driveshafts

1 The driveshaft removal and refitting details are the same as for petrol-engined models. Some later 1.8 litre models may be fitted with an inner driveshaft fitted with a tripod-type joint rather than the ball-type joint normally used. This modification is made to the left and right hand driveshaft to reduce overrun rumble.

2 When assembling the tripod-type joint, the joint housing must be packed with 95 grammes of the specified grease and a new circlip fitted to secure the inner joint.

3 Whenever the driveshafts have been removed or detached from the transmission it is advisable to renew the driveshaft oil seal in the transmission housing. After the driveshaft is refitted and the vehicle is standing level, the oil level in the transmission should be checked and if necessary, the level topped up with the specified grade of oil.

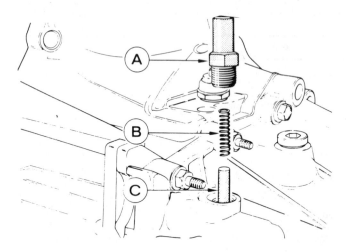

Fig. 4.1 Selector shaft locking components – remove to drain (Sec 2)

A Cap nut   B Spring   C Detent pin

2.4 Transmission oil filler/level plug (arrowed)

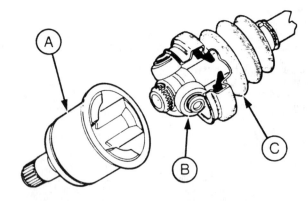

4.2 Tripod-type driveshaft joint fitted to some later 1.8 litre models (Sec 4)

A Joint bellhousing
B Driveshaft and tripod joint unit
C Rubber gaiter

Chapter 5 Braking system

Contents

Specifications

General

System type .... Discs front, drums rear; hydraulic operation with servo assistance. Handbrake mechanical to rear wheels

Adjustment .... Automatic in use

Front (disc) brakes

Disc diameter:
    Fiesta .... 221.0 mm (8.70 in)
    Escort/Orion .... 239.5 mm (9.43 in)
Disc thickness:
    New .... 10.0 mm (0.39 in)
    Minimum .... 8.7 mm (0.34 in)
Disc run-out (fitted) .... 0.15 mm (0.006 in) max
Pad lining thickness .... 1.5 mm (0.06 in) min

Rear (drum) brakes

Drum diameter:
    Fiesta .... 177.8 mm (7.00 in)
    Escort/Orion .... 180.0 mm (7.09 in)
Shoe lining thickness .... 1.0 mm (0.04 in) min

Hydraulic system

Type .... Dual circuit, diagonally split
Fluid type/specification .... Hydraulic fluid to Ford spec Amber SAM 6C 9103 A or C (Duckhams Universal Brake and Clutch Fluid)

Torque wrench setting

	Nm	lbf ft
Vacuum pump to cylinder head	18 to 22	13 to 16

1 General description

The braking system is conventional in design. The brake pedal operates disc brakes at the front, drums at the rear, by means of a dual circuit hydraulic system and with servo assistance. The handbrake operates on the rear wheels only, by means of cables. Both front and rear brakes are self-adjusting in normal use.

Because there is no throttling of the inlet manifold on the Diesel engine, it is not a suitable source of vacuum for servo operation. Vacuum is therefore derived from a separate vacuum pump, driven by an eccentric on the tail of the camshaft.

Except as noted in this Chapter, overhaul and repair procedures are as described in the appropriate manual for petrol-engined vehicles.

2 Maintenance and inspection

1 Maintenance is as described for petrol-engined vehicles, with the following additions.

2 At every major service interval, inspect the vacuum pump for oil leaks, security and condition of hoses and security of mountings. Rectify as necessary.

3 At the same intervals, check the operation of the pump as follows.

4 With the engine stopped, operate the footbrake several times to destroy any residual vacuum in the servo. Keep the brake pedal depressed and start the engine. The pedal should be felt to move downwards as the vacuum pump operates on the servo – if not, there is

a fault in the pump, the servo or their connecting pipe (not forgetting the non-return valve).

5   A defective vacuum pump must be renewed – no spares are available.

3 Vacuum pump – removal and refitting

1   Disconnect the battery earth lead.

2   Disconnect the breather hoses, then unbolt and remove the camshaft cover. Note the location of the reinforcing strips. Those bolts without reinforcing strips have washers.

3   Turn the engine (eg by applying a gear and turning a front wheel) until the vacuum pump cam lobe is pointing away from the pump. The vacuum pump is mounted on the flywheel end of the engine (refer to page 4, item 12).

4   Unscrew the vacuum pipe union from the pump (photo). Plug the hole to keep dirt out.

5   Disconnect the pump oil return hose (photo). Be prepared for oil spillage.

6   Remove the pump upper securing bolt. Slacken the lower bolt a few turns, tilt the pump and slide it upwards to remove it. Recover the sealing ring.

7   Commence refitting by placing a new sealing ring in the groove on the pump flange (photo).

8   Tilt the pump and engage its slotted lower mounting over the slackened lower bolt (photo).

9   Insert the upper bolt. Tighten both bolts progressively to the specified torque.

10 Reconnect the pump oil return hose, using new clips if necessary.

11 Remove the blanking plug. Refit the vacuum pipe union and tighten it.

12 Refit the camshaft cover, using a new gasket if necessary. Tighten the bolts to the specified torque (see Chapter 1 Specifications). Reconnect the breather hoses.

13 Reconnect the battery earth lead.

14 Start the engine and check for correct operation of the pump as described in the previous Section.

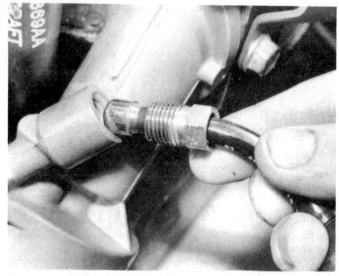

3.4 Disconnecting the vacuum pipe from the pump

3.5 Disconnecting the vacuum pump oil return hose

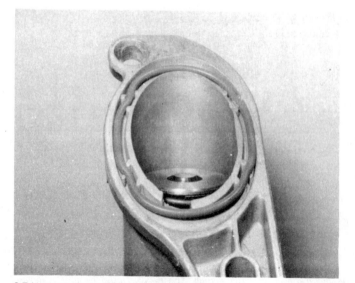

3.7 Vacuum pump flange with O-ring fitted

3.8 Fitting the pump over the lower bolt

Chapter 6 Suspension and steering

Contents

Specifications

General

Suspension type:
Front, all models	Fully independent, MacPherson struts
Rear, Fiesta	Semi-independent, five-point linkage
Rear, Escort/Orion (except Van)	Fully independent, wishbone and tie-bar
Rear, Escort Van	Axle tube and leaf springs
Steering type, all models	Rack and pinion

Front suspension alignment

Fiesta:
Castor, nominal	+0° 30'
Castor, tolerance	−0° 30' to +1° 45'
Camber, nominal	+1° 45'
Camber, tolerance	+0° 45' to +2° 45'
Toe, nominal	3.0 ± 1.0 mm (0.12 ± 0.04 in, or 0° 30' ± 0° 10') toe-out
Toe, tolerance	0 to 6 mm (0 to 0.24 in, or 0° 00' to 1° 00') toe-out

Escort/Orion:
Castor, nominal (except Estate and Van)	+2° 15'
Castor, nominal (Estate)	+2° 45' standard, +2° 15' heavy duty
Castor, nominal (Van)	+1° 39' (35), +1° 19' (55)
Castor, tolerance	+1° 00'
Camber, nominal (except Estate and Van)	0° 00' standard, +0° 30' heavy duty
Camber, nominal (Estate)	+0° 30'
Camber, nominal (Van)	−0° 17'
Camber, tolerance	±1° 00'
Toe, nominal	2.5 mm ± 1 mm (0.10 ± 0.04 in) toe-out
Toe, tolerance	0.5 mm (0.02 in) toe-in to 5.5 mm (0.22 in) toe-out

Rear suspension alignment

Fiesta .... Not stated

Escort/Orion (except Van) – according to ride height:

	Toe setting (± 0° 52')	Camber (± 1° 00')
349 to 372 mm	0° 08'	−1° 05'
373 to 396 mm	0° 15'	−0° 30'
397 to 420 mm	0° 30'	−0° 14'
421 to 438 mm	0° 50'	+0° 52'
439 to 450 mm	1° 15'	+1° 22'

Escort Van .... Not stated

Tyre pressures, cold, in bar (lbf/in²)

	Normal load*		Full load†	
	Front	Rear	Front	Rear
Fiesta:				
Hatchback	1.9 (28)	1.9 (28)	2.1 (31)	2.3 (33)
Van	1.6 (23)	1.8 (26)	2.1 (31)	2.3 (33)
Orion	1.8 (26)	2.0 (29)	2.0 (29)	2.3 (33)
Escort:				
Hatchback and Estate	1.8 (26)	2.0 (29)	2.0 (29)	2.3 (33)
Van:				
155 R 13 tyres	1.8 (26)	1.8 (26)	1.8 (26)	2.6 (38)
165 R 13 tyres	1.8 (26)	1.8 (26)	1.8 (26)	3.0 (44)

* Normal load is defined as up to three passengers, or a load of up to 170 kg (375 lb) plus driver
† On Fiesta only, full load pressures may be used under all conditions to achieve maximum fuel economy

1 Introduction

Suspension and steering systems are identical to those found on the equivalent petrol-engined vehicles. Various components may be uprated to take account of the increased weight of the Diesel engine – for instance, the Diesel Fiesta shares a special tie-bar bracket with the XR2.

Should the pre-1985 Escort and Orion models suffer from the suspension bottoming under certain road conditions, or exhibit excessive front tyre wear, the uprated struts and coil springs fitted to later models may be substituted for the original components.

Maintenance, inspection and repair procedures are as given in the appropriate manual for petrol-engined vehicles. Refer also to the Specifications in this Chapter.

2 Wheels and tyres – general care and maintenance

Wheels and tyres should give no real problems in use provided that a close eye is kept on them with regard to excessive wear or damage. To this end, the following points should be noted.

Ensure that tyre pressures are checked regularly and maintained correctly (photo). Checking should be carried out with the tyres cold and not immediately after the vehicle has been in use. If the pressures are checked with the tyres hot, an apparently high reading will be obtained owing to heat expansion. Under no circumstances should an attempt be made to reduce the pressures to the quoted cold reading in this instance, or effective underinflation will result.

Underinflation will cause overheating of the tyre owing to excessive flexing of the casing, and the tread will not sit correctly on the road surface. This will cause a consequent loss of adhesion and excessive wear, not to mention the danger of sudden tyre failure due to heat build-up.

Overinflation will cause rapid wear of the centre part of the tyre tread coupled with reduced adhesion, harsher ride, and the danger of shock damage occurring in the tyre casing.

Regularly check the tyres for damage in the form of cuts or bulges, especially in the sidewalls. Remove any nails or stones embedded in the tread before they penetrate the tyre to cause deflation. If removal of a nail *does* reveal that the tyre has been punctured, refit the nail so that its point of penetration is marked. Then immediately change the wheel and have the tyre repaired by a tyre dealer. Do *not* drive on a tyre in such a condition. In many cases a puncture can be simply repaired by the use of an inner tube of the correct size and type. If in any doubt as to the possible consequences of any damage found, consult your local tyre dealer for advice.

Periodically remove the wheels and clean any dirt or mud from the inside and outside surfaces. Examine the wheel rims for signs of rusting, corrosion or other damage. Light alloy wheels are easily damaged by 'kerbing' whilst parking, and similarly steel wheels may become dented or buckled. Renewal of the wheel is very often the only course of remedial action possible.

The balance of each wheel and tyre assembly should be maintained to avoid excessive wear, not only to the tyres but also to the steering and suspension components. Wheel imbalance is normally signified by vibration through the vehicle's bodyshell, although in many cases it is particularly noticeable through the steering wheel. Conversely, it should be noted that wear or damage in suspension or steering

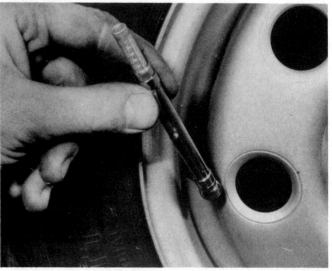

2.0 Checking a tyre pressure

components may cause excessive tyre wear. Out-of-round or out-of-true tyres, damaged wheels and wheel bearing wear/maladjustment also fall into this category. Balancing will not usually cure vibration caused by such wear.

Wheel balancing may be carried out with the wheel either on or off the vehicle. If balanced on the vehicle, ensure that the wheel-to-hub relationship is marked in some way prior to subsequent wheel removal so that it may be refitted in its original position.

General tyre wear is influenced to a large degree by driving style – harsh braking and acceleration or fast cornering will all produce more rapid tyre wear. Interchanging of tyres may result in more even wear, but this should only be carried out where there is no mix of tyre types on the vehicle. However, it is worth bearing in mind that if this is completely effective, the added expense of replacing a complete set of tyres simultaneously is incurred, which may prove financially restrictive for many owners.

Front tyres may wear unevenly as a result of wheel misalignment. The front wheels should always be correctly aligned according to the settings specified by the vehicle manufacturer.

Legal restrictions apply to the mixing of tyre types on a vehicle. Basically this means that a vehicle must not have tyres of differing construction on the same axle. Although it is not recommended to mix tyre types between front axle and rear axle, the only legally permissible combination is crossply at the front and radial at the rear. When mixing radial ply tyres, textile braced radials must always go on the front axle, with steel braced radials at the rear. An obvious disadvantage of such mixing is the necessity to carry two spare tyres to avoid contravening the law in the event of a puncture.

In the UK, the Motor Vehicles Construction and Use Regulations apply to many aspects of tyre fitting and usage. It is suggested that a copy of these regulations is obtained from your local police if in doubt as to the current legal requirements with regard to tyre condition, minimum tread depth, etc.

Chapter 7 Electrical system

For modifications, and information applicable to later models, see Supplement at end of manual

Contents

Specifications

General
System type .... 12 V, negative earth

Battery
Type .... Lead acid
Capacity .... 63 Ah nominal
Rating (cold cranking/reserve capacity) 610 A/110RC

Alternator
Make and type .... Lucas A127/45, A127/55, or Mitsubishi
Nominal rated output (at 13.5 V and 6000 engine rpm):
    A127/45 .... 45 A
    A127/55 and Mitsubishi .... 55 A
Regulating voltage:
    Lucas .... 13.7 to 14.6
    Mitsubishi .... 13.7 to 14.6
Rotor winding resistance:
    Lucas .... 3.2 ($\pm$ 5%)
    Mitsubishi .... 2.7 to 3.1
Brush wear limit:
    Lucas .... 5.0 mm (0.20 in) protrusion
    Mitsubishi .... 5.0 mm (0.20 in) protrusion

Starter motor
Make and type .... Bosch 1.7 kW short frame or reduction gear
Brush wear limit .... 8 mm (0.32 in) long
Commutator refinishing limit .... 32.8 mm (1.29 in) diameter
Armature endfloat .... 0.3 mm (0.012 in)

Torque wrench settings

	Nm	lbf ft
Starter motor bracket to block	20	15
Starter motor to transmission	35 to 45	26 to 33

1 General description

The electrical system follows conventional automobile practice: 12 volt, negative earth, with power being supplied by an alternator driven from the crankshaft pulley. A lead acid battery provides a reserve of power for starting the engine, and for situations where the demand on the system temporarily exceeds the alternator output.

Except as noted in this Chapter, repair and overhaul procedures are as described in the relevant manual for petrol-engined vehicles. The main differences are in the starting and charging system, both of which are uprated to cope with the heavier demands of the Diesel engines.

Two types of starter motor are fitted. The first type is a larger version of a petrol engine starter. The second type is unusual in having permanent magnets instead of field windings, and carries a planetary reduction gear set between the armature and the pinion. Both these features contribute to the motor's low size and weight.

2 Maintenance and inspection

1   At alternate major service intervals, check the tension and condition of the alternator/water pump drivebelt. Refer to Chapter 2, Section 11.

2   At the same intervals, clean the battery terminals as follows. Disconnect the terminals, earth (negative) first (photo). Clean the terminals with a wire brush or abrasive paper. Remove stubborn deposits with a solution of bicarbonate of soda and an old toothbrush – do not let any solution get into the battery. Coat the terminals with petroleum jelly or proprietary anti-corrosive compound, then refit and tighten them.

3   Keep the top of the battery clean and dry. Periodically inspect its tray for corrosion, and make good as necessary.

2.2 Disconnecting the battery earth terminal

4   Other maintenance work on the battery is considered in the next Section.

5   At all times, be careful to keep fuel and coolant out of the alternator and starter motor. Diesel fuel has a more damaging effect on some electrical components than petrol.

3 Battery – maintenance and charging

1   The battery fitted as original equipment requires no maintenance, other than having the terminals and top kept clean as deescribed in the previous Section.

2   Other types of battery may be fitted as replacements. Unless otherwise instructed, check the electrolyte level at every major service interval, either by removing the cell covers or by observing the level through the translucent case. The plate separators in each cell should be covered to a depth of approximately 6 mm (0.25 in). Top up if necessary using clean distilled or de-ironized water. Refit the cell covers and mop up any spillage.

3   If a battery hydrometer is available, it is instructive to measure the state of charge of the battery occasionally. Electrolyte is sucked up from each cell in turn, a reading is taken and the electrolyte returned to the cell. Typical readings are as follows:

State of charge	Hydrometer reading
Full	1.27 to 1.29
Half	1.20 to 1.22
Zero	1.11 to 1.13

4   If one cell has a much lower hydrometer reading than the others, this may be a sign of approaching cell failure. Alternatively, electrolyte may have been lost from that cell at some time and the deficiency made up with water instead of with electrolyte. Consult a Ford dealer or battery specialist if electrolyte replenishment seems necessary – do not attempt to mix it yourself.

5   In normal use the battery should not require charging from an external source, unless the vehicle is laid up for long periods, when it should be recharged every six weeks or so. If vehicle use consists entirely of short runs in darkness it is also possible for the battery to become discharged. Otherwise, a regular need for recharging points to a fault in the battery or elsewhere in the charging system.

6   Domestic battery chargers of low output (say up to 6 A) can safely be used with the battery connected and in the vehicle. Charging at a higher rate should only be done under carefully controlled conditions; the battery must be disconnected from the vehicle wiring, and should preferably be removed completely. Rapid or 'boost' charging should be avoided if possible.

4 Alternator – removal and refitting

1   Access to the alternator is from below. Raise the vehicle on ramps, or drive it over a pit.

2   Disconnect the battery earth (negative) lead.

3   Unplug the electrical connectors from the alternator. It will be necessary to remove the end cover for access to the main connector, which is secured by a spring clip (photo).

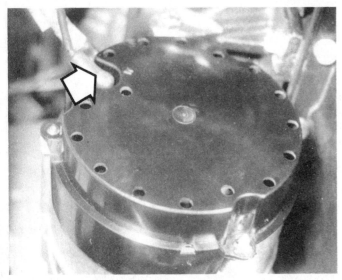

4.3A Alternator warning light connector (arrowed)

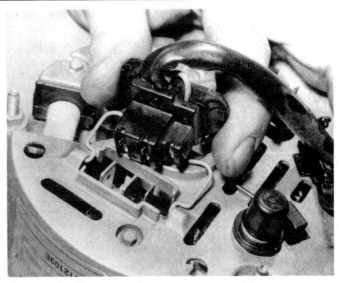

4.3B Unplugging the alternator main connector

4.4 Alternator pivot and adjusting strap fastenings (arrowed)

4   Slacken the alternator pivot and adjusting strap nuts and bolts. Pivot the alternator towards the engine and remove the drivebelt (photo).

5   Support the alternator. Remove the pivot and adjusting strap nuts and bolts. Withdraw the alternator from under the vehicle.

6   Do not drop the alternator, it is fragile. Also protect it from entry of coolant, fuel or other fluids.

7   Commence refitting by securing the alternator to its mountings. Leave the pivot and adjusting strap nuts and bolts finger tight.

8   Refit and tension the drivebelt as described in Chapter 2, Section 11.

9   Refit the electrical connectors and the end cover.

10 Reconnect the battery earth lead. Run the engine and check that the 'no charge' warning light goes out. If not, check that the diode in the warning light circuit is connected the right way round (photo).

5   Alternator – brush renewal

Lucas

1   Remove the alternator as described in the previous Section.

2   Remove the three screws which secure the voltage regultor/brush carrier to the rear of the alternator (photo). Remove the regulator/carrier unit, at the same time disengaging the field connector.

3   Measure the length of the brushes protruding from the carrier (photo). If they are at or below the specified minimum, a new regulator/carrier unit, complete with brushes, must be fitted.

4   Before refitting, clean the alternator slip rings with a petrol-moistened cloth.

5   Fit the regulator/carrier unit to the alternator, placing the brushes onto the slip rings and engaging the field connector.

6   Insert and tighten the three securing screws.

7   Refit the alternator to the vehicle.

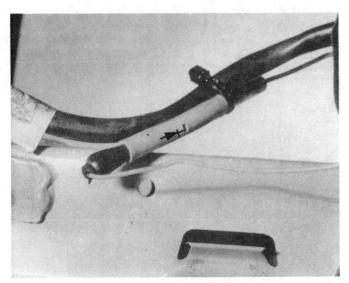

4.10 Warning light diode (clipped to harness between starter and alternator) must be connected the right way round

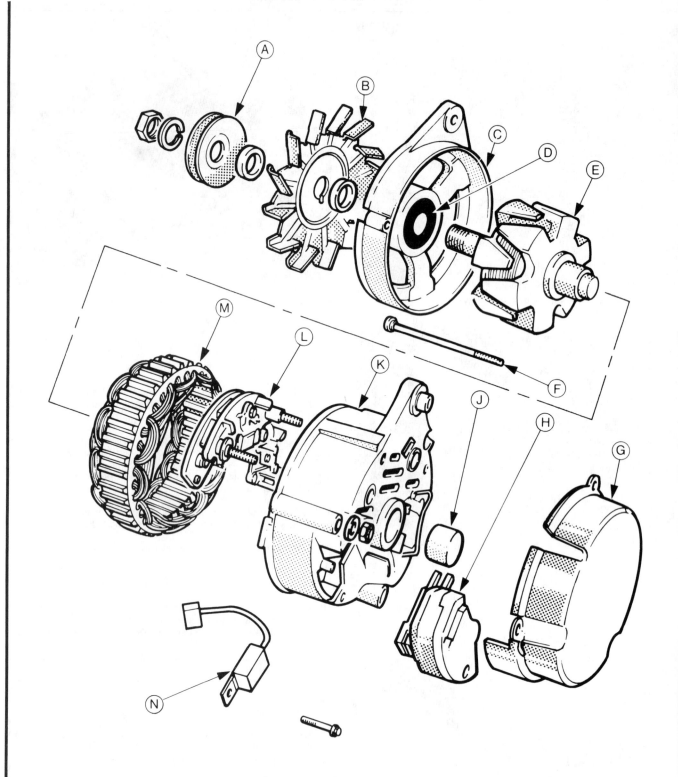

Fig. 7.1 Exploded view of Lucas alternator (Sec 5)

A Pulley
B Fan
C Drive end housing
D Drive end bearing
E Rotor

F Through-bolt
G Cover
H Voltage regulator/brush
   carrier

J Slip ring end bearing
K Slip ring end housing
L Diode plate (rectifier)

M Stator
N Radio interference
   suppressor

5.2 Voltage regulator/brush carrier securing screws (arrowed)

5.3 Voltage regulator/brush carrier removed

Mitsubishi
8   Refer to relevant manual for petrol-engined vehicle.

---

6   Starter motor – removal and refitting

1   The starter motor is removed from below. Raise the vehicle on ramps, or drive it over a pit.

2   Disconnect the battery earth (negative) lead.

3   Disconnect the main lead and the command lead from the starter motor solenoid (photos).

4   Remove the bolt which secures the tail bracket to the block (photo). (On some models there may be two such bolts.)

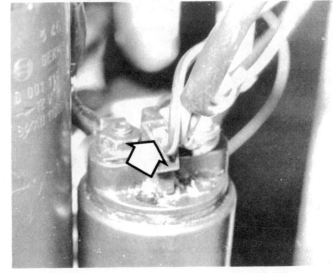

6.3A Starter motor command lead (arrowed)

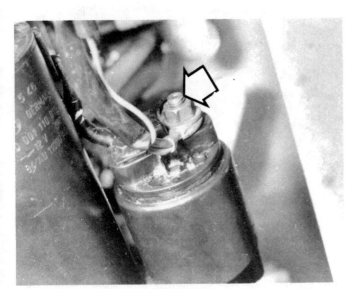

6.3B Starter motor main lead (arrowed)

6.4 Starter motor tail bracket bolt (arrowed)

5   Support the motor and remove the three bolts which secure it to the transmission (photo). Remove the motor.

6   When refitting, leave the tail bracket-to-motor nuts loose until the motor and bracket bolts have been fitted and tightened.

7   Tighten the motor-to-transmission bolts to the specified torque. Tighten the bracket-to-block bolts(s) next, and finally tighten the bracket-to-motor nuts.

8   Reconnect the command and main leads to the solenoid.

9   Reconnect the battery and check for correct operation.

7   Starter motor – brush renewal

1   Remove the starter motor as described in the previous Section. Remove the tail bracket (photo).

2   Disconnect the link lead from the solenoid terminal (photo).

3   Remove the two screws which secure the armature end cap. Remove the cap, the C-washer and plain washer(s) (photo). Wipe away grease from the end of the armature shaft.

4   Remove the two through-bolts or studs. If the stud nuts are inaccessible, lock two nuts onto the end of the stud and use them to unscrew it (photos).

5   Remove the commutator end cover to expose the brushgear (photo).

6   Carefully withdraw the brushplate from the commutator. The brushes will be released with some force: to avoid damage, unclip them by pressing their holders towards the commutator as the brushplate is withdrawn.

7   Remove the old brushes and fit the new ones. On the reduction gear motor, the brushes are handled in pairs, each pair sharing a clip

6.5 Removing a starter motor-to-transmission bolt

7.1 Tail bracket securing nuts (arrowed). Note correct fitting of bracket – it can be fitted 180° out

7.2 Disconnecting the link lead from the solenoid terminal

7.3 Removing the C-washer (arrowed) from the end of the armature shaft

7.4A Using the tail bracket nuts, locked together, to unscrew a stud

7.4B Removing a stud – note cup washer (arrowed)

7.5 Starter motor with commutator end cover removed

which fits over the brushplate (photo). On the short frame motor, the brush leads must be removed from the stand-off connectors and the clips on the new leads soldered to the connectors (Fig. 7.2).

8 Clean the commutator with a rag moistened in petrol or other suitable solvent. If this does not remove burn marks or other damage, refer to the next Section.

9 Fit the brushplate over the commutator. Either clip the brushes in place after locating the brushplate, or use a tube of suitable diameter to keep the brushes retracted during fitting (photo). Either way it is a fiddly business.

10 Refit the commutator end cover and secure it with the through-bolts or studs.

11 Refit the plain washer(s) to the end of the armature shafts and secure with the C-washer. Apply some grease to the shaft, then refit and secure the cap.

7.7 Brushgear fitted to reduction gear type motor

Fig. 7.2 Brushplate and brushes – short frame starter motor (Sec 7)

1   *Stand-off connector*   2   *Clip*

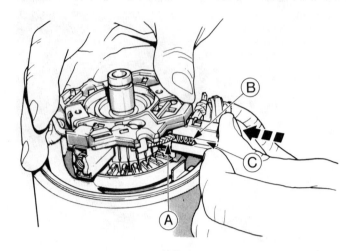

Fig. 7.3 Fitting the brushes after locating the brushplate (Sec 7)

A   Brush   C   Holder
B   Spring

7.9 Using a socket to keep the brushes retracted

12 Reconnect the link lead to the solenoid. Refit the tail bracket, making sure that it is the right way round, but only tighten its nuts finger tight for now.

13 Refit the starter motor as described in the previous Section.

8   Starter motor – overhaul

1   Complete overhaul of a well-used motor is unlikely to be an economic proposition, since the cost of the new parts needed may well exceed the cost of a new or reconditioned motor. However, most parts can be renewed, so in the event of premature failure of one part the motor can be repaired.

2   Remove the starter motor as described in Section 6. Clean it externally if necessary.

3   Remove the brushgear as described in the previous Section.

Short frame type
Note: Refer to Figs. 7.4, 7.5, 7.6, 7.8 and 7.9

4   Remove the three screws which secure the solenoid. Withdraw the solenoid yoke and spring; unhook and remove the plunger.

5   Remove the field winding yoke by carefully tapping the drive end housing off it. The armature, pinion etc can be freed from the drive end housing. Note the location of the rubber plug.

6   To remove the pinion and one-way clutch from the shaft, carefully grip the armature (**not** the clutch) in a vice with padded jaws. Use a tube and hammer to drive the thrust collar down the shaft to expose the spring clip. Remove the thrust collar and clip, then pull off the clutch and pinion.

Reduction gear type
Note: Refer to Chapter 8, Fig. 8.29, and to Figs. 7.7 and 7.9 of this Chapter.

7   With the brushgear removed, the field yoke and armature can be pulled off the drive end housing. Draw the armature out of the yoke, against the pull of the field magnets (photo). Be careful with the yoke – the magnets are fragile.

8   Remove the three screws which secure the solenoid. Withdraw the solenoid, unhooking its plunger from the operating arm (photos).

9   The drive end components can now be withdrawn from the drive end housing (photo). Note the location of the rubber plug.

10 The pinion and one-way clutch can be removed as described in paragraph 6 (photos).

All types
11 Inspect all components for wear and damage. The armature shaft bushes can be renewed if necessary. If there are signs that the commutator has been touching pole pieces, bush wear may be suspected.

12 Simple continuity checks can be made on the armature and (when applicable) the field windings, using a multi-meter or a battery and test lamp. Special test equipment is required for thorough checking, however.

13 A burnt or otherwise damaged commutator can sometimes be reclaimed by machining, providing that the refinishing limit is not exceeded. This is specialist work. Be wary of using abrasives to clean the commutator, as particles may become embedded in the copper.

14 Renewal of individual field coils or magnets is not possible without special equipment, even if the parts are available.

15 Commence reassembly by fitting the clutch and pinion to the armature or planet gear shaft. Fit the thrust collar and a new spring clip to the shaft, then use a couple of spanners to lever the collar over the clip (photo).

16 On the reduction gear (DW) type motor, apply a little silicone-based grease to the reduction gears (photo). When refitting the armature to the yoke, insert the retaining plate and twist it clockwise to position it as shown in Fig 7.7.

17 Reassemble the motor in the reverse order to that followed when dismantling. Note how the solenoid plunger is fitted to the operating arm on the short frame motor (Fig 7.8).

18 Refit the brushgear as described in the previous Section. Adjust the armature endfloat as near zero as possible, without preloading, by adding or subtracting plain washers under the C-washer. Push the armature towards the commutator end to take up any slack when checking endfloat.

19 Refit the starter motor as described in Section 6.

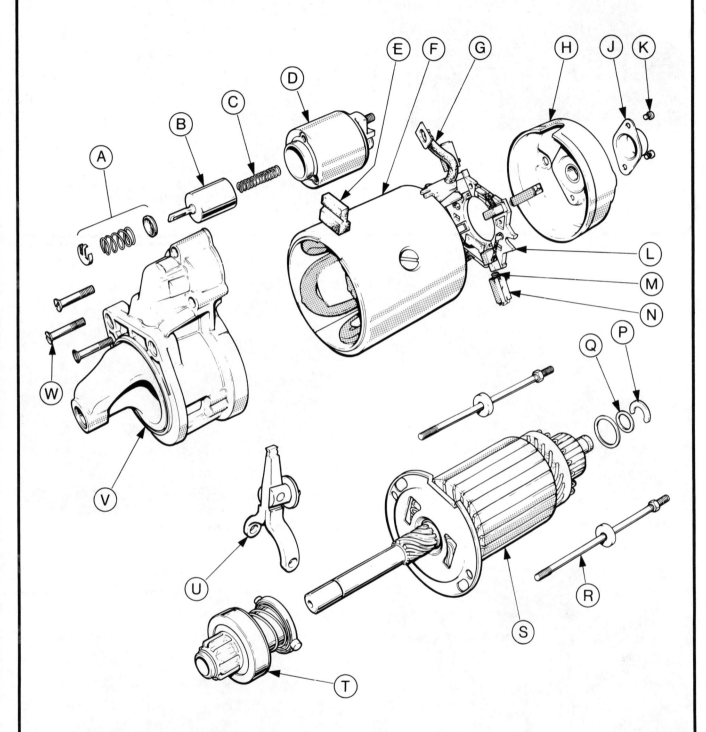

Fig. 7.4 Exploded view of Bosch short frame starter motor (Sec 8)

A	Operating arm retaining components	F	Field winding yoke	M	Spring	S
B	Plunger	G	Link lead	N	Brush holder	T
C	Spring	H	Commutator end cover	P	C-washer	U
D	Solenoid yoke	J	Armature cap	Q	Plain washer	V
E	Rubber plug	K	Cap screw	R	Through-stud	W
		L	Brushplate			

A Operating arm retaining
   components
B Plunger
C Spring
D Solenoid yoke
E Rubber plug

F Field winding yoke
G Link lead
H Commutator end cover
J Armature cap
K Cap screw
L Brushplate

M Spring
N Brush holder
P C-washer
Q Plain washer
R Through-stud

S Armature
T Pinion and clutch
U Operating arm
V Drive end housing
W Screw

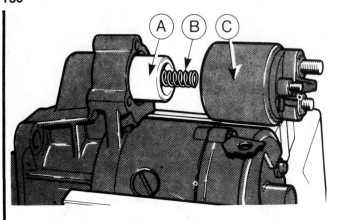

Fig. 7.5 Removing the solenoid – short frame motor (Sec 8)

A Plunger
B Spring

C Yoke

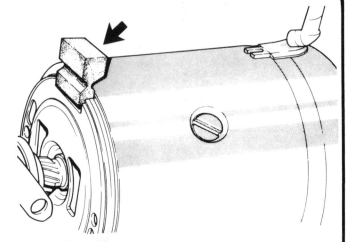

Fig. 7.6 Correct position of rubber plug (arrowed) – short frame motor (Sec 8)

8.7 Removing the armature from the yoke

8.8A Removing a solenoid securing screw

8.8B Unhooking the solenoid plunger from the operating arm

8.9 Drive end components and housing

8.10A Using a tube and hammer to drive down the thrust collar

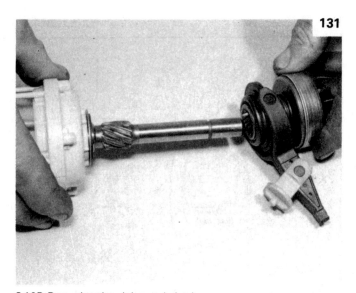

8.10B Removing the pinion and clutch

8.15 Levering the collar over the spring clip

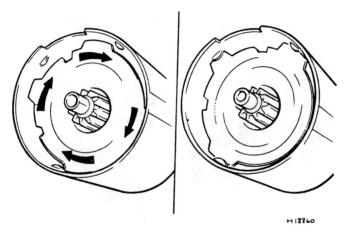

Fig. 7.7 Twist armature retaining plate clockwise into correct position in yoke – reduction gear (DW) motor (Sec 8)

8.16 Reduction gears exposed

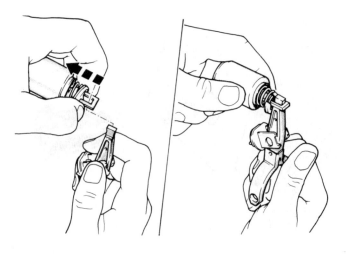

Fig. 7.8 Fitting the solenoid plunger to the operating arm – short frame motor (Sec 8)

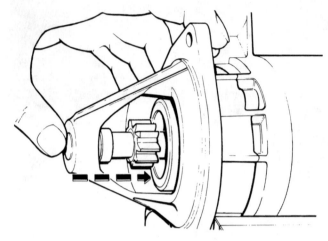

Fig. 7.9 Push the armature in the direction arrowed before adjusting the endfloat (Sec 8)

9 Glow plug warning light unit – renewal

Fiesta

1   Remove the instrument cluster, as described in the appropriate manual for petrol-engined vehicles.

2   Remove the warning light unit securing screw from the printed circuit board. Withdraw the warning light unit.

3   Fit the new unit and secure it with the screw. (The LED cannot be renewed separately).

4   Refit the instrument cluster and check for correct operation.

Escort/Orion

5   Carefully prise the warning light unit out of the panel.

6   Extract the bulbholder from the lens and renew the bayonet fitting bulb.

7   Reassemble the light unit and push it home.

10 Engine oil level sensor – removal and refitting

1   The oil level sensor is only fitted to high level models with the auxiliary warning system. It is located on the rear face of the block at the flywheel end, more or less opposite the dipstick.

2   Access to this side of the engine is not good. It may be improved by removing the air cleaner.

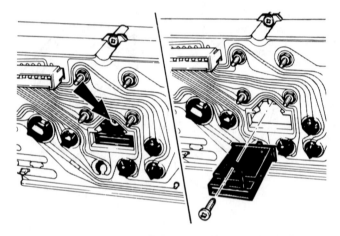

Fig. 7.10 Glow plug warning light removal – Fiesta. Securing screw is arrowed (Sec 9)

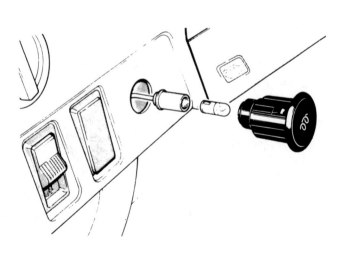

Fig. 7.11 Glow plug warning light unit – Escort/Orion (Sec 9)

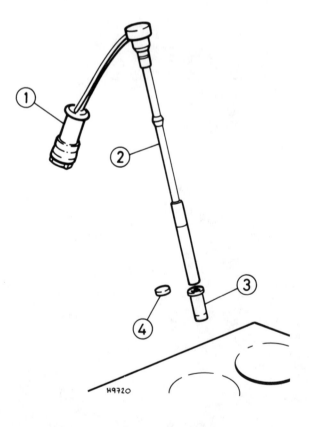

Fig. 7.12 Engine oil level sensor (Sec 10)

1 Wiring plug	3 Guide tube
2 Sensor	4 Blanking plug

3   Unplug the sensor from the wiring harness and withdraw it from its tube. If a new sensor is not to be fitted immediately, fit a blanking plug – this is essential if the engine is to be run.

4   Fit the new sensor and press it home in its tube. Connect the wiring harness plug.

5   Switch on the ignition and check for correct operation.

6   Refit any other disturbed components.

11 Fusible links – description and renewal

1   Apart from the starter motor feed lead (which also carries the alternator output), the entire electrical system is protected by two fusible links. One link protects the preheater system, which is otherwise unfused; the other protects the remaining circuits. Each link consists of a length of wire, attached to the battery positive terminal at one end and soldered into the wiring harness at the other (photo). If the current passing through the link exceeds a certain value, the link will melt and break the circuit.

2   Should a link melt, this can only be due to a serious short-circuit. The short **must** be found and rectified before the link is renewed. The job should be entrusted to a Ford dealer or other competent specialist.

3   Do not attempt to repair a melted link using ordinary insulated wire. Although the electrical system will work, the protection afforded by the link will be missing. Should a short-circuit occur again, serious damage or even fire could result.

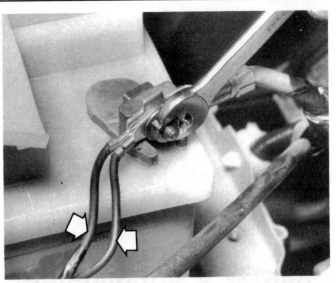

11.1 Fusible links (arrowed) are attached to the battery positive terminal

12   Wiring diagrams – general

The wiring diagrams in this manual are supplementary to the main universal diagrams for the petrol-engined variants. Refer to the diagrams at the end of Chapter 8 for circuits unique to the Diesel model, and to the appropriate manual for the petrol-engined vehicles for the other circuits.

Chapter 8 Supplement:
Revisions and information on later models

Contents

1   Introduction

General

This Supplement contains information which is additional to, or a revision of, that contained in the preceding seven Chapters of this manual and, where Diesel-engined versions differ, of that contained in the appropriate manual for the petrol-engined vehicle. To use the Supplement to its best advantage, it is therefore recommended that it is always referred to before the appropriate one of the manual's preceding seven Chapters; information or procedures not given here or in Chapters 1 to 7 will be as described in the appropriate manual for the petrol-engined vehicle.

Since first publication of this manual, the Ford 1.6 litre Diesel engine received few modifications apart from the substitution of a CAV RotoDiesel fuel injection system in July 1986 for the Bosch system used on earlier models. In September 1988 a 1.8 litre engine was introduced; this being fitted with either Bosch or CAV RotoDiesel fuel injection systems. Note that changes general to all models in a range will be documented in the appropriate manual for the petrol-engined vehicle.

Project vehicles

The vehicle used in the preparation of this Supplement, and appearing in some of the photographic sequences, was a 1989-model Fiesta 1.8D Van (Bosch fuel injection system). Additional work was carried out and photographed on a 1992-model Escort 1.8D Van (CAV RotoDiesel fuel injection system); also used was a 1992-model Orion LX (1.8 litre Diesel, CAV RotoDiesel fuel injection system).

2   Specifications

The Specifications given below are revisions of, or supplementary to, those at the beginning of the preceding Chapters.

1.6 litre engine
General
Maker's designation for later Escort/Orion models.. LTC

1.8 litre engine
General
Maker's designation:
    Fiesta... RTC, RTD, RTG
    Escort/Orion .... RTC, RTD, RTE, RTF, RTH
Note: *RTG and RTH engines are fitted with catalytic converters*
Bore and stroke (nominal) .... 82.5 x 82.0 mm
Cubic capacity .... 1753 cc
Maximum power (DIN) .... 44 kW (60 PS) @ 4800 rpm
Maximum torque (DIN) .... 110 Nm (81 lbf ft) @ 2500 rpm

Cylinder block
Cylinder bore diameter:
    Class A.. 82.500 to 82.515 mm
    Class B.. 82.515 to 82.530 mm
    Class C.. 82.660 to 82.675 mm
    Class D.. 82.675 to 82.690 mm
    Class E (first rebore)... 83.000 to 83.015 mm
    Class F (second rebore) .... 83.500 to 83.515 mm

Crankshaft
Main bearing journal diameter:
    Additional (1.00 mm) undersize .... 53.470 to 53.490 mm
Big-end bearing journal diameter:
    Additional (0.50 mm) undersize .... 48.470 to 48.490 mm

Pistons
Piston diameter (measured at 90° to gudgeon pin bore):
    Class A.. 82.460 to 82.475 mm
    Class B.. 82.475 to 82.490 mm
    Class C.. 82.620 to 82.635 mm
    Class D.. 82.635 to 82.650 mm
    Class E (first rebore)... 82.961 to 82.979 mm
    Class F (second rebore) .... 83.461 to 83.479 mm
Piston protrusion at TDC .... 0.500 to 0.840 mm

Piston rings
Clearance in groove (top compression) .... 0.09 to 1.22 mm
End gap (fitted):
    Top compression.. 0.35 to 0.500 mm
    Second compression.. 0.35 to 0.500 mm
    Oil control... 0.25 to 0.450 mm

Camshaft
Cam lift:
    Inlet.. 9.0 mm
    Exhaust... 10.0 mm

Underbonnet view of a 1.8 litre Fiesta Diesel

1 Coolant expansion tank
2 Suspension strut turret
3 Plastic section of the inlet manifold
4 Wheel brace
5 Brake fluid reservoir
6 Camshaft cover
7 Oil filler cap
8 Air intake duct from air cleaner
9 Fuel filter

10 Brake pressure regulator
11 Air cleaner
12 Fuel injection pump
13 Radiator cooling fan
14 Top hose bleed screw
15 Vacuum pump
16 Battery
17 Washer fluid reservoir cap

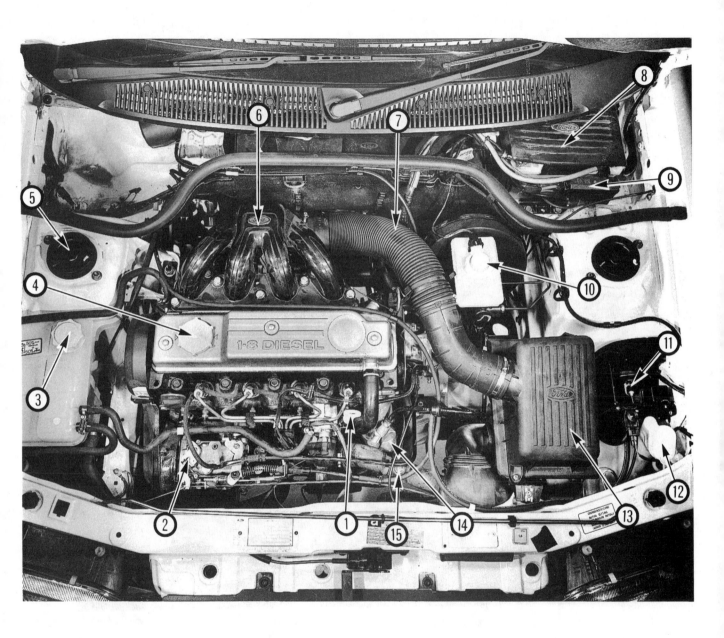

Underbonnet view of a 1.8 litre Escort Diesel

1   Engine oil level dipstick
2   Fuel injection pump
3   Coolant expansion tank
4   Engine oil filler cap
5   Suspension strut turret
6   Plastic section of the inlet manifold
7   Air intake duct from air cleaner
8   Battery

9   Engine compartment relays
10   Brake fluid reservoir
11   Engine upspeed control unit
12   Washer fluid reservoir cap
13   Air cleaner unit
14   Vacuum pump
15   Top hose bleed screw

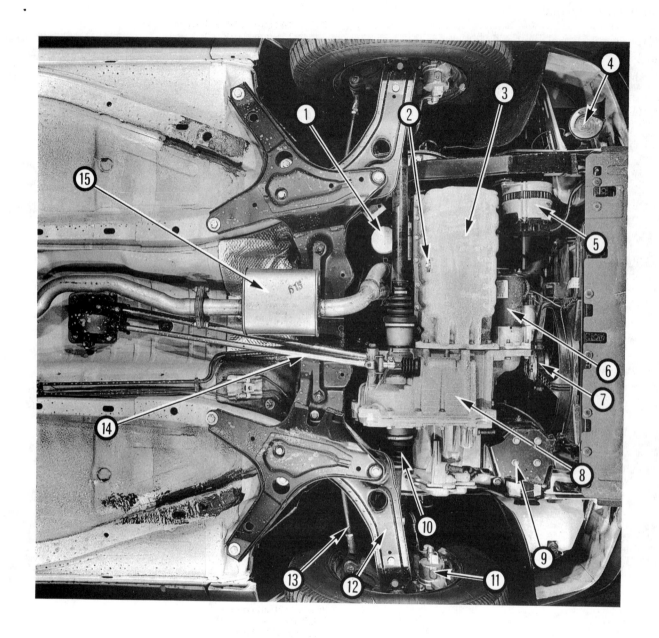

Under-side view of the front end of a 1.8 litre Escort Diesel

1   Engine oil filter
2   Engine oil drain plug
3   Engine oil sump (aluminium type shown)
4   Horn
5   Alternator
6   Starter motor
7   Radiator cooling fan
8   Transmission

9   Engine/transmission mounting
10   Driveshaft
11   Front brake caliper
12   Suspension arm
13   Track rod
14   Gearchange linkage
15   Exhaust system

Valve timing
Inlet opens .... 6° BTDC
Inlet closes .... 32° ABDC
Exhaust opens .... 57° BBDC
Exhaust closes .... 7° ATDC

Valve clearances (cold)
Inlet .... 0.30 to 0.40 mm (0.012 to 0.016 in)
Exhaust .... 0.45 to 0.55 mm (0.018 to 0.022 in)

Valves
Valve length:
    Inlet .... 107.05 to 107.15 mm
    Exhaust .... 109.15 to 109.25 mm
Valve head diameter:
    Inlet .... 36.40 to 36.60 mm
    Exhaust .... 31.90 to 32.10 mm
Valve stem diameter – standard:
    Inlet .... 7.82 to 7.97 mm
    Exhaust .... 7.81 to 7.96 mm
Valve stem diameter – first oversize:
    Inlet .... 8.02 to 8.17 mm
    Exhaust .... 8.01 to 8.16 mm
Valve stem diameter – second oversize:
    Inlet .... 8.22 to 8.37 mm
    Exhaust .... 8.21 to 8.36 mm

Cylinder head gasket
Thickness identification:
    Standard bores .... 2 to 4 teeth
    Oversize bores .... 2 to 4 holes
Selection according to piston protrusion:
    0.500 to 0.680 mm .... 2 teeth or holes
    0.681 to 0.740 mm .... 3 teeth or holes
    0.741 to 0.840 mm .... 4 teeth or holes

Cylinder head
Distortion limit .... 0.08 mm overall
Swirl chamber projection .... 0.000 to 0.061 mm
Note: *For details of diameters, depths and dimensions 'A', 'B' and 'C', referred to in the following, see Chapter 1, Section 11 and Figs. 1.23 and 1.24*
Swirl chamber seat dimensions:
    Standard:
        Diameter A .... 31.250 to 31.280 mm
        Diameter B .... 27.530 to 27.660 mm
        Depth C .... 4.938 to 5.034 mm
    Oversize:
        Diameter A .... 31.550 to 31.580 mm
        Diameter B .... 27.830 to 27.960 mm
        Depth C .... 5.233 to 5.284 mm
Valve seat dimensions:
    Standard:
        Diameter A (inlet) .... 38.000 to 38.003 mm
        Depth B (inlet) .... 8.300 to 8.500 mm
        Diameter A (exhaust) .... 33.000 to 33.030 mm
        Depth B (exhaust) .... 8.800 to 9.000 mm
    Class A (oversize):
        Diameter A (inlet) .... 38.200 to 38.230 mm
        Depth B (inlet) .... 8.600 to 8.800 mm
        Diameter A (exhaust) .... 32.200 to 33.230 mm
        Depth B (exhaust) .... 9.100 to 9.300 mm
    Second oversize:
        Diameter A inlet .... 38.400 to 38.430 mm
        Depth B inlet .... 8.900 to 9.100 mm
        Diameter A exhaust .... 33.400 to 33.430 mm
        Depth B exhaust .... 9.400 to 9.600 mm

Lubrication system
Oil capacity:
    With filter .... 4.5 litres (7.9 pints)
    Without filter .... 4.1 litres (7.2 pints)
Oil pressure:
    At 750 rpm .... 0.75 bar (11 lbf/in^2)
    At 2000 rpm .... 1.50 bars (22 lbf/in^2)
Oil filter .... Champion C115
Oil pressure relief valve setting .... 2.0 to 4.0 bars
Oil pump inner-to-outer rotor maximum clearance .... 0.174 mm

Torque wrench settings

	Nm	lbf ft
Main bearing cap bolts:		
Stage 1	27	20
Stage 2 (angle-tighten)	75°	75°
Big-end bearing cap bolts:		
Stage 1	30	22
Stage 2 (angle-tighten)	60°	60°
Stage 3 (angle-tighten)	20°	20°
Crankshaft rear oil seal retainer	21	15
Engine front plate	28	21
Oil pump	25	18
Auxiliary shaft thrustplate	10	7
Auxiliary shaft oil seal carrier	25	18
Auxiliary shaft sprocket bolt	50	·37
Sump pan bolts	9	7
Flywheel bolts:		
Stage 1	20	15
Stage 2 (angle-tighten)	45°	45°
Stage 3 (angle-tighten)	45°	45°
Belt tensioner bolt	55	41
Crankshaft pulley vibration damper centre bolt	180	133
Cylinder head bolts (Imperial thread and hexagonal head):		
Stage 1	30	22
Stage 2	92	68
Stage 3 (wait at least two minutes and then angle-tighten)	90°	90°
Cylinder head bolts (M12 and Torx T70 head):		
Stage 1	10	7
Stage 2	100	74
Stage 3		
a)	Unscrew number 1 bolt 180°	
b)	Tighten number 1 bolt to 70 Nm (52 lbf ft)	
c)	Further tighten the number 1 bolt 120°	
Stage 4	Repeat stage three with each of the remaining bolts in sequence	
Camshaft sprocket bolts:		
M6	10	7
M8	33	24
Toothed belt idler pulley	51	38
Vacuum pump	25	18
Camshaft cover	4	3
Camshaft bearing cap	22	16
TDC timing pin plug	27	20
Oil drain plug	28	21
Oil pick-up pipe bracket bolts	25	18
Engine mountings:		
Fiesta:		
Engine mounting bolt (to apron panel)	50	37
Engine mounting nut (to side member)	70	52
Engine bracket to cylinder block	90	66
Escort/Orion:		
Engine/transmission bolts	40	30
Engine mounting-to-cylinder block bracket	125	92
Front mounting brace-to-engine	70	52
Front mounting brace-to-crossmember	70	52
Engine mounting bracket-to-cylinder head	70	52
Engine mounting panel-top-apron panel	85	63

Cooling system – 1.8 litre engine

Coolant

Type/specification (see text)	Soft water, and antifreeze to Ford spec ESD-M97B-49A	
Capacity - approximate:		
Fiesta	9.3 litres (16.4 pints)	
Recommended concentration of antifreeze:		
For normal topping-up	50%	
At coolant renewal	40%	
Protection at recommended concentration:	**40%**	**50%**
Slush point	– 25°C (– 13°F)	– 40°C (– 40°F)
Solidifying point	– 30°C (– 22°F)	– 48°C (– 54°F)
Specific gravity at recommended concentration and 15°C/59°F (without other additives)	1.061	1.084

Thermostat

Opening commences	85° to 89°C (185° to 192°F)
Fully-open temperature	102°C (216°F)

Water pump

Drive	From back of camshaft drivebelt

Alternator drive

Type .... Flat 'polyvee' belt from crankshaft

	New	Used
Drivebelt tension (cold belt, using tension gauge):		
Without power-assisted steering – conventional (slotted-link) belt adjustment	350 to 450 N (79 to 101 lbf)	250 to 350 N (56 to 79 lbf)
Without power-assisted steering – rack-and-pinion belt adjustment	550 to 650 N (124 to 146 lbf)	350 to 450 N (79 to 101 lbf)
With power-assisted steering	550 to 650N (124 to 146 lbf)	400 to 500 N (90 to 112 lbf)

Note: *A 'used' drivebelt (V-belt or 'polyvee' type) is defined as one that has been run for at least 10 minutes. Tension gauge readings are nominal and are given for reference only where rack-and-pinion adjustment is found – if procedure is followed exactly (see text), correct drivebelt tensioning should be automatic*

Torque wrench settings

	Nm	lbf ft
Thermostat housing to cylinder head	17 to 21	12 to 15
Camshaft drivebelt cover spacer stud-to-water pump	6 to 8	4 to 6
Radiator bottom mounting bolts – September 1990-on Escort/Orion models...	20 to 27	15 to 20
Alternator mounting bracket-to-cylinder block bolts................	41 to 51	30 to 38
Alternator pivot bolts and nuts	18 to 25	13 to 18
Adjuster link-to-(alternator/pump) mounting bracket bolt and nut	21 to 28	15 to 21
Alternator drivebelt adjustment – slotted-link adjuster		
Alternator-to-adjuster link bolt and nut.......................	18 to 25	13 to 18
Alternator drivebelt adjustment – rack-and-pinion adjuster:		
Adjuster nut – new drivebelt	15	11
Adjuster nut – used drivebelt	10	8
Adjuster centre lockbolt	18 to 25	13 to 18
Alternator/power-assisted steering pump drivebelt adjustment:		
Adjuster nut..	8	6
Adjuster centre lockbolt...	18 to 25	13 to 18

Fuel and exhaust systems – 1.8 litre engine

General

Glow plugs	Champion CH147
Air filter:	
Fiesta models...	Champion U557
Escort/Orion models	Champion U560
Fuel filter:	
Bosch	Champion L134
CAV RotoDiesel..	Champion L131 or L137

Fuel

Fuel capacity.. 42 to 55 litres (9.2 to 12.0 gallons) according to model

Injection pump

Make and type...	Bosch VE or CAV RotoDiesel
Rotation (viewed from crankshaft pulley end)...................	Clockwise
Drive	By toothed belt from crankshaft

Injectors (Bosch)

Needle seat leakage/Injector dribble .... Holds 125 bars (1813 lbf/in^2) for 10 seconds

Note: *This applies to all later 1.6 litre engines as well as 1.8 litre units with the Bosch system*

Adjustment data

Idle speed	850 ± 50 rpm
Injection pump timing (see text)...................................	By timing page, at TDC

Torque wrench settings

	Nm	lbf ft
Fuel injection pump-to-engine front plate	18 to 28	13 to 21
Fuel injection pump-to-rear support bracket	18 to 22	13 to 16
Fuel injection pump support bracket-to-cylinder block.............	18 to 27	13 to 20
Fuel injection pump sprocket bolts...................................	20 to 25	15 to 18
Fuel shut-off solenoid – CAV RotoDiesel pump	16 to20	12 to 15
Exhaust Gas Recirculation vacuum regulator valve-to-pump bolts..........	2 to 3	1 to 2
Fuel filter bracket-to-cylinder head/lifting eye	40 to50	30 to 37
Inlet and exhaust manifold-to-cylinder head fasteners:		
Studs..	10 to 14	7 to 10
Nuts and bolts..	18 to 25	13 to 18
Exhaust Gas Recirculation valve-to-inlet manifold Allen bolts..................	17 to 22	12 to 16
Exhaust Gas Recirculation valve exhaust supply pipe bolts	20 to 25	15 to 18
Exhaust downpipe-to-manifold flange nuts – Escort/Orion with catalytic converter..	31 to 44	23 to 32
Exhaust downpipe-to-centre section U-bolt nuts – Fiesta	48 to 64	35 to 47
Catalytic converter flange joint nuts – all models:		
Front	48 to 64	35 to 47
Rear	35 to 40	26 to 30

Clutch, transmission and driveshafts – 1.8 litre engine

Clutch

Type..	Single dry plate, 'low lift' diaphragm spring, cable-actuated
Driven plate diameter...	220 m
Driven plate lining thickness – nominal	3.23 mm
Pedal stroke – nominal	145 mm

Transmission

Final drive ratio...	3.59:1

Torque wrench settings

	Nm	lbf ft
Clutch pressure plate to flywheel..	25 to 34	18 to 25

Braking system

General

System type	Ventilated front discs fitted to all Escort/Orion models, September 1990-on

Front disc brakes

Disc diameter – all models...	240 mm
Disc nominal thickness – new:	
Solid disc..	10 mm
Ventilated disc..	20 mm
Disc minimum thickness:	
Solid disc..	8 mm
Ventilated disc..	18 mm
Disc maximum run-out – installed	0.10 mm

Rear drum brakes

Drum nominal diameter – new:	
Fiesta...	180.0 mm
Escort Van models...	228.6 mm
All other Escort models, Orion models...............................	203.0 mm
Drum maximum diameter:	
Fiesta...	181.0 mm
Escort Van models...	229.6 mm
All other Escort models, Orion models...............................	204.0 mm

Suspension and steering

General

Rear suspension type..	Semi-independent, with twist beam rear axle, fitted to revised Fiesta models from February 1989-on and to revised Escort/Orion models (except Vans) from September 1990-on

Front suspension alignment

Note: *The following settings are for a vehicle at kerb weight - ie, unladen but with all lubricants and fluids. On Fiesta models before 1990 (model year) the nominal settings are with 3.0 litres of fuel in the tank; in all other cases, settings are for a full fuel tank. See a Ford dealer for a precise identification of the model year of the vehicle in question*

Fiesta (except Van) - up to 1990 model year:

Castor, nominal..	+ 0° 18'
Castor, tolerance	– 0° 42' to + 1° 18'
Camber, nominal..	+ 0° 12'
Camber, tolerance	– 1° 03' to + 1° 27'
Toe, nominal	– 3,00 mm (toe-out) to + 3.0 mm (toe-in)/– 0° 30' (toe-out) to + 0° 30' (toe-in)
Toe, tolerance..	0.00 mm (toe-in) ± 1.0 mm/0° 00' (toe-in) ± 0° 10'

Fiesta (except Van) - 1990 to early 1992 model years:

Castor, nominal..	+ 0° 53'
Castor, tolerance	– 0°22' to + 2° 08'
Camber, nominal..	– 0° 08'
Camber, tolerance	– 1° 28' to + 1° 12'
Toe, nominal	– 4.5 mm (toe-out) to + 0.5 mm (toe-in/– 0° 45' (toe out) to + 0° 05' (toe-in)
Toe, tolerance..	– 2.0 mm (toe-out) ± 1.0 mm/0° 20' (toe-out) ± 0° 10'

Fiesta (except Van) - early 1992-on model years:

Castor, nominal..	+ 0° 52'
Castor, tolerance	– 0° 23' to + 2° 07'
Camber, nominal..	– 0° 09'
Camber, tolerance	– 1° 29' to + 1° 11'
Toe, nominal	– 4.5 mm (toe-out) to + 0.5 mm (toe-in)/– 0° 45' (toe-out) to + 0° 05' (toe-in)
Toe, tolerance..	– 2.0 mm (toe-out) ± 1.0 mm/0° 20' (toe-out) ± 0° 10'

Front suspension alignment (continued)

Fiesta Van up to 1990 model year:
- Castor, nominal .... + 0° 23′
- Castor, tolerance .... – 0° 37′ to + 1° 23′
- Camber, nominal .... + 0° 25′
- Camber, tolerance... – 0° 50′ to + 1° 40′
- Toe, nominal .... – 3.0 mm (toe-out) to + 3.0 mm (toe-in)/– 0° 30′ (toe-out) to + 0° 30′ (toe-in)
- Toe, tolerance .... 0.0 mm (toe-in) ± 1.0 mm/0° 00′ (toe-in) ± 0° 10′

Fiesta Van 1990 to early 1992 model years:
- Castor, nominal .... + 0° 51′
- Castor, tolerance .... – 0° 24′ to + 2° 06′
- Camber, nominal .... – 0° 03′
- Camber, tolerance... – 1° 23′ to + 1° 17′
- Toe, nominal .... – 4.5 mm (toe-out) to + 0.5 mm (toe-in)/– 0° 45′ (toe-out) to + 0° 05′ (toe-in)
- Toe, tolerance .... – 2.0 mm (toe-out) ± 1.0 mm/0° 20′ (toe-out) ± 0° 10′

Fiesta Van early 1992-on model years:
- Castor, nominal .... + 0° 53′
- Castor, tolerance .... – 0° 22′ to + 2° 08′
- Camber, nominal .... – 0° 06′
- Camber, tolerance... – 1° 26′ to + 1° 14′
- Toe, nominal .... – 4.5 mm (toe-out) to + 0.5 mm (toe-in)/– 0° 45′ (toe-out) to + 0° 05′ (toe-in)
- Toe, tolerance .... – 2.00 mm (toe-out) ± 1.0 mm.0° 20′ (toe-out) ± 0° 10′

Escort (except Van), Orion:
- Castor, nominal... 0° 00′
- Castor, tolerance .... – 1° 15′ to + 1° 15′
- Camber, nominal .... – 0° 15′
- Camber, tolerance... – 1° 36′ to + 1° 04′
- Toe, nominal .... – 4.5 mm (toe-out) to + 0.5 mm (toe-in)/– 0° 45′ (toe out) to + 0° 05′ (toe-in)
- Toe, tolerance .... – 2.0 mm (toe-out) ± 1.0 mm/0° 20′ (toe-out) ± 0° 10′

Escort Van:
- Castor, nominal .... – 0° 48′
- Castor, tolerance .... – 2° 03′ to + 0° 27′
- Camber, nominal .... – 0° 22′
- Camber, tolerance... – 1° 42′ to + 0° 58′
- Toe, nominal .... – 4.5 mm (toe-out) to + 0.5 mm (toe-in)/– 0° 45′ (toe-in) to + 0° 05′ (toe-in)
- Toe, tolerance .... – 2.0 mm (toe-out) ± 1.0 mm/0° 20′ (toe-out) ± 0° 10′

Rear suspension alignment

Note: *The following settings are for a vehicle at kerb weight – ie, unladen but with all lubricants and fluids, including a full fuel tank. See a Ford dealer for a precise identification of the model year of the vehicle in question*

Fiesta – up to 1990 model year:
- Camber, nominal .... – 1° 01′
- Camber, tolerance.. – 2° 01′ to – 0° 31′
- Toe, nominal .... + 0.2 mm (toe-in)
- Toe, tolerance .... + 2.2 mm (toe-in) to – 1.8 mm (toe-out)

Fiesta (except Courier Van) – 1990-on model years:
- Camber, nominal.. – 1° 00′
- Camber, tolerance.. – 2° 00′ to – 0° 30′
- Toe, nominal .... + 2.3 mm (toe-in)
- Toe, tolerance .... + 3.0 mm (toe-in) to + 4.3 mm (toe-in)

Fiesta Courier Van:
- Camber, nominal.. – 0° 24.5′
- Camber, tolerance.. – 0° 34.5′ to – 0° 14.5′
- Toe, nominal .... + 1.35 mm (toe-in)
- Toe, tolerance .... + 0.85 mm (toe-in) to + 1.85 mm (toe-in)

Escort/Orion:
- Camber, nominal.. – 1° 00′
- Camber, tolerance.. – 2° 00′ to – 0° 30′
- Toe, nominal .... + 2.00 mm (toe-in)
- Toe, tolerance .... 0.0 mm (parallel) to + 4.0 mm (toe-in)

Tyre pressures – cold

	Normal load – bars (lbf/in^2)		Full load – bars (lbf/in^2)	
	Front	Rear	Front	Rear
Fiesta:				
145 SR 13 tyres	2.0 (29)	1.8 (26)	2.5 (36)	2.8 (41)
155/70 SR 13 tyres...	2.2 (32)	1.8 (26)	2.5 (36)	2.8 (41)
Escort Van:				
'40' (165 TR 13 tyres)	2.0 (29)	1.8 (26)	2.3 (33)	3.0 (44)
'60' (165 RR 13 tyres)	2.0 (29)	1.8 (26)	2.3 (33)	3.5 (51)
All other Escort and Orion models	2.0 (29)	1.8 (26)	2.3 (33)	2.8 (41)

Torque wrench settings

	Nm	lbf ft
Power-assisted steering pump bracket-to-cylinder block bolts	41 to 58	30 to 43
Drivebelt adjuster/alternator fasteners..	See 'Cooling system' Specifications	

Electrical system

Battery

Rating cold cranking/reserve capacity)... 500 A/75 RC, 590 A/90 RC, 600 A/110 RC or 650 A/130 RC depending on year and model

Alternator

Make and type .... Bosch K1-55A or K1-70A, Lucas/Magneti Marelli A127/55 or A127/70, or (only vehicles with power-assisted steering) Mitsubishi A002T

Nominal rated output .... 55 A or 70 A, depending on year and model

Note: *For alternator specifications and servicing procedures not given in Chapter 7 (and Section 4 of this Chapter) of this manual, refer to the relevant manual for the petrol-engined vehicle.*
Where a Magneti Marelli A127 alternator is encountered, note that these are simply renamed Lucas units, all procedures and specifications are exactly the same as those given for Lucas A127 alternators

Starter motor

Make and type .... Bosch DW (1.8 kW), Bosch EV (2.2 kW), or Lucas/Magneti Marelli M80R (1.8 kW) – all with four brushes and reduction gears

Commutator refinishing limit – Lucas Magneti Marelli M80R .... Not available
Armature endfloat – Lucas/Magneti Marelli M80R...................................... 0.25 mm (0.010 in)

Note: *For starter motor specifications and servicing procedures not given in Chapter 7 (and Section 8 of this Chapter) of this manual, refer to the relevant manual for the petrol-engined vehicle.*
Where a Magneti Marelli M80R starter motor is encountered, note that these are simply renamed Lucas units; all procedures and specifications are exactly the same as those given for Lucas M80R starter motors.

3   Engine (1.8 litre)

PART A: GENERAL

Description

1   Although essentially an increased-capacity version of the 1.6 litre unit, there are several major differences which are described in the following paragraphs.

2   Refer to the Specifications at the beginning of this Supplement for details of changed dimensions and tolerances.

3   The cylinder bore diameters are increased, and the undersides of the pistons are cooled by oil jets.

4   The oil pump is mounted externally, and is driven by an auxiliary shaft.

5   Two toothed drivebelts are used, one to drive the fuel injection pump and the other to drive the camshaft, the oil pump auxiliary shaft and the water pump.

6   The inlet manifold consists of an upper moulded plastic section bolted to a cast aluminium alloy lower section.

7   The engine mountings have been designed to reduce vibration, and the air cleaner is remotely-sited from the engine.

Modifications and notes

8   Some modifications have been made to the 1.8 litre engine since its introduction and these include the following (photos).

(a)   *The sump pan is now cast in aluminium and is bolted to the clutch housing at its transmission end*
(b)   *An oil baffle is now fitted above the camshaft to improve lubrication*
(c)   *Cylinder head bolts modified from Imperial thread with hex-agonal head to metric thread with Torx head. The tightening sequence differs according to bolt type (see Specifications)*
(d)   *An Exhaust Gas Recirculation (EGR) system is fitted to later engines, the details of which are discussed in Section 5, part C of this Chapter*
(e)   *Both the camshaft and the fuel injection pump drivebelts* **must**

be renewed as a matter of course at the reduced interval specified in 'Routine maintenance' at the front of this manual
(f)   *Depending on the exact date of manufacture of the vehicle, a modified camshaft sprocket may be available to prevent prema-ture wear (and perhaps breakage) of the camshaft drivebelt. Whenever the camshaft drivebelt cover is removed, check whether the sprocket has any red paint marks on it; if no marks are found it may be necessary to replace the sprocket with the modified item. Any Ford dealer will be able to identify exactly the vehicle's date of manufacture and to decide accordingly whether a modified sprocket is required*

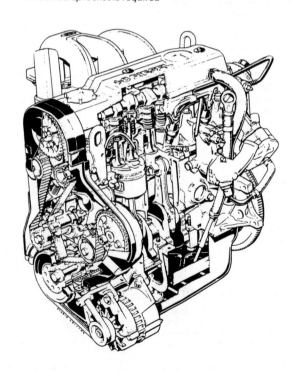

Fig. 8.1 Cutaway view of Ford 1.8 Diesel engine (Sec 3)

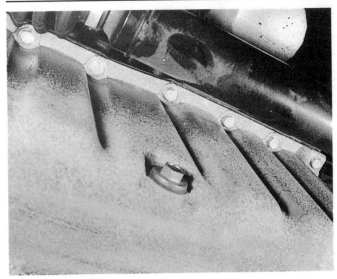

3A.8A Aluminium sump showing retaining bolts to the block ...

3A.8B ... and transmission (later models)

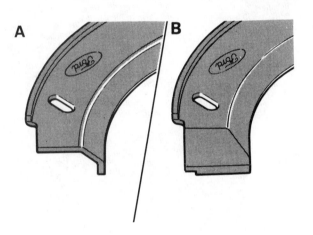

Fig. 8.2 Identifying camshaft drivebelt cover dust shields (Sec 3)

A   Old type   *B   New type*

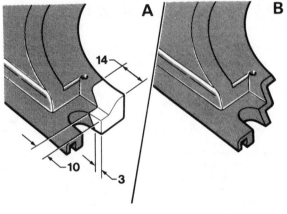

Fig. 8.3 Modifying camshaft drivebelt cover to accept new-type dust shield (Sec 3)

A   Area to be cut away –   *B   The cover modified*
dimensions in mm

(g)   *The dust shield at the bottom of the camshaft drivebelt cover has been modified to improve its dust-excluding properties, so preventing premature wear (and perhaps breakage) of the camshaft drivebelt. Whenever the cover is removed, check the dust shield with reference to Fig. 8.2; if it is of the old type, measure and note the location of the retaining screws inside the slots, remove the shield and use a small saw to cut away the drivebelt cover as shown in Fig. 8.3. Obtain a new-type dust shield and fit it to the cover using the original screws at the points noted before removal.*

(h)   *If it is ever suspected that any of the pistons have contacted their respective valves (usually as a result of camshaft drivebelt slipping or breakage), be particularly careful to check the pistons for indentations on their crowns and for signs of scuffing or other damage to their lands or skirts, the piston rings and cylinder bores for signs of scuffing and the valves for signs of bending. Check carefully all these points and renew any component that is thought to have been damaged before the engine is reassembled, or poor engine performance, excessive smoke emission and oil consumption, higher than normal noise levels and eventual piston seizure may result. Note that the above procedure will require a full engine strip and, possibly, a full overhaul; this must be carried out to ensure the engine's future reliability, economy and performance*

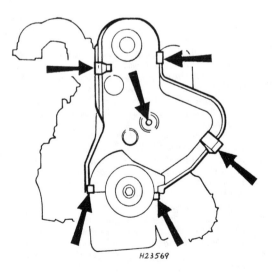

H23569

Fig. 8.4 Location of camshaft drivebelt cover fastenings (Sec 3)

3B.1 Camshaft oil baffle (arrowed) fitted to later engines

PART B: OPERATIONS POSSIBLE WITH ENGINE IN VEHICLE

Valve clearances – checking and adjustment

1 Refer to Section 7 of Chapter 1, noting the following points (photo):

   (a) *The camshaft cover is secured by three bolts on all engines*

   (b) *When the camshaft cover is removed to reveal an oil baffle (later engines only), unscrew the six retaining nuts and withdraw the baffle, then refit the nuts (which also secure the camshaft bearing caps), tightening them to the specified torque wrench setting*

   (c) *Check the valve clearances, noting the revised clearances given in the Specifications Section of this Chapter; adjust by fitting shims of different thickness where required*

   (d) *Unscrew the six nuts, refit the baffle, then tighten all ten camshaft bearing cap nuts to the specified torque wrench setting and refit the camshaft cover*

Camshaft and fuel injection pump drivebelts – renewal

2 Begin by carrying out the following preliminary dismantling procedures (photo):

   (a) *Jack up the front right-hand side of the vehicle and support it on axle stands placed at the points shown in the appropriate manual for petrol-engined models*

   (b) *Disconnect the battery earth (negative) lead*

   (c) *Detaching the shield(s) and/or cover(s) as necessary, remove the alternator/water pump drivebelt as described in Section 4 of this Chapter*

   (d) *On Fiesta models (Escort/Orion as well, depending on the task to be carried out and the tools available) the front right-hand roadwheel and the wheel arch liner should also be removed refer to the appropriate manual for petrol-engined models*

   (e) *With the engine still in the vehicle, it will probably be necessary to remove the alternator (Chapter 7, Section 4) and, if fitted, the power-assisted steering pump (Section 7 of this Chapter) to reach the TDC pin hole plug and to insert a timing pin*

   (f) *Improved access may be gained by unbolting the coolant expansion tank and, if fitted, the power-assisted steering fluid reservoir on Escort/Orion models so that these can be moved aside (without disconnecting them) as required. On Fiesta models the air cleaner assembly must be removed as described in Section 5, part C of this Chapter*

   (g) *Where applicable, slacken the engine lifting eye retaining nut(s) or bolt(s) and swing it clear of the drivebelt cover; where a throttle damper is fitted which will prevent the removal of the cover, this must first be removed   see Section 5, part C of this Chapter*

3 Working under the vehicle, unscrew the front (vertical) retaining bolt and the rear (horizontal) pivot bolt, then withdraw the drivebelt

3B.2 Removing the cover as described in text

3B.4 Removing plastic fuel deflector from alternator mounting bracket

lower cover from the crankshaft pulley/vibration damper (see photos 5C.24A and B).

4 If not already removed, detach the plastic fuel deflector from the alternator mounting bracket (photo).

5 Returning to the engine compartment, release the three camshaft drivebelt cover retaining clips and unscrew the single (central) retaining bolt, then manoeuvre the cover upwards and withdraw it (photos).

6 Using the bolt in the centre of the crankshaft pulley vibration damper, turn the crankshaft in the normal direction of rotation, until the drilling in the injection pump flange (CAV) or the recess (Bosch) is aligned with the drilling in the pump housing. This gives the TDC position for pistons 1 and 4 (photo).

7 Release the belt tensioner and then remove the camshaft drivebelt. If the injection pump drivebelt is to be renewed, then its tensioner should be removed and the belt withdrawn.

8 Align the camshaft sprocket and the injection pump sprocket, so that the drillings and the recess in the sprockets are aligned with the drillings in the cylinder head and the pump housing.

9 A special pin will now be required to time the camshaft sprocket and the injection pump sprocket. If a CAV pump is fitted, then pins number 23-019 will time both sprockets, but if a Bosch pump is fitted, pin

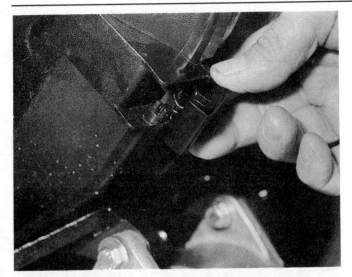

3B.5A Toothed belt cover clip

3B.5B Toothed belt cover bolt

3B.5C Removing the upper cover ...

3B.5D ... to provide access to the drive belt (Escort)

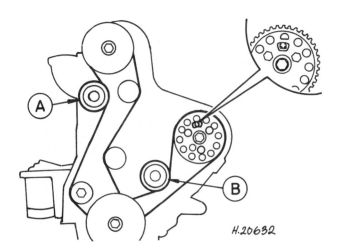

Fig. 8.5 Drivebelts with crankshaft at TDC - Nos 1 and 4 pistons (Sec 3)

A   Camshaft drivebelt
    tensioner
B   Fuel injection pump
    drivebelt tensioner

3B.6 Toothed belt and sprocket identification (engine removed)

1   Camshaft sprocket
2   Idler sprocket
3   Fuel pump sprocket
4   Fuel pump belt tensioner
5   Crankshaft pulley vibration damper
6   Auxiliary shaft sprocket
7   Water pump sprocket
8   Camshaft belt tensioner

3B.12A Fuel pump sprocket timing 'pin'

3B.12B Camshaft sprocket timing 'pin'

3B.13A TDC pin hole plug

3B.13B Screwing in the TDC setting pin

number 23-029 will be required for the pump sprocket, and one pin 23-019 for the camshaft sprocket.

10   Twist drills will serve as substitute pins, but they must be in unworn condition, and be long enough to enter the holes in the pump or cylinder head. A drill of 9.5 mm diameter will be required for the Bosch type pump, plus one of 6.0 mm diameter for the camshaft sprocket.

11   Two drills of 6.0 mm diameter will be required for the CAV type pump (one for the camshaft sprocket and one for the pump).

12   Insert the appropriate timing pins (photos).

13   Screw in the TDC setting pin referred to in Chapter 1, Section 9. Make sure that the crankshaft is in contact with the timing pin (photos).

14   Fit the new injection pump drivebelt so that it is taut between the crankshaft and pump sprockets, and the directional arrows are pointing the correct way.

15   Slacken the injection pump sprocket bolts half a turn, and also slacken the belt tensioner bolts half a turn. Allow the belt tensioner to snap against the belt. Retighten all the slackened bolts, but make sure that the bolts are not at the ends of their slots, otherwise any further adjustment would be impossible.

16   Fit the new camshaft drivebelt, with the directional arrows correct for normal crankshaft rotational directional. The belt should be slack on the tensioner side and taut between sprockets.

17   Slacken the camshaft sprocket bolts and the tensioner bolts half a turn. Allow the tensioner to snap against the belt.

18   Retighten all slackened bolts. Remove all the timing pins, and turn the crankshaft through two revolutions in the normal direction of rotation, until the slot in the injection pump sprocket is at the highest point (12 o'clock).

19   Now turn the crankshaft anti-clockwise until the slot in the injection pump sprocket is at the 11 o'clock position.

20   Screw in the TDC setting pin.

21   Slowly turn the crankshaft clockwise until the crankshaft contacts the timing pin.

22   Insert the timing pins in the camshaft and the injection pump sprockets.

23   Slacken the bolts (through half a turn) that secure the camshaft and injection pump sprockets and the belt tensioners.

24   Depress both drivebelts on the taut side opposite to the tensioners, and then release them.

25   Retighten all slackened bolts.

26   Remove all timing pins and screw in the TDC pin hole plug.

27   Refit the belt covers.

28   Refit and tension the alternator drivebelt as described in Section 4 of this Chapter, then refit all components removed for better access.

29   Reconnect the battery.

Cylinder head – removal and refitting

30   Carry out the operations described in Chapter 1, Section 10, paragraphs 1 to 12 and those outlined in paragraphs 2 and 4 of this Section. On models fitted with an EGR system it will also be necessary to disconnect the two hoses from the vacuum regulating valve (located on the fuel injection pump).

31   Slacken and remove the alternator drivebelt.

32   Remove the toothed belt lower and upper covers (paragraphs 3 and 5 above).

33   Remove the alternator cover, and unscrew the TDC pin hole plug.

34   Turn the crankshaft by means of the pulley vibration damper centre bolt until the slot in the injection pump sprocket reaches the 11 o'clock position.

35   Screw in the TDC setting pin.

36   Turn the crankshaft until it makes contact with the timing pin.

37   Slacken the centre bolt of the camshaft sprocket through half a turn.

38   Unbolt and remove the camshaft belt tensioner and take off the belt.

39   Unbolt and remove the camshaft sprocket, tapping it off its tapered seat if necessary using a plastic hammer.

40   Remove the camshaft belt idler pulley, using a Torx bit to unscrew its securing bolt.

41   Remove the toothed belt backing plates, and also the side belt cover.

42   Remove the fuel injectors and heat shields (Chapter 3).

43   Disconnect the wiring loom and remove the glow plugs.

44   Disconnect the ventilation system hoses, unscrew the three fixing bolts and take off the rocker cover and the gasket.

45   Unscrew the cylinder head bolts in the reverse order to refitting (see Fig. 1.19, Chapter 1). As new bolts will be required when refitting the cylinder head, it is important to note which type of bolts are used. The earlier 1.8 litre engines were fitted with hexagon head bolts having an imperial thread, whilst later models (1992 model year on) have an M12 thread and a Torx T70 head.

46   Remove the cylinder head, but retain the gasket.

47   Three possible thicknesses of cylinder head gasket are available for the 1.8 litre engine according to the piston protrusion, the details of which are given in the Specifications for the cylinder head at the start of this Chapter.

48   Before fitting the cylinder head, make sure that the groove on the camshaft rear eccentric is parallel with the upper surface of the cylinder head, and the larger segment is uppermost (photo).

3B.48 Camshaft rear eccentric groove (arrowed)

49   Fit the new selected gasket and use new cylinder head bolts. Make sure that the centralising dowel sleeves are located at bolt holes 8 and 10, and the word TOP/OBEN is visible.

50   Fit the cylinder head (photo), screw in the new bolts (lightly oiled), and tighten as indicated in the Specifications (according to type) in the sequence shown in Fig. 1.19, Chapter 1.

51   Screw in and connect the glow plugs.

52   Fit the injectors with new heat shields.

53   The curved (convex) side of the shield should be towards the cylinder head.

54   Fit the toothed belt rear backing plates.

55   Fit and tension a new camshaft drivebelt as described in the preceding sub-section.

56   Fit the drivebelt upper cover, the lower cover, and the alternator cover.

57   Fit and tension the alternator drivebelt as described in Section 4 of this Chapter, then refit all components removed for access.

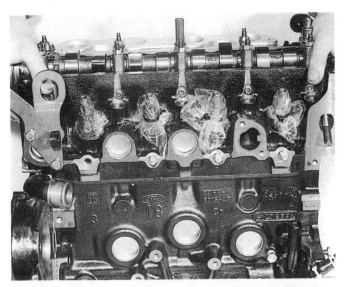

3B.50 Lowering cylinder head onto block – note injectors protected against dirt

3B.81A Oil pump gasket

3B.81B Fitting the oil pump

58   Reconnect the exhaust pipe to the manifold.

59   Check the valve clearances.

60   Fit the rocker cover with gasket, and reconnect the ventilation hoses.

61   Reconnect the fuel line and filter. Use new line seals if a CAV pump is used.

62   Fit the thermostat housing, with a new gasket, and the dipstick bracket.

63   Connect the coolant hoses and injection pipes, and also the leak-off pipes.

64   Reconnect all electrical leads.

65   Reconnect the vacuum pump hoses.

66   Fit and connect the air cleaner.

67   Fill the cooling system, as described in Chapter 2.

68   Connect the battery and top-up the engine oil if necessary.

69   The fuel system can be primed, and air bled out (as much as possible) as described in Part A of Section 5.

Cylinder head – dismantling, overhaul and reassembly
70   The operations are essentially as described in Chapter 1 for the 1.6 litre engine, but it is necessary to use an exhaust manifold gasket when reassembling, even if one was not fitted originally (new engine). Also make sure that the plastic expansion sleeve is located on the upper right-hand end manifold stud. Note also that on later models, an oil baffle is fitted above the camshaft to improve lubrication (photo 3B.1).

71   The vacuum pump must be fitted with a new O-ring seal.

Oil seals – renewal
72   Refer to Chapter 1, Section 13, but observe the following points.

73   Time, and tension, the drivebelts as described in paragraphs 5 to 26 of Part B of this Chapter.

74   Apply thread-locking fluid to the drivebelt cover spacer stud on the water pump.

Crankshaft front oil seal
75   Access to the seal can only be obtained after removing the

vibration damper and the two toothed bolts, and pulling the belt sprocket off the front of the crankshaft. A puller may be required for this.

Camshaft – removal and refitting
76   Refer to Chapter 1, Section 8.

Oil pump – removal and refitting
77   Drain the engine oil.

78   Disconnect the battery negative lead.

79   Unscrew and discard the oil filter cartridge.

80   Unscrew the four bolts and withdraw the oil pump from the engine crankcase.

81   Before refitting, pour engine oil into the pump to prime it, and use a new flange gasket (photos).

82   A worn oil pump should be renewed complete.

Pistons and connecting rods – removal and refitting
83   Refer to Chapter 1, Section 18.

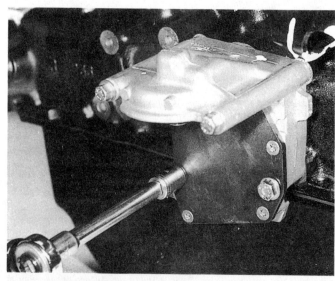

3B.81C Tightening the oil pump bolts

3B.84A Sump gasket in position

3B.84B Sump gasket lug engaged in recess (arrowed)

Sump pan – removal and refitting

84 The operations are similar to those described in Chapter 1, Section 14, but when fitting the sump pan, make sure that the lug on the gasket (flywheel side) engages in the recess in the crankshaft oil seal retainer (photos). Note that when an aluminium sump pan is used, it bolts direct to the clutch housing at the transmission end and there is no bottom cover plate fitted.

PART C: ENGINE AND TRANSMISSION REMOVAL

Engine – method of removal

1 The engine is removed together with the transmission in a downward direction and withdrawn from underneath the front of the vehicle.

2 Unless an inspection pit is available, ensure that the vehicle can eventually be raised sufficiently to allow the engine/transmission to be withdrawn from underneath. Axle stands will be required to ensure that the vehicle is suitably supported when raised. Ensure that the stands are correctly positioned according to model and are positioned as shown in the appropriate manual for petrol-engine models.

Engine and transmission – removal

3 Disconnect the battery earth lead.

4 Although not essential, removal of the bonnet will provide additional access during subsequent operations. If removing the bonnet, the insulating sheet must be removed from the underside of the bonnet and the washer fluid hose detached. Bonnet removal is otherwise as described in the appropriate manual for the model concerned.

5 Remove the air cleaner casing (Section 5, Part C). Although not strictly necessary, the removal of the plastic upper section of the inlet manifold (Section 5, Part C) will provide additional clearance and prevent the risk of its damage.

6 Drain the engine oil (Section 2 of Chapter 1).

7 Where possible, drain the oil from the transmission unit. For details, refer to the appropriate petrol-engined manual for the model concerned. In some instances a drain plug or alternative may not exist, in which case it will not be possible to drain the oil from the transmission until later when the driveshafts are removed.

8 Drain the cooling system as described in Chapter 2, Section 4, then detach and remove the coolant top and bottom hoses from the engine and radiator.

9 Detach the coolant expansion tank hoses at the cylinder head and thermostat housing.

3C.13A Earth strap and wiring harness connection to the transmission

3C.13B Reversing light switch and lead connector

10   Disconnect the heater feed and return hoses from the distribution pipe and the cylinder head. Although not strictly necessary, removal of the radiator, fan and shroud will provide additional clearance during engine removal and prevent the possibility of it being damaged. Refer to Section 4 for details.

11   Disconnect the throttle cable from the fuel pump. Refer to Chapter 3, Section 15.

12   Where applicable, disconnect the idle upspeed operating cable at its connection to the injection pump. Refer to Section 5, Part C in this Chapter for further details.

13   Disconnect the following electrical leads (photos)

    (a)   *Temperature gauge sender*
    (b)   *Oil pressure switch*
    (c)   *Cooling fan thermoswitch*
    (d)   *Glow plug feed*
    (e)   *Injection pump fuel shut-off solenoid*
    (f)   *Oil level sensor*
    (g)   *Earth strap to transmission*
    (h)   *Reversing light lead from switch on transmission*

When disconnecting the earth strap from the top face of the flywheel housing, also disconnect the adjacent wiring harness.

14   Disconnect the fuel inlet hose from the fuel filter and the return pipe from the injection pump. Where applicable, when disconnecting the fuel pipe from the pump, detach it at the in-line hose connector to minimise the possibility of dirt entering the fuel system. The connecting tube is secured by compression clips. Plug or cap the hoses and unions to keep fuel in and dirt out.

15   Disconnect the servo vacuum hose from the vacuum pump and detach the vacuum hose.

16   Press the clutch lever to the rear and, with the tension taken from the cable, release it from the lever. Withdraw the clutch cable rearwards through its locating bracket on the transmission and position it out of the way.

17   Undo the retaining nut and disconnect the speedometer cable from the top face of the transmission and position it out of the way.

18   Undo the two retaining bolts securing the transmission bracket to the mounting on the front crossmember (photo).

19   Raise and support the front of the vehicle on axle stands at a height allowing for the engine/transmission unit to be subsequently withdrawn from underneath the front of the vehicle.

3C.18 Remove the two transmission mounting bolts (arrowed)

20   Unbolt and withdraw all cover(s) and/or shield(s) protecting the crankshaft pulley/vibration damper (Section 4, paragraphs 22 and 23).

21   Note their connections and detach the wiring from the alternator and starter motor. Release the cable ties and move the wiring harness out of the way.

22   Undo the retaining nuts and detach the exhaust downpipe from the manifold and the exhaust system.

23   Place the gear lever in 4th gear, then disconnect the selector rod from the transmission by loosening the clamp and sliding it along the rod.

24   Unscrew the retaining bolt and disconnect the stabiliser rod from the transmission. As it is detached collect the flat washer located between the rod and transmission. Tie the shift rod and the stabiliser rod up out of the way.

25   Disconnect the track control (suspension) arm balljoint from the spindle carrier each side as described in the appropriate petrol-engined manual for the model concerned.

26   Disconnect the track (tie) rod balljoint from the steering arm on the left-hand side by unscrewing the retaining nut and using a balljoint separator to release the tapered joint.

27   Remove both driveshafts as described in the relevant petrol-engined manual for the vehicle concerned but note that in some instances (depending on model), it may not be possible to drain the transmission oil and it is therefore necessary to prepare for some oil loss as the driveshafts are withdrawn from the transmission. Position a suitable container under the transmission and withdraw the driveshafts. When the right hand shaft is removed, plug its aperture in transmission to prevent further oil loss when the transmission is removed. When the left-hand shaft is removed, insert a wooden or plastic plug in its aperture to prevent the differential side gears from being dislodged and further oil leakage.

28   With the driveshafts withdrawn, tie the shafts up to the suspension member to support them and prevent the CV joints from being strained. The inner joint must not be angled more than 20°, the outer joint more than 45°.

29   Attach lifting tackle to the engine, using the lifting eyes provided. Take the weight of the engine and transmission unit.

30   Disconnect the right-hand engine mounting according to type (photo):

    Escort/Orion: *Unscrew and remove the nuts from the top of the right-hand mounting. Undo the two nuts (at the top end) and the single bolt (at the bottom end) and detach the engine mounting brace on the right-hand side*

    Fiesta: *Working through the access hole in the right-hand wheel arch, undo the single retaining bolt and nut and disconnect the right-hand mounting from the body*

31   Undo the two retaining bolts and disconnect the forward transmission mounting from the underbody on the left-hand side (photo).

32   The forward transmission mounting on later models has an additional anti-vibration block attached between the mounting and the transmission. If this block is to be removed, note that the orientation arrow (viewed from the top) faces towards the front to ensure correct refitting (photos).

33   The engine and transmission should now be ready for removal. Check that all attachments and fittings are clear and not in a position where they may impede removal and get damaged in the process.

34   Arrange for an assistant to help guide the power unit down through the engine compartment to ensure that associate components and fittings are not damaged as it is withdrawn. If possible, lower the combined unit onto an engine trolley so that it can be more easily withdrawn from under the front of the vehicle.

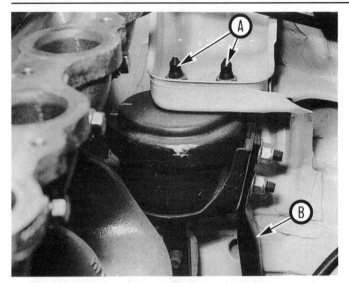

3C.30 Right-hand engine mounting nuts (A) and strut (B) (Escort/Orion)

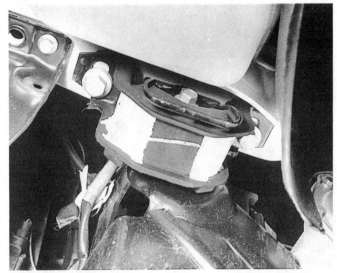

3C.31 Transmission mounting on the front left-hand side (Escort/Orion)

3C.32A Underside view of the anti-vibration block fitted to the front left mounting

3C.32B Arrow on top face of anti-vibration block indicates direction of fitting

35   Carefully lower the combined engine/transmission unit and withdraw it from under the vehicle.

36   If the vehicle is to be moved whilst the engine is out, temporarily reconnect the front suspension components and ensure that the driveshafts are suitably supported so that they can rotate without being damaged.

Engine and transmission – separation
37   Refer to Chapter 1, Section 23, but note that the starter motor and its support bracket are secured by four bolts, the engine bracket by three bolts. On steel sump models, the flywheel cover plate is secured by three bolts. The aluminium sump used on later models is secured to the base of the crankcase by 16 bolts and to the clutch bell housing by two bolts (see photos 3A.8A and 3A.8B).

38   If still in position, unbolt and remove the plastic upper section of the inlet manifold and collect the four O-ring seals.

Engine dismantling – general
39   Refer to Chapter 1, Section 24.

Engine – complete dismantling
40   Unbolt and remove the exhaust manifold. If this is the first time that the engine has been dismantled, then no exhaust manifold gasket will be found, but one will be required at reassembly.

41   Unbolt and remove the clutch assembly from the flywheel.

42   Unbolt and remove the flywheel.

43   Release the tension, and then remove the alternator drivebelt.

44   Unscrew the bolts, release the clips, and take off the upper and lower camshaft toothed belt covers.

45   Using a spanner on the crankshaft pulley bolt, turn the crankshaft in the normal direction of rotation until the drilling in the injection pump flange (CAV) or the recess (Bosch) is aligned with the drilling in the pump housing. This indicates TDC on Nos 1 and 4 pistons.

46   Remove the camshaft belt tensioner and spring. A Torx bit will be required for the spring bolt. Take off the camshaft drivebelt.

47   Unbolt and remove the crankshaft pulley vibration damper. To prevent rotation of the crankshaft while unscrewing the bolt, screw two bolts into the flywheel mounting flange, and place a long lever between them (photo).

48   Remove the injection pump belt tensioner and its spring, and then take off the drivebelt.

49   Using a Torx bit, remove the camshaft belt idler pulley.

3C.47 Method of locking crankshaft

3C.82 No 12 Torx socket and big-end bearing cap bolt

50   Unbolt and remove the camshaft belt sprocket, but only unscrew the outer bolts.

51   Unbolt and remove the belt cover backing plates.

52   Unscrew the three bolts and remove the fuel injection pump belt sprocket.

53   Detach the leak-off pipes from the injectors and the injection pump.

54   Disconnect the pipes from the injectors and the injection pump. Cap the openings to prevent the entry of dirt. Lift the pipe assembly away.

55   Disconnect the fuel line from the fuel filter.

56   Unbolt and remove the injection pump bracket.

57   Extract the Torx screws and remove the fuel injection pump, complete with fuel line.

58   Unbolt and remove the alternator, with its adjuster link.

59   Unbolt and remove the alternator bracket.

60   Pull off the crankcase ventilation system hoses from the camshaft cover, cylinder block and inlet manifold.

61   Remove the fuel filter with its bracket, and the engine lifting eye.

62   Disconnect the vacuum pump oil return hose from the cylinder block, and then unscrew the two bolts and remove the vacuum pump from the cylinder head.

63   Disconnect the coolant hoses from the coolant pump and thermostat housing.

64   Unbolt and remove the thermostat housing.

65   Unscrew the fuel injectors, using a deep socket.

66   Extract the heat shields. These should be renewed on reassembly.

67   Disconnect the glow plug wiring loom and unscrew the glow plugs.

68   Unscrew the three bolts and take off the camshaft cover and gasket.

69   Unscrew and remove the cylinder head bolts in the reverse sequence to tightening (refer to Fig 1.19, Chapter 1).

70   Remove the cylinder head and gasket.

71   Unscrew and discard the oil filter.

72   Unscrew the four bolts and remove the oil pump from the cylinder block.

73   Unscrew the bolt and remove the auxiliary shaft sprocket.

74   Remove the three bolts and take off the auxiliary shaft oil seal carrier with seal.

75   Unscrew the auxiliary shaft thrustplate bolts, and withdraw the shaft with thrustplate.

76   Unbolt and remove the coolant pump.

77   Unscrew the sump pan bolts, and remove the pan.

78   Remove the belt sprocket from the crankshaft, using a puller if necessary.

79   Using a Torx bit, remove the engine front plate screws and withdraw the plate.

80   Unbolt and remove the crankshaft rear oil seal carrier.

81   Invert the engine, and unbolt and remove the oil pick-up pipe and bracket.

82   Check that the big-end bearing caps and connecting rods are marked 1 to 4, from the camshaft belt end of the engine. Using an internally-splined Torx socket, unscrew the big-end bearing cap bolts and remove them (photo).

83   Withdraw the piston/rod assemblies out of the top of the cylinder block.

84   If the original shells are to be used again, keep them taped to their respective caps or rods.

85   Unbolt the main bearing caps (numbered 1 to 5 from the camshaft belt end of the engine) and remove them. If the original shells are to be used again, keep them taped to their respective caps.

86   The piston-cooling oil jets are inserted into the cylinder block, projecting upwards from Nos 1 to 4 main bearings. These must be removed if the lubricating system is to be effectively and thoroughly cleaned at overhaul; see your local Ford dealer or engine reconditioning specialist for details.

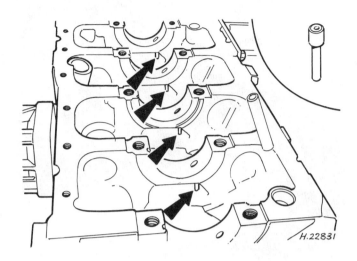

Fig. 8.6 Location of piston-cooling oil jets (Sec 3)

PART D: ENGINE OVERHAUL, REASSEMBLY AND REFITTING

Examination and renovation – general
Refer to Chapter 1, Section 26.

Engine components – examination and renovation
Refer to Chapter 1, Section 27.

Engine reassembly – general
Refer to Chapter 1, Section 28.

Engine – complete reassembly

1   Position the block so that access to the bottom end is clear, and then wipe clean the main bearing shell seats in the block. Do not forget to check that the oil jets are clear and securely refitted.

2   Fit the bearing shells to the crankcase, noting that No 1 is of twin-shell type, with a lubrication groove in each shell. All the other main bearings incorporate a lubrication groove in the crankcase shell only.

3   Fit the plain shells into the bearing caps.

4   Fit the thrustwashers on both sides of No 3 main bearing, so that the oil grooves are visible.

3D.6A Tightening a main bearing cap bolt

3D.6B Angle-tightening a main bearing cap bolt

3D.9A Pushing oil pick-up pipe into crankcase hole   note O-ring seal (arrowed)

3D.9B Tightening oil pick-up pipe bracket bolt

3D.10 Tightening crankshaft rear oil seal retainer bolt

3D.11 Tightening an engine front plate bolt

3D.13A Crankshaft inner sprocket showing O-ring seal (arrowed)

3D.13B Fitting crankshaft inner sprocket

5   Lower the crankshaft into place and oil the journals. Locate the main bearing caps with their shells, so that their numbered position is correct, and the triangular mark has its apex towards the camshaft belt end of the engine. No 1 cap must be flush with the block.

6   Screw in new main bearing cap bolts (lightly oiled), and tighten to the specified torque (photos).

7   Measure the crankshaft endfloat by levering the crankshaft back and forth, and using feeler blades or a dial gauge. If the endfloat is not within the specified limits, then dismantling must be carried out, and the thrustwashers changed for ones of different thickness.

8   Fit the pistons/connecting rods in their correct cylinder bores, as described in Chapter 1, Section 18. Tighten the big-end bearing cap bolts as specified.

9   Fit the oil pick-up pipe and bracket. Make sure that the O-ring is correctly seated (photos).

10   Using a new gasket, fit the crankshaft rear oil seal retainer, with a new oil seal. Make sure that the retainer is flush with the edge of the cylinder block. Grease the seal lips (photo).

11   Using a new gasket, fit the engine front plate, making sure that its

3D.13C Fitting crankshaft outer sprocket/damper assembly

3D.15 Tightening a coolant pump bolt

3D.16 Inserting the auxiliary shaft

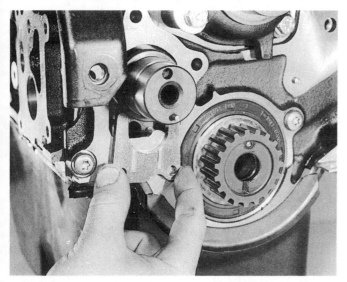

3D.17 Auxiliary shaft thrustplate

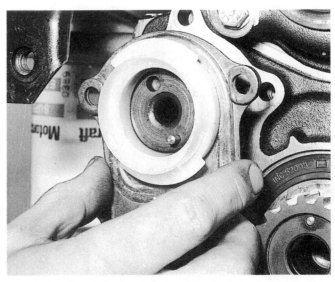

3D.18A Auxiliary shaft oil seal retainer with plastic installer

3D.18B Tightening auxiliary shaft oil seal retainer bolts

3D.18C Auxiliary shaft oil seal retainer with installer removed

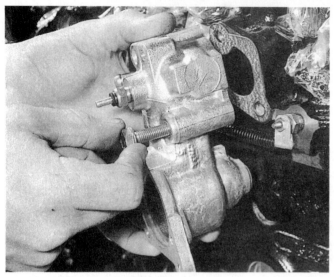

3D.24A Fitting the thermostat housing ...

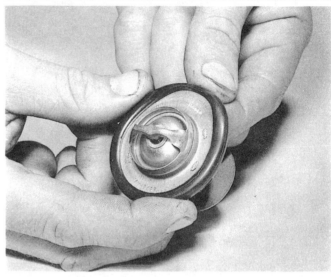

3D.24B ... thermostat seal ring ...

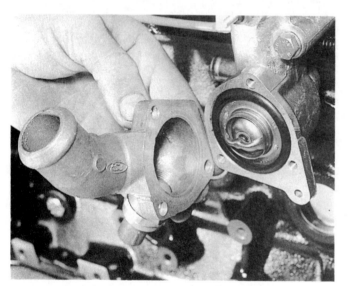

3D.24C ... and refit the cover

3D.24D Lower end of the dipstick guide tube

edge is flush with the edge of the cylinder block, and that the vibration damper is centred in the hole in the plate (photo).

12   Draw a new crankshaft front oil seal into place, using a suitable piece of tubing and the vibration damper centre bolt as an installer.

13   Fit the drivebelt sprocket fully onto the front of the crankshaft, making sure that the positioning dowel engages correctly, and that the O-ring seal is in good condition. Fit the vibration damper/pulley, engaging the vee in its cut-out. Tighten the fixing bolt to the specified torque (photos).

14   Fit the sump pan and its gasket, as described earlier in this supplement.

15   Using a new gasket, fit the coolant pump (photo).

16   Oil the bearings, and fit the auxiliary shaft (photo).

17   Fit the thrustplate so that the oil grooves are visible (photo).

18   Fit a new auxiliary shaft/oil seal assembly, which is supplied complete with a retainer. A plastic installer is provided, to prevent damage to the oil seal lips as it is pushed over the step on the shaft, but

3D.24E Tightening dipstick guide tube upper bracket bolt

insulating tape will serve as an alternative. Grease the seal lips before fitting the retainer plate (photos).

19   Fit the oil pump as described in paragraph 81 of Part B.

20   Smear oil on the sealing ring of a new oil filter and screw it on hand-tight.

21   Check the piston protrusion, select a cylinder head gasket, and fit the cylinder head as described earlier in this Section, and after reference to Chapter 1, Sections 18 and 29. Remember that no subsequent retightening of the cylinder head bolts is required.

22   Screw in the glow plugs and connect the wiring, with the black coiled end towards flywheel.

23   Fit the fuel injectors, using new heat shields. Tighten the injectors to the specified torque.

24   Using a new gasket, fit the thermostat housing, and assemble its component parts. Fit the dipstick guide tube (photos).

25   Fit the coolant hose to the coolant pump, so that the white mark on the hose is aligned with the cast mark on the pump.

26   Connect the coolant distribution pipe, and then push it into its spring clip on the side member.

27   Fit the alternator bracket, the alternator and adjuster strap (photos).

28   Fit the fuel deflector, fuel pump and bracket (photos).

29   Connect the fuel injection pipes, and also the leak-off pipes (photos).

30   Fit the vacuum pump (using a new O-ring seal) in the following way. Screw in the lower bolt, fit the pump, and then screw in the upper bolt. Tighten both bolts equally. Connect the oil return hose (photos).

31   Fit the fuel filter, bracket and engine lifting eye to the cylinder head (photo).

32   Connect the fuel outlet hose to the fuel filter (photo).

33   Fit the toothed belt backing plates (photo).

34   Fit the camshaft sprocket and belt tensioner, and also the idler sprocket (photos).

3D.27A Fit the alternator bracket ...

3D.27B ... and then the alternator

3D.28A Fitting the fuel injection pump

3D.28B Fuel injection pump rear bracket

3D.29A Connecting a fuel injector pipe union

3D.29B Fuel injector pipe arrangement

3D.29C Fuel pipes at the injection pump

3D.30A Fitting the vacuum pump

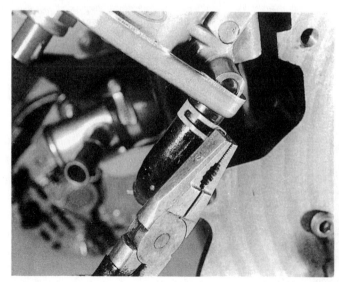
3D.30B Vacuum pump oil return hose

3D.31 Bosch fuel filter

3D.32 Connecting fuel outlet hose to Bosch filter

3D.33 Toothed belt backing plate

3D.34A Camshaft sprocket and fixing bolts

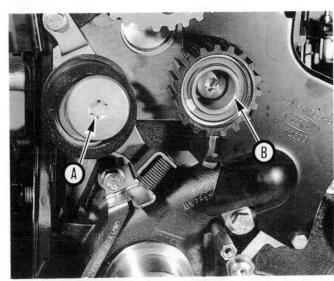

3D.34B Camshaft belt tensioner (A) and idler sprocket (B)

3D.34C Tightening idler sprocket Torx bolt

3D.35 Toothed belt lower side cover

3D.37 Fuel injection pump belt tensioner

3D.38A Auxiliary shaft sprocket

3D.38B Tightening auxiliary shaft sprocket bolt. Note oil filter strap wrench used to prevent rotation of sprocket

3D.42 Engine rear plate (arrowed)

35   Fit the lower side cover (photo).

36   Fit the injection pump sprocket.

37   Fit the injection pump belt tensioner, locked in its retracted position (photo).

38   Fit the auxiliary shaft sprocket, making sure that the locating dowel is correctly engaged (photos).

39   Fit and tension the drivebelts as described earlier in this Supplement (Part B, paragraphs 6 to 26).

40   Fit the upper and lower belt covers, making sure that the drivebelt cover spacer stud on the water pump is secure by applying thread-locking fluid.

41   Fit and tension the alternator drivebelt (Section 4 of this Chapter).

42   Locate the engine rear plate on its dowels (photo).

43   Fit the flywheel, using new bolts, and tightening to the specified torque. The flywheel can only be fitted in one position, as the bolt holes are offset (photos).

44   Fit the clutch assembly, remembering to centralise the driven plate.

45   Check the valve clearances and adjust if necessary, as described in Chapter 1 with reference to paragraph 1, Section B of this Chapter.

46   Fit the camshaft cover, with a new gasket (photos).

47   Reconnect the crankcase ventilation system hoses (photos).

48   Fit the exhaust manifold, with a new gasket.

49   It is recommended that the plastic upper section of the inlet manifold is fitted after the engine is in the vehicle, but cover the inlet ports now, to prevent the entry of dirt.

Engine – refitting to transmission
50   Offer the transmission to the engine, rocking it slightly until the locating dowels engage fully. Do not allow the weight of the transmission to hang upon the input shaft once it is engaged in the clutch.

3D.43A Torque-tightening flywheel bolts

3D.43B Angle-tightening flywheel bolts

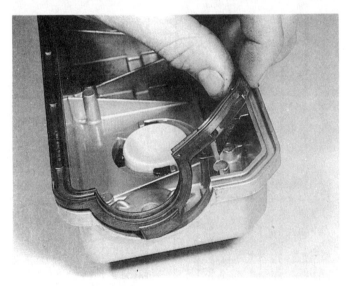

3D.46A Camshaft cover gasket

3D.46B Fitting camshaft cover

3D.47A Crankcase vent hoses

3D.47B Crankcase vent hose at camshaft cover

3D.54A Engine/transmission ready for installation

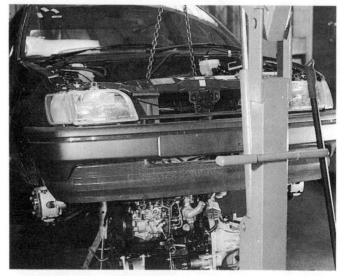

3D.54B Engine/transmission being hoisted into the vehicle

3D.56A Bearer for transmission flexible mountings (Fiesta)

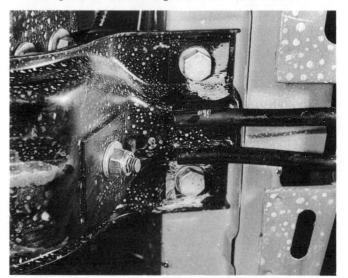

3D.56B Bearer bolts at towing hook end (Fiesta)

51   Refit and tighten securely the engine-to-transmission bolts.

52   Bolt on the starter motor and bracket.

53   Bolt on the flywheel cover plate (where fitted) and the right-hand mounting, if removed.

Engine and transmission – refitting

54   With the front of the vehicle raised and securely supported, place the engine/transmission on a suitable trolley, and slide it under the engine compartment (photos).

55   Attach a suitable hoist, and carefully lift the engine/transmission until the right-hand mounting bolts can be inserted.

56   Reconnect the engine and transmission mountings. On the Fiesta model bolt the transmission flexible mounting to the bearer, then bolt the bearer to the body (photos). On Escort models, reconnect the right-hand engine mounting strut.

57   As soon as the engine/transmission is secure, remove the lifting gear.

58   Reconnect the gearchange stabiliser rod to the transmission, noting the location of the plain washer (photo).

59   Reconnect the gearchange rod. To do this, have the lever inside the vehicle, and the transmission selector rod, in 4th gear. Insert a thin rod through the cut-outs in the plastic housing below the gear lever, under the vehicle. The rod should be inserted with its end inclined upwards, so that it passes through the hole in the lever dog, and then pulled to the horizontal position (photo).

60   Slide the gearchange rod clamp over the joint, and then tighten the clamp pinch-bolt (photo).

61   Check that all gears can be selected.

62   Connect the electrical leads to the starter motor (photo).

63   Connect the leads to the alternator (photos).

64   Fit the driveshafts as described in the appropriate workshop manual for your vehicle. Make sure that the dummy shafts have been removed from the transmission.

65   Fit the roadwheels.

66   Reconnect the exhaust downpipe to the manifold, and the front section, or the complete exhaust system, to its rubber hangers (photo).

67   Refit the radiator and bolt the fan assembly into position (if removed), and reconnect the wiring plug.

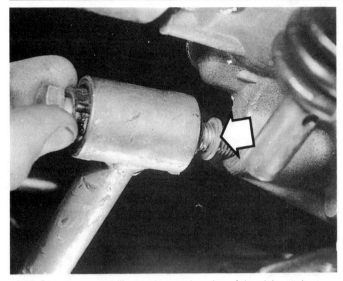

3D.58 Gearchange stabiliser rod – note location of the plain washer (arrowed)

3D.59 Locking rod (arrowed) to hold gear lever in 4th gear

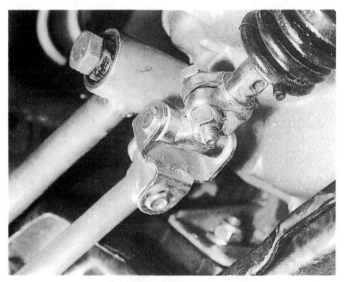

3D.60 Gearchange rod joint and clamp

3D.62 Starter motor connections

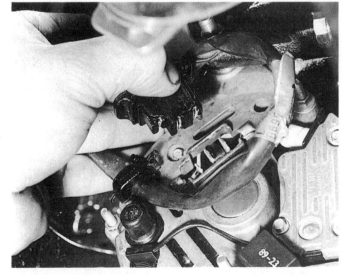

3D.63A Alternator connector plug

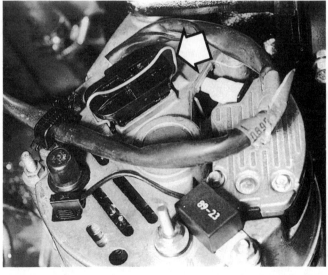

3D.63B Alternator connector plug retaining spring clip (arrowed)

3D.66 Always renew gasket when reconnecting exhaust downpipe to manifold

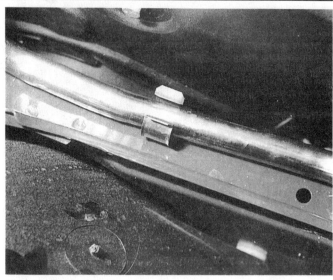

3D.69 Coolant distribution pipe in clip

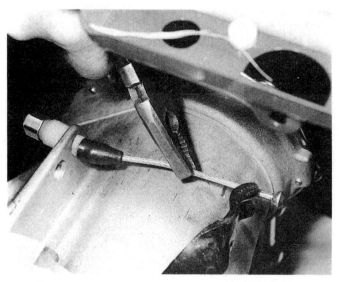

3D.70 Connecting the clutch cable

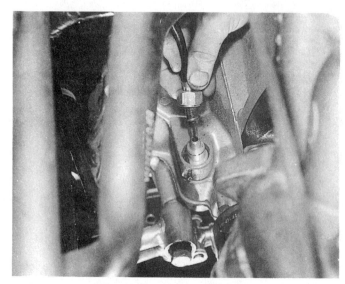

3D.71 Connecting the speedometer drive cable

3D.72A Connecting the brake servo hose to the vacuum pump

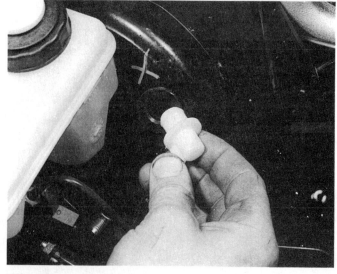

3D.72B Connecting the brake servo hose to the servo

3D.75A Oil pressure switch (arrowed) and cable

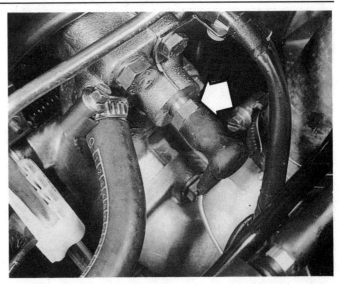

3D.75B Coolant temperature switch (arrowed) and cable on thermostat housing (Fiesta)

3D.76 Connecting the throttle cable

3D.79 Alternator rear cover

68   Connect the coolant hoses, the heater hoses and the expansion tank hoses to the cylinder head and thermostat housing.

69   Where applicable, reconnect and clip the metal coolant distribution pipe (photo).

70   Connect the clutch operating cable (photo).

71   Connect the speedometer cable to the transmission (photo).

72   Connect the vacuum pipe from the brake servo to the vacuum pump (photos).

73   Connect the fuel inlet and return hoses.

74   Connect the transmission earth strap.

75   Connect the electrical leads to the following (photos):

Oil pressure switch
Coolant temperature switch
Fuel injection pump fuel shut-off solenoid and cold start device
Glow plug feed
Radiator fan thermoswitch

76   Connect the throttle cable (photo).

77   Using new sealing rings, bolt on the plastic upper section of the inlet manifold.

78   Fit the air cleaner casing, the filter element and lid, and connect the air inlet hose.

79   Fit the protective cover to the rear of the alternator (photo).

80   Support the vehicle on a workshop, or substantial hydraulic or screw type jack placed under the front mounting point and remove the axle stands.

81   Lower the vehicle to the ground.

82   Fill the engine and transmission with the specified quantities and grade of oil (photo).

83   Fill and bleed the cooling system, as described in Chapter 2.

84   Reconnect the battery.

85   Refit the bonnet and connect the washer tube.

3D.82 Filling the engine with oil

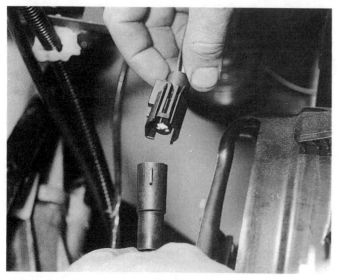

4.5A Radiator fan and motor removal (Fiesta) – disconnect motor wiring ...

4.5B ... unscrew top mounting bolt ...

Engine – initial start-up after overhaul

86   The operations are as described in Chapter 1, Section 32. The fuel system can be primed, and air bled out (as much as possible) as described in Part A of Section 5.

---

4   Cooling system – 1.8 litre engine

Coolant renewal – general

1   Ford now recommend the use of their Motorcraft Super Plus 4 antifreeze and state that if it is used in the recommended concentration, unmixed with any other type of antifreeze or additive, it can remain in the system for a maximum period of four years before being renewed. At that time the system must be drained and thoroughly reverse-flushed before the fresh coolant mixture is poured in.

2   This time interval is correct at the time of writing, but may be extended in the future **only** for vehicles which have been properly serviced as outlined above; see your local Ford dealer for the latest recommendation.

3   Owners who use any other type of antifreeze should continue to use the interval given in Routine maintenance at the front of this manual.

Radiator fan and motor – removal and refitting

4   The fasteners securing the fan shroud to the radiator vary slightly according to model.

5   On Fiesta models, the shroud is secured by a single bolt at the top and by pegs into locating slots at the bottom (photos).

6   On Escort/Orion models, the shroud is secured by two nuts at the top and by clips on the radiator at the bottom.

Radiator – removal and refitting

7   On Fiesta and early Escort/Orion models radiator removal and refitting is essentially as described in Section 9 of Chapter 2; note the differences (where applicable) outlined in paragraphs 5 or 6 above and paragraph 8 below.

8   On all Escort/Orion models, note that the hose from the coolant expansion tank must also be disconnected before the radiator can be removed.

9   On the revised (September 1990-on) range of Escort/Orion models, note that the radiator is now secured by rubber mountings at the top and bottom, the bottom mountings being clamped by a support bracket that is bolted to the body from underneath. To remove the radiator, proceed as follows.

4.5C ... and withdraw fan and shroud from bottom mounting pegs

10   Drain the cooling system (Chapter 2).

11   Remove its retaining screw and unclip the air cleaner intake duct from the air cleaner assembly and the body.

12   Remove the radiator fan and shroud as described in Chapter 2, noting the differences outlined in paragraph 6 above.

13   Disconnect all three coolant hoses from the radiator, taking care not to damage its unions as noted in Chapter 2.

14   Raise the front of the vehicle and support it securely on axle stands placed at the points shown in the appropriate manual for petrol-engined models.

15   Working underneath the vehicle, unbolt the radiator support bracket; if the mounting bolts cannot be reached, remove the splash shield from the radiator by drilling out the eight securing rivets (note that this will have to be done anyway if the radiator is to be renewed).

16   Pull the radiator downwards out of its top retaining lugs and withdraw it from under the vehicle. If the radiator is to be renewed, remove the splash shield, support bracket, rubber mountings and side deflectors.

17   Refitting is the reverse of the removal procedure, referring to the notes outlined in Section 9 of Chapter 2. If the splash shield was detached, refit it using new rivets.

Auxiliary drivebelt

General
18   The alternator, located in the front right-hand corner of the engine compartment, is driven from the crankshaft pulley by a flat 'polyvee'-type of drivebelt.

19   With the alternator pivoting on a mounting bracket bolted to the cylinder block, its drivebelt is tensioned either by a conventional arrangement (slotted adjusting link) or, on all models built after May 1991 (build code LM), by a rack-and-pinion system.

20   The rack-and-pinion system can be fitted to earlier 1.8 litre models, if the drivebelt is thought to be noisy or, if it is thought to have worn excessively and difficulty is experienced in adjusting it correctly. See a local Ford dealer for details.

21   On models with power-assisted steering, the pump and alternator are both mounted on a bracket that is bolted to the cylinder block and driven (from the crankshaft pulley) by the same flat 'polyvee'-type of drivebelt; drivebelt adjustment is by the rack-and-pinion system (Fig. 8.7).

Preliminary operations — all models
22   Before any drivebelt servicing operations can be undertaken, adequate access must first be gained by jacking up the front right-hand side of the vehicle and supporting it on axle stands placed at the points shown in the appropriate manual for petrol-engined models. Disconnect the battery earth (negative) lead.

23   The splash shield and/or cover protecting the drivebelt and adjuster components must now be removed. On all models there should be either a cover immediately over the alternator pulley, secured by three bolts (or plastic quarter-turn fasteners) screwed vertically into the body side member, or a splash shield secured by two bolts at the right-hand end of the engine or to the inner wing panel; on some models, both cover/shield(s) may be fitted. On Fiesta models (Escort/Orion as well, depending on the task to be carried out and the tools available) the front right-hand roadwheel and the wheel arch liner should also be removed — refer to the appropriate manual for petrol-engined models.

24   The method of drivebelt adjustment is easily identifiable from the accompanying photographs and illustrations; proceed according to the relevant sub-Section below.

Drivebelt check and renewal – all models
25   Once the drivebelt and adjuster components are fully accessible, rotate the crankshaft as necessary to inspect the full length of the belt

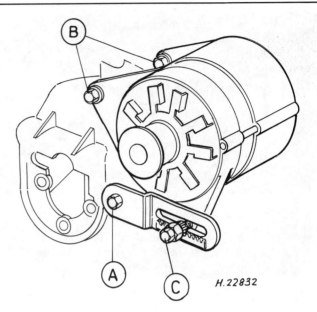

Fig. 8.7 Alternator mountings and drivebelt adjustment details – models with power-assisted steering (Sec 4)

A   *Adjuster link-to-mounting*   B   *Alternator pivot bolts and nuts*
      bracket bolt (and nut)   C   *Adjuster centre lockbolt*

checking for signs of cracks, splitting and fraying, or for signs of wear or damage such as glazing (shiny patches) or separation on the belt plies. Renew the belt if worn or damaged and check the condition and security of the pulleys, the mounting bracket and adjuster components and their fasteners.

26   To renew the belt, unclip and withdraw (where fitted) the plastic fuel deflector from the alternator mounting bracket. Slacken the two pivot bolts and nuts at the top of the alternator, then the adjuster link bolts and nuts— where rack-and-pinion adjustment is fitted, slacken the adjuster's centre lockbolt.

27   Move the alternator towards the engine until the drivebelt can be slipped off the pulleys – where rack-and-pinion adjustment is fitted, rotate the adjuster nut anti-clockwise.

28   Fit the new drivebelt, ensuring that it is routed correctly and settled in the pulley grooves, then tension the drivebelt as described in the relevant sub-Section below.

Alternator only - slotted-link adjustment
29   To check the drivebelt's tension Ford recommend the use of a tension gauge, but state that the procedure outlined in paragraph 8 of Chapter 2, Section 11, will serve as an acceptable substitute if a tension gauge is not available.

30   Proceed as described in Chapter 2; on tightening the alternator fasteners, tighten first the adjuster link bolts and nuts, then the alternator pivot bolts and nuts (drivebelt end first), noting the torque wrench settings specified in this Chapter (photo).

31   On completion, refit all other components removed and reconnect the battery.

Alternator only - rack-and-pinion adjustment
Note: *This procedure requires the use of a torque wrench (preferably two) and a 22 mm crowfoot adaptor.*
Note that there is no 'check' as such of the drivebelt's tension (except by tension gauge, if required to check the adjuster's operation) - the tension checking and adjusting procedures are one and the same, as described below.

32   Slacken the two pivot bolts and nuts at the top of the alternator, then the adjuster link-to-mounting bracket bolt and nut and finally the adjuster's centre lockbolt (photo).

4.30 Alternator mountings and drivebelt adjustment alternator only, slotted-link adjustment

4.32 Alternator mountings and drivebelt adjustment alternator only, rack-and-pinion adjustment

33   Using a torque wrench with a crowfoot adaptor, tighten the adjuster nut to the torque setting appropriate to the drivebelt's condition. This will cause the adjuster nut to rotate clockwise so that, with its pinion teeth engaging the adjuster link's rack teeth, the alternator will be moved automatically to the appropriate position for correct drivebelt tension.

34   While maintaining the pressure on the nut, tighten securely (preferably using a second torque wrench to tighten the bolt to the setting specified) the adjuster's centre lockbolt (photo).

35   Tighten to their specified torque wrench settings first the adjuster link-to-mounting bracket bolt and nut, then the alternator pivot bolts and nuts (drivebelt end first).

36   Refit all other components removed and reconnect the battery.

Alternator and power-assisted steering pump
Note: *This procedure ideally requires the use of a torque wrench (preferably two) and a 22 mm crowfoot adaptor.*
Note that there is no 'check' as such of the drivebelt's tension (except by tension gauge, advisable if a torque wrench is not used to set the adjustor) the tension checking and adjusting procedures are one and the same, as described below

| A | Adjuster link | C | Adjuster centre lockbolt |
| B | Adjuster nut | | |

37   Slacken the two pivot bolts and nuts at the top of the alternator, then the adjuster link-to-mounting bracket bolt and nut and finally the adjuster's centre lockbolt.

38   Using a torque wrench with a crowfoot adaptor, tighten the adjuster nut to the specified torque setting. This will cause the adjuster nut to rotate clockwise so that, with its pinion teeth engaging the adjuster link's rack teeth, the alternator will be moved automatically to the appropriate position for correct drivebelt tension. While maintaining the pressure on the nut, tighten securely (preferably using a second torque wrench to tighten the bolt to the setting specified) the adjuster's centre lockbolt.

39   If the necessary torque wrench(es) and adaptor are not available or cannot be used because of poor access, tighten the adjuster nut using an ordinary spanner until one of the nut's pinion teeth engages in the centre groove (the eighth from either end) of the adjuster link's rack, then securely tighten the centre lockbolt (Fig. 8.8). If this method is used, the drivebelt's tension should be checked as soon as possible with a tension gauge and adjusted accordingly; the expected readings being given in the Specifications Section of this Chapter.

4.34 Hold adjuster nut as specified torque setting using torque wrench and crowfoot adaptor, then tighten adjuster centre lockbolt

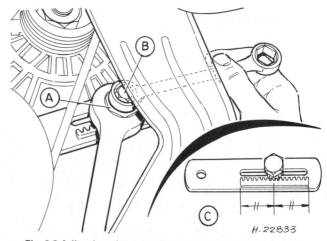

Fig. 8.8 Adjusting alternator/power-assisted steering pump drivebelt (Sec 4)

A	Adjuster nut	C	Adjuster nut pinion tooth
B	Adjuster centre lockbolt		engaged with adjuster link rack
			centre groove

4.58A Clean mating surfaces thoroughly before refitting water pump

4.58B Align white paint mark on hose with pump casting's raised rib as shown

40   Tighten securely, to their specified torque wrench settings if possible, first the adjuster link-to-mounting bracket bolt and nut, then the alternator pivot bolts and nuts (drivebelt end first).

41   Refit all other components removed and reconnect the battery.

Modified coolant expansion tank hose

42   If at any time, symptoms are encountered in the cooling system which lead you to suspect a blown cylinder head gasket or even a cracked cylinder head, and a compression test indicates that the engine is sound, a modified hose is available to solve the problem.

43   Available through your local Ford deliver, the hose replaces that which runs from the thermostat housing to the coolant expansion tank and incorporates a restrictor at the thermostat end.

44   To fit the modified hose, slacken the clips at each end and disconnect it from its unions; if you work quickly, there will be no need to drain the system. Renew the clips if necessary.

45   Fit the modified hose, restrictor next to the thermostat, and secure it with the clips, then top up the coolant expansion tank to the 'MAX' mark. Start the engine and run it up to normal operating temperature as described in Section 6 of Chapter 2, topping up the level if required. If an airlock is thought to have occurred, use the top hose bleed screw to purge out the trapped air.

Water pump – removal and refitting

46   On the 1.8 litre engine, the water pump is driven from the back of the camshaft drivebelt. Note that Ford recommend that the drivebelt is renewed whenever the water pump is renewed. To renew the pump, proceed as follows.

47   Start by carrying out the (applicable) preliminary dismantling procedures described in paragraphs 2 to 5 of Section 3, Part B.

48   Drain the cooling system, disconnect the expansion tank hoses and the coolant hose from the water pump; note the white paint mark on the hose which should be aligned with the guide mark on the pump casting on refitting (Chapter 2).

49   Remove the camshaft drivebelt as described in Section 2, Part B of this Chapter.

50   Using a Torx bit, unbolt and remove the idler pulley.

51   Unscrew the two bolts next to the injection pump sprocket which secure the drivebelt backing plate, then withdraw the backing plate.

52   Carefully slacken the tensioner pulley adjusting bolt and remove the tensioner spring, then swing the pulley upwards and retighten the bolt.

53   Unbolt and remove the tensioner spring bracket, noting that the two bolts also secure the water pump.

54   Unscrew the drivebelt cover spacer stud, then unscrew the two remaining pump securing bolts and withdraw the water pump.

55   Remove the pump gasket and carefully clean the cylinder block mating surface, also that of the pump, if it is to be refitted.

56   Note that a worn or damaged pump cannot be reconditioned; it must be renewed complete. Check the condition of the coolant hoses and clips, renewing them if there is any doubt about their condition.

57   Obtain a new camshaft drivebelt; this must be renewed as a matter of course whenever the water pump is renewed. Considering the amount of work required to renew the drivebelts, and the fact that they must be renewed anyway if liquids such as coolant, oil or Diesel fuel are allowed to contaminate them, owners are advised to consider renewing both drivebelts on a precautionary basis whenever the pump is disturbed.

58   On reassembly, fit the gasket to the pump mating surface and offer up the pump to the cylinder block. Engage the coolant hose on to the pump union, ensuring that the hose's white paint mark aligns with the raised rib on the pump casting (photos).

59   Ensuring that the tensioner spring bracket is correctly located, refit the pump's four retaining bolts and tighten them to their specified torque wrench setting, then tighten securely the coolant hose clip.

60   Applying one or two drops of a thread-locking compound (Ford recommend Loctite 242) to its threads, refit the drivebelt cover spacer stud, tightening it to its specified torque wrench setting.

61   Refit the drivebelt backing plate, tightening only loosely its two bolts at this stage.

62   Slacken the tensioner pulley adjusting bolt, refit the tensioner spring, then swing the pulley until the spring is fully compressed and retighten the bolt.

63   Check that all timing pegs are fully engaged in the crankshaft and in the camshaft and fuel injection pump sprockets, slacken the camshaft sprocket bolts and fit the (new) camshaft drivebelt so that the sprocket bolts are in the middle of their slots.

4.66A Refill cooling system ...

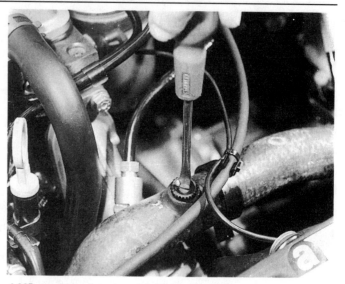

4.66B ... and bleed out trapped air at top hose bleed screw

64   Refit the idler pulley, tightening its Torx bolt to the specified torque wrench setting, then tighten securely the backing plate bolts.

65   The remainder of the procedure is as described in Part B of Section 3 of this Chapter, paragraph 17 onwards.

66   When all disturbed components have been correctly refitted and adjusted (where applicable), refill the cooling system, start the engine and run it to normal operating temperature, then switch off and allow it to cool down (photos). Inspect the engine for coolant leaks and rectify if required, then top up the system.

5 Fuel and exhaust systems

PART A: ALL MODELS

1   This part is concerned with fuel filter maintenance and other fuel system procedures applicable to all models irrespective of engine size.

2   All engines covered in this manual use either the Bosch or the CAV RotoDiesel injection systems. In all cases, the filter assembly is bolted to the left-hand end of the cylinder head, above the clutch bellhousing.

3   Early 1.6 litre engines with Bosch systems are fitted with filter assemblies which incorporate a separate element, while later versions with the Bosch system use filter assemblies with a 'spin-on' cartridge (Fig. 8.12'B'). 1.8 litre engines with Bosch systems are fitted with clamp-fixing cartridge filters (Fig. 8.9). Procedures concerning the CAV RotoDiesel filter assembly are the same for all engines with that system (Fig. 8.12'A').

4   Use the accompanying photographs and illustrations, if necessary, to identify the type of filter fitted, then refer to the relevant sub-Section below for details of the task to be undertaken.

Draining water from the fuel filter

Note: *Before starting any work on the fuel filter, obtain a suitable container into which it can be drained and place rags or similar material under the filter assembly to catch any spillages.* **Do not** *allow Diesel fuel to leak into the clutch bellhousing or it will contaminate the clutch driven plate friction material   this will cause severe clutch slip which can be cured only by the renewal of the clutch plate and the degreasing of all fouled surfaces. Similarly, Diesel fuel should* **never** *be allowed to contaminate components such as the alternator and starter motor, the coolant hoses and engine mountings, and any wiring.*
When working on the filter, always take great care to examine the condition of all rubber seals, copper sealing washers, etc; these should be

renewed if there is the slightest doubt about their condition. On reassembly, carefully ensure that all seals are correctly located and that they are not distorted on being tightened; any imperfect seal will allow air to be drawn into the system

1.6 litre engine   early-type Bosch (separate element) filter
5   Refer to Chapter 3, Section 4. If no fuel emerges at first, use the procedure given in paragraph 10 below.

1.6 litre engine   later-type Bosch ('spin-on' cartridge) filter
6   Disconnect the battery earth lead.

7   In addition to taking the precautions noted above to catch any fuel spillages, connect a tube to the drain spigot on the base of the fuel filter. Place the other end of the tube in a clean jar or can.

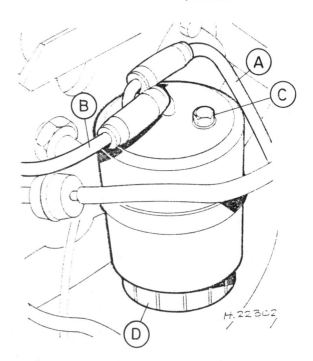

Fig. 8.9 1.8 litre engine fuel filter   Bosch clamp-fixing cartridge type (Sec 5)

A Fuel inlet hose	C Vent screw
B Fuel outlet hose	D Drain cock

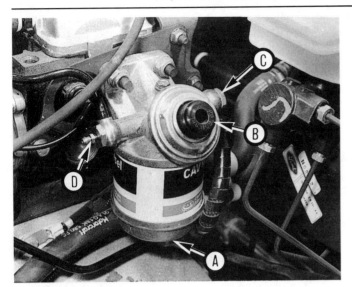

5A.14 CAV RotoDiesel fuel filter

A   Water drain cock   C   Fuel inlet hose banjo union
B   Hand-priming pump   D   Bleed nipple

8   Open the drain cock by unscrewing the knurled wheel.

9   Allow the filter to drain until clean fuel, free of dirt or water, emerges from the tube (approximately one-quarter of a pint/100 cc is usually sufficient). Close the drain cock and remove the tube, containers and rag, mopping up any spilt fuel.

10   If, as often happens, no fuel emerges on opening the drain cock, slacken the vent screw on the filter head to allow sufficient air into the filter for fuel to flow. If this does not work, remove the filter cartridge (see paragraphs 21 to 25 below) and check it carefully until the reason for the lack of flow can be identified and is cured. It is unwise simply to probe the drain cock with a piece of wire in an attempt to clear the obstruction; the small seals in the drain cock may be damaged or dislodged. Note that the system may require bleeding (see paragraphs 48 to 51 below) if the vent screw is disturbed or the filter unscrewed.

11   On completion, dispose safely of the drained fuel and reconnect the battery earth lead. Check carefully all disturbed components to ensure that there are no leaks (of air or fuel) when the engine is restarted.

1.8 litre engine   Bosch clamp-fixing cartridge filter
12   Proceed as described in paragraphs 6 to 11 above, noting that on this filter the vent screw is the single (slotted, hexagon-headed) screw on the top of the filter itself. Access to the fuel filter assembly may be much improved on Escort-Orion models if the duct from the air cleaner to the inlet manifold is first removed.

1.6 and 1.8 litre engines   CAV RotoDiesel filter
13   Disconnect the battery earth lead.

14   On Escort/Orion models with 1.8 litre engines, access to the fuel filter assembly may be much improved if the duct from the air cleaner to the inlet manifold is first removed (photo).

15   In addition to taking the precautions noted above to soak up any spilt fuel, connect a tube to the drain spigot (where fitted) on the base of the fuel filter. Place the other end of the tube in a clean jar or can.

16   Open the drain cock either by unscrewing the knurled wheel/thumbscrew or by using a spanner, as appropriate (photo).

17   Allow the filter to drain until clean fuel, free of dirt or water, emerges from the tube (approximately one-quarter of a pint/100 cc is usually sufficient). Close the drain cock and remove the tube, containers and rag, mopping up any split fuel.

18   If, as often happens, no fuel emerges on opening the drain cock,

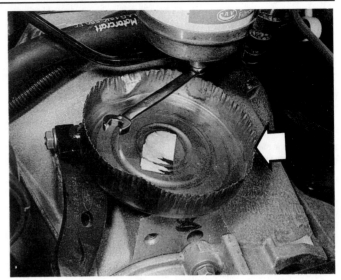

5A.16 Draining water from CAV RotoDiesel fuel filter – note use of container (arrowed) to prevent spillage

either operate the hand-priming pump to get fuel flowing or slacken the bleed nipple on the filter outlet union to allow sufficient air into the filter for fuel to flow. If this does not work, remove the filter element (see paragraphs 34 to 40 below) and check the element and bowl carefully until the reason for the lack of flow can be identified and is cured. In some cases, it would appear that the drain cock passage in the bowl was never made on manufacture; in such cases, either the filter element must be removed at each draining interval so that any water or foreign matter can be tipped out of the filter bowl, or the necessary replacement parts must be obtained so that the drain cock can be used as described above. It is unwise simply to probe the drain cock with a piece of wire in an attempt to clear the obstruction; the small seals in the drain cock may be damaged or dislodged. Note that the system may require bleeding (see paragraphs 52 to 55 below) if the bleed nipple is disturbed or the filter dismantled.

19   On completion, refit the air cleaner duct (if removed), dispose safely of the drained fuel and reconnect the battery earth lead. Check carefully all disturbed components to ensure that there are no leaks (of air or fuel) when the engine is restarted.

Fuel filter (element) renewal
Note: *Before starting any work on the fuel filter, wash or wipe clean the filter assembly and the area around it, removing all traces of dirt from the filter's components and its hose unions; it is essential that no dirt or other foreign matter is allowed into the system. Next, refer to the note at the beginning of the previous sub-section and take precautions accordingly to catch any fuel spillages.*

1.6 litre engine   early-type Bosch (separate element) filter
20   Refer to Chapter 3, Section 4.

1.6 litre engine   later-type Bosch ('spin-on' cartridge) filter
21   Drain the filter as described in paragraphs 6 to 11 above, but allow it to drain completely.

22   Using a chain or strap wrench, unscrew the filter cartridge from the filter head and remove it, taking care to spill as little as possible of any remaining fuel.

23   Check that both seals on the top of the new filter cartridge are correctly located in the groove and retainer provided (as applicable) and ensure that its drain cock is closed. Smear the seals with clean fuel and screw on the new cartridge, tightening it by hand only (or as directed by the manufacturer).

24   Reconnect the battery earth lead and restart the engine. Considerable cranking may be required to bleed the air from the system (see paragraphs 48 to 51 below); to spare the battery, this time may be reduced by filling the filter with clean fuel via the vent screw opening on the filter head but, as noted above, it is essential that no dirt is

introduced into the system and that no Diesel fuel is poured over vulnerable components when doing this.

25   On completion, dispose safely of the old filter and the drained fuel. Check carefully all disturbed components to ensure that there are no leaks (of air or fuel) when the engine is restarted.

1.8 litre engine   Bosch clamp-fixing cartridge filter
26   Drain the filter as described in paragraphs 6 to 12 above, but allow it to drain completely.

27   Note carefully the orientation of the fuel inlet and outlet hoses and the filter vent screw. Clean them thoroughly (see note above) and obtain new hose clamps and/or flexible hoses if the condition of those fitted is in any way suspect.

28   Releasing the clamps with pliers, disconnect the fuel inlet and outlet hoses from the filter stubs. Plug or cap hoses and unions to keep fuel in and dirt out.

29   Slacken the clamp screw and withdraw the filter from its bracket, taking care to spill as little as possible of any remaining fuel.

30   Fit the new filter to the clamp, aligning its stubs with the hoses as noted on removal and observing any directional markings on the filter. Fit the new flexible hoses and/or clamps (if required), then connect the hoses to the filter and fasten them securely with the clamps.

31   Tighten the filter mounting clamp screw, but be careful not to over-tighten it (nominal torque wrench setting of 1.5 to 2.5 Nm/1 to 2 lbf ft **only**), or the filter may be crushed. Check that the drain cock is closed.

32   Reconnect the battery earth lead and restart the engine. Considerable cranking may be required to bleed the air from the system (see paragraphs 48 to 51 below); to spare the battery, this time may be reduced by filling the filter with clean fuel via its vent screw opening but, as noted above, it is essential that no dirt is introduced into the system and that no Diesel fuel is poured over vulnerable components when doing this.

33   On completion, dispose safely of the old filter and the drained fuel. Check carefully all disturbed components to ensure that there are no leaks (or air or fuel) when the engine is restarted.

1.6 and 1.8 litre engines   CAV RotoDiesel filter
34   Drain the filter as described in paragraphs 13 to 19 above, but allow it to drain completely.

35   Support the filter bowl and unscrew the through-bolt from the filter head. Withdraw the filter bowl and the element, taking care to spill as little as possible of any remaining fuel (photo).

36   Using a small mirror and a torch if necessary, check that all seals are removed from above and below the filter element, from the through-bolt and from (the underside of) the filter head. Precise details of seal type and location will vary according to engine and model, as well as depending on the make of filter element used, but **all** these seals must be renewed as a matter of course before the filter is reassembled; usually they will be supplied with the new element.

37   Wipe clean the filter head and bowl. Check that the drain cock in the filter bowl is clean, that its seals are in good condition and correctly located, then tighten it securely closed.

38   Ensuring that all seals are renewed, fitted as noted on removal and are correctly located, refit the element to the filter head, followed by the filter bowl, then ensure that the seals above and below the element are not distorted or dislodged as the through-bolt is refitted and tightened securely.

39   Reconnect the battery earth lead, bleed the system (see paragraphs 52 to 55 below), then restart the engine.

40   On completion, dispose safely of the old filter and the drained fuel. Check carefully all disturbed components to ensure that there are no leaks (of air or fuel) when the engine is restarted.

5A.35 CAV RotoDiesel fuel filter

A   Fuel filter assembly
     mounting nuts

B   Filter element retaining
     through-bolt
C   Fuel outlet hose banjo union

Fuel filter assembly – removal and refitting
Note: *Before starting work, carefully read the notes at the beginning of the previous two sub-sections concerning catching any spilt Diesel fuel, checking seals, etc., and the need for cleanliness in general*

1.8 litre engine   Bosch clamp-fixing cartridge filter
41   Proceed as described in paragraphs 26 to 33 above.

All other types
42   Drain the filter as described in paragraphs 5 to 11, or 13 to 19 (as appropriate) above, but allow it to drain completely.

43   Unscrew the fuel inlet and outlet hose banjo union bolts. Note carefully the location of the copper sealing washers at each union, check them meticulously for scratches or distortion and renew them if there is any doubt at all about their condition. Plug or cap hoses and unions to keep fuel in and dirt out.

44   Unscrew the mounting nuts and withdraw the filter assembly from the vehicle, taking care to spill as little as possible of any remaining fuel.

45   On refitting, tighten the mounting nuts securely, to the specified torque wrench setting, if given. Ensure that the copper sealing washers are located correctly on each side of each union and tighten securely the union banjo bolts; again, use the specified torque wrench setting, if given.

46   Reconnect the battery earth lead, bleed the system (see the appropriate paragraphs below and, on 1.6 litre engines with the Bosch system, the note in paragraph 24 above), then restart the engine.

47   On completion, check carefully all disturbed components to ensure that there are no leaks (of air or fuel) when the engine is restarted.

Bleeding air from the fuel system
Note: *Before starting work, carefully read the notes at the beginning of the previous two sub-sections concerning catching any spilt Diesel fuel, checking seals, etc., and the need for cleanliness in general.*
*Note also that the bleeding procedure varies only according to the make of system fitted; details are the same for 1.6 and 1.8 litre engines. The valve fitted between the filter and the pump on later 1.8 litre engines is used at the factory **only**, to fill and bleed the system on production; it is of little value after that, but check regularly that it is tightly closed.*

Bosch system
48   As this system is intended to be 'self-bleeding', no hand-priming pump or separate bleed screws/nipples are fitted.

49   When any part of the system has been disturbed therefore, air must be purged from the system by cranking the engine on the starter motor until it starts; when it has started, keep the engine running for approximately 5 minutes to ensure that all air has been removed from the system. To minimise the strain on the battery and starter motor when trying to start the engine, crank it in 10-second bursts, pausing for 30 seconds each time, until the engine starts.

50   Depending on the work that has been carried out, it may be possible partially to prime the system so as to spare the battery by reducing as much as possible the amount of cranking time required to start the engine; refer to paragraphs 24 and 32 above.

51   If a hand-operated vacuum pump is available, this can be connected to the pump's fuel return union and used to suck fuel through the supply lines and filter; this will obviously save the battery a good deal of work. If a long length of clear plastic tubing is used to connect the vacuum pump to the injection pump union, it will be easier to see when fuel emerges free from air bubbles. Do not forget to energise the fuel shut-off solenoid by switching on the 'ignition', to position 'II' so that fuel can pass through the pump.

CAV RotoDiesel system
52   This system is fitted with a hand-priming pump, operated by depressing repeatedly the black button on the top of the filter assembly. If air has entered the system always purge it from the filter bleed nipple first, then (if required) from the pump union and the injector pipes. **Always** ensure that rags are placed underneath the bleeding point to catch the spilt fuel; as noted above, Diesel fuel must **not** be allowed to contaminate vulnerable components, especially the clutch, alternator and starter motor.

53   To bleed air from the system as far as the fuel filter, slacken the bleed nipple on the filter outlet union and operate the hand-priming pump until fuel emerges free from air bubbles. Tighten securely the bleed nipple, mop up any spilt fuel and operate the hand-priming pump until increased resistance is felt.

54   If air has reached the fuel injection pump, energise the fuel shut-off solenoid by switching on the 'ignition' (to position 'II'), slacken the pump's fuel return union and operate the hand-priming pump until fuel emerges free from air bubbles. Tighten securely the union banjo bolt, mop up any spilt fuel and operate the hand-priming pump until increased resistance is felt. Switch off the 'ignition'.

55   Finally, start the engine and keep it running for approximately 5 minutes to ensure that all air is removed from the system.

All models
56   If air has entered the injector pipes, slacken each union at the injectors and crank the engine until fuel emerges, then tighten securely all unions and mop up the spilt fuel. Start the engine and keep it running for a few minutes to ensure that all air has been expelled.

Fuel contamination
57   If, at any time, sudden fuel filter blockage, poor starting or otherwise unsatisfactory engine performance should be traced to the appearance of black sludge or slime within the fuel system, this may be due to corrosion caused by the presence of various micro-organisms in the fuel. These can live in the fuel tank if water is allowed to remain there in significant quantities, their waste products causing corrosion of steel and other metallic components of the fuel system.

58   If a vehicle's fuel system is thought to be contaminated in this way, immediately seek the advice of a Ford dealer or Diesel specialist; thorough and extensive treatment is required to cure the problem and to prevent it from occurring again.

59   **Note:** *If you are considering treating the vehicle on a DIY basis, read carefully the 'Safety First!' section at the front of this manual and remember that Diesel fuel is more irritating to the skin than petrol, also that it is harmful to the eyes. Besides the use of barrier cream to protect exposed skin, consider using lightweight disposable gloves and eye protection; also, change out of fuel-soaked clothing as soon as possible. Clean up spillages as quickly as possible to avoid accidents and protect tarmac surfaces by putting down plastic sheets or newspaper. Do not re-use contaminated fuel; dispose safely of all fuel that is thought to be contaminated, with all that used for flushing. Most local authorities now have oil disposal facilities or will be able to advise how you can dispose of waste fuel in a responsible fashion.*

60   First drain and remove the fuel tank, flush it thoroughly with clean Diesel fuel and use a torch to examine as much as possible of its interior; if the contamination is severe the tank must be steam-cleaned internally and then flushed again with clean Diesel fuel.

61   Disconnect the fuel feed and return hoses from the injection pump, remove the fuel filter (element) and flush through the system's feed and return lines with clean Diesel fuel.

62   Renew the fuel filter (element), refit the fuel tank and reconnect the fuel lines, then fill the tank with clean Diesel fuel and bleed the system as described above. Watch carefully for signs of the problem occurring again.

63   While it is unlikely that such contamination will be found beyond the fuel filter, if it is thought to have reached the injection pump, the pump may require cleaning; this is a task **only** for the local Bosch or CAV RotoDiesel (as appropriate) agent. **Do not** attempt to disturb any part of the pump (other than the few adjustments detailed in this manual) or to clean it yourself.

64   The most common cause of excessive quantities of water being in the fuel is condensation from the water vapour in the air. Diesel tanks (whether underground storage tanks or that in the vehicle) are more susceptible to this problem than petrol tanks because of petrol's higher vapour pressure; its formation in the vehicle's tank can be minimised by keeping the tank as full as possible at all times and by using the vehicle regularly.

65   Note that proprietary additives are available to inhibit the growth of micro-organisms in vehicle fuel tanks or storage tanks.

66   If you buy all your fuel from the same source and suspect that to be the source of the contamination, the owner or operator should be advised; otherwise the risk of taking on contaminated fuel can be minimised by using only reputable filling stations which have a good turnover.

PART B: 1.6 LITRE ENGINE

CAV RotoDiesel system – general
1   This system was fitted instead of the Bosch version used on earlier models. The components of the two systems are not interchangeable, the major differences being outlined below to assist in identification.

2   This section highlights differences between the Bosch and CAV systems. Any fuel system component which is not detailed here is fully covered in Chapter 3.

Injector
3   The differences between Bosch and CAV RotoDiesel type injectors are shown in Fig. 8.10

Injector fuel pipes
4   The pipes of both systems look similar but they have different bore sizes. To identify a pipe, insert a new twist drill of specified diameter into the pipe bore.

Bosch pipe internal diameter: 2.0 mm
CAV RotoDiesel pipe internal diameter: 2.5 mm

Fuel filter
5   The different fuel filters are shown in Fig. 8.12. The CAV filter incorporates a hand primer on the upper casing.

6   Refer to Part A of this Section for details of filter servicing.

Fuel injection pump
7   The CAV RotoDiesel fuel injection pump is identified by the two large octagonal plugs on the side of the pump body (Fig. 8.13).

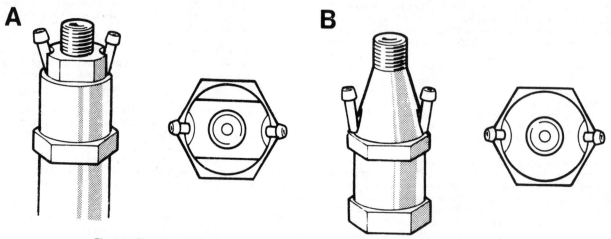

Fig. 8.10 Showing differences between CAV RotoDiesel (A) and Bosch (B) fuel injectors (Sec 5)

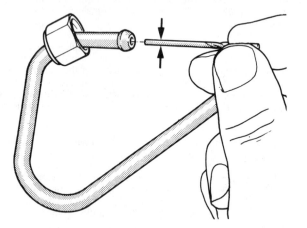

Fig. 8.11 Using a drill bit to check the bore diameter of a fuel injector pipe (Sec 5)

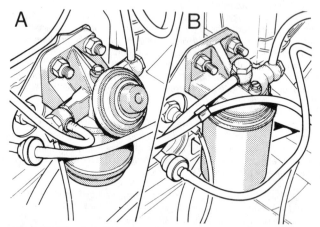

Fig. 8.12 Showing differences between CAV RotoDiesel (A) and Bosch (B) fuel filters (Sec 5)

Note: *Bosch filter shown in 'spin-on' cartridge type fitted to 1.6 litre engines*

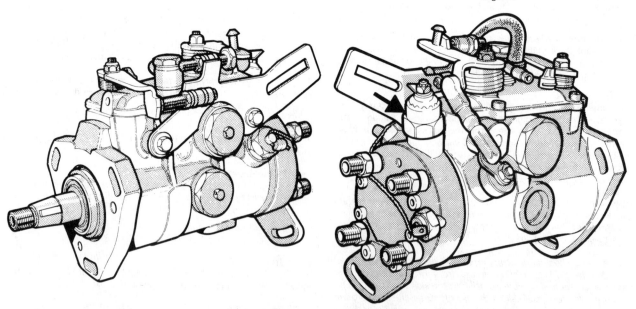

Fig. 8.13 CAV RotoDiesel fuel injection pump (Sec 5)

Note: *Fuel shut-off solenoid arrowed*

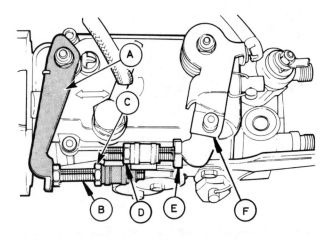

Fig. 8.14 Idle speed and anti-stall adjustment – CAV RotoDiesel fuel injection pump (Sec 5)

A   Idle speed/stop lever
B   Idle speed adjusting screw
C   Locknut
D   Locknut
E   Anti-stall adjustment screw
F   Throttle lever

CAV RotoDiesel injection pump – idle speed and anti-stall adjustment

Note: *A special (spacer) service tool (23-016) will be required for these operations; if not available, this can be replaced by the (careful) use of spacers. – see Fig. 8.16. See also Chapter 3, Section 5, paragraph 1.*

8   Have the engine at normal operating temperature and check the idle speed.

9   If the idle speed exceeds 910 rpm, slacken the idle speed screw locknut (C in Fig. 8.14) and adjust the idle speed screw until the engine idles at 880 ± 30 rpm. Tighten the locknut.

10   Insert a 2.0 mm thick spacer between the adjusting screw and the idle stop lever as shown in Fig. 8.15. The idle speed should fall by approximately 100 rpm. No change in speed indicates the need for anti-stall adjustment; see paragraphs 12 to 18.

11   If the engine idle speed when originally checked was less than 850 rpm, insert a 2.0 mm thick spacer between the adjusting screw and the idle stop lever. If the engine speed does not alter, carry out the anti-stall adjustment described in paragraphs 12 to 18. If the speed alters when the spacer is inserted, then the idle speed should be set to specification as described in paragraph 9.

Anti-stall adjustment

12   Make sure that the engine is at normal operating temperature. Fit the special service (spacer) tool (23-016) or suitable alternatives, plus a 1.0 mm thick feeler blade (to a total thickness of 4.0 mm) between the anti-stall screw and the throttle lever (Fig. 8.16).

13   Insert a 3.0 mm thick spacer between the head of the idle speed screw and the idle stop lever as shown in Fig. 8.15.

14   Release the locknut on the anti-stall adjustment screw, start the engine and turn the anti-stall adjustment screw until the engine is idling at between 900 ± 100 rpm.

15   Remove the 3.0 mm spacer and check that the idle stop lever returns to make contact with the head of the idle speed adjuster screw.

16   Remove the special service tool (23-016) or alternative(s).

17   Release the locknut on the idle speed adjusting screw and turn the screw until the engine idles at 880 ± 30 rpm.

18   Stalling and slow engine deceleration should not occur if the idle and anti-stall adjustments have been correctly carried out. However, if

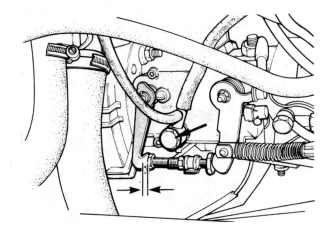

Fig. 8.15 Idle speed adjustment – CAV RotoDiesel fuel injection pump – insert spacer between idle speed/stop lever and idle speed adjusting screw at point indicated (Sec 5)

Note: *Fuel return banjo union arrowed*

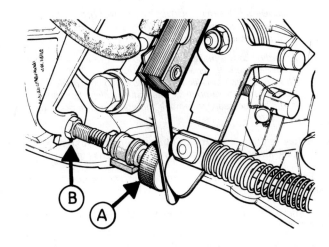

Fig. 8.16 Anti-stall adjustment – CAV RotoDiesel fuel injection pump (Sec 5)

A   Service tool (spacer) 23-016 and 1.0 mm feeler blade – total thickness 4.0 mm – inserted between throttle lever and anti-stall adjustment screw
B   Insert spacer (thickness according to engine – refer to text) between idle speed/stop lever and idle speed adjusting screw

stalling continues, turn the anti-stall adjusting screw by **no more than** one quarter of a turn clockwise. If slow deceleration is a problem, turn the anti-stall adjusting screw (again, by not more than) one quarter of a turn (maximum) anti-clockwise.

CAV RotoDiesel injection pump fuel shut-off solenoid – removal and refitting

19   Disconnect the battery and check that the ignition key is in the 'O' position, or removed from the ignition switch.

20   Disconnect the lead from the solenoid terminal then clean the exterior of the solenoid.

21   Using a deep socket or box spanner, unscrew and remove the solenoid from the injection pump.

22   Refitting is a reversal of removal, but use a new O-ring if the old one is in anything but perfect condition. Tighten the solenoid to its specified torque wrench setting.

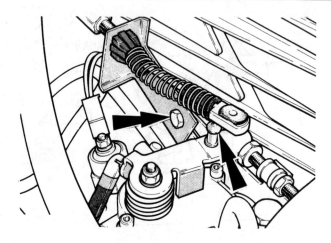

Fig. 8.17 Disconnecting throttle cable from CAV RotoDiesel fuel injection pump (Sec 5)

Unclip cable end from throttle lever pin (arrow), then unscrew bolt (arrow) to release cable bracket from pump

CAV RotoDiesel injection pump – removal and refitting

23   The procedures are basically as described in Chapter 3, Section 8. Note the following points during removal:

    (a)   According to the makers there is no need to drain the cooling system or move the coolant vent hose
    (b)   There is no separate electrical feed to a cold start device
    (c)   It is necessary to remove the alternator shield, when fitted
    (d)   It will be necessary to remove the pump rear support bracket completely

24   Before refitting, drain the fuel from the pump (if applicable) by removing the lower of the two plugs in the side of the pump.

25   Before refitting the rear support bracket, set the pump timing as described below.

26   Prime a new pump with clean fuel via the fuel return banjo connection.

27   Before attempting to start the engine, prime the system as described in Part A of this Section, then bleed any trapped air out when the engine is restarted.

CAV RotoDiesel injection pump – timing

28   For these operations a dial gauge, a TDC gauge pin and a dial gauge holding fixture will be required. The TDC pin is described in Chapter 1, Section 9; the dial gauge fixture (Ford tool No 21-100) can probably be dispensed with if the radiator and cooling fan are removed to improve access.

29   Injection pump timing will only be required if the pump has been removed and refitted, or the crankshaft pulley vibration damper bolt has been disturbed. Whenever the sprocket bolt is slackened, it is possible for the sprocket to move very slightly in relation to the crankshaft – hence the need to check the injection pump timing.

30   If timing is being carried out for a reason other than pump removal or refitting, take off the camshaft drivebelt cover and alternator shield and remove the TDC gauge pin hole blanking plug.

31   Turn the crankshaft in a clockwise direction until the injection pump sprocket and front cover timing marks are in alignment.

32   Remove the lower plug from the side of the pump body. Be prepared to catch any released fuel and prevent it from entering the alternator.

33   Fit the TDC gauge pin into its hole, then fit the dial gauge and its holding fixture to the fuel injection pump.

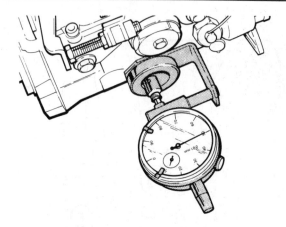

Fig. 8.18 Checking CAV RotoDiesel fuel injection pump (static) timing (Sec 5)

34   Turn the crankshaft clockwise until the dial gauge stops moving and then zero the gauge.

35   Continue turning the crankshaft until the crankshaft locks against the TDC pin. The dial gauge should register 1.40 ± 0.07 mm (0.055 ± 0.003 in).

36   If the gauge reading is outside the specified range, release the pump mounting nuts and bolts and rotate the pump until the correct reading is indicated on the gauge.

37   Now turn the crankshaft anti-clockwise until the pump sprocket and front cover marks are in alignment. Tighten the pump nuts and bolts.

38   Repeat the operations described in paragraphs 34 and 35 to check the setting.

39   Remove the dial gauge, holding fixture and TDC pin. Refit the plug.

40   Fit the alternator plastic fuel deflector and camshaft drivebelt cover where applicable.

Glow plug relay (October 1986 on)

41   As from October 1986, a modified controller relay has been fitted to increase glow duration at cold starting.

42   Earlier models may be fitted with the later type relay if cold starting is a problem, this assumes that injection pump timing and all other factors (starter motor, fuel supply, etc.) are in order.

Draining water from fuel filter

43   Refer to Part A of this Section.

Fuel filter (element) renewal

44   Refer to Part A of this Section.

Fuel filter assembly – removal and refitting

45   Refer to Part A of this Section.

Bleeding air from fuel system

46   Refer to Part A of this Section.

PART C: 1.8 LITRE ENGINE

Air cleaner element – renewal

1   Open and support the bonnet. On Fiesta models, disconnect the air intake duct from the manifold (photo).

2   Release the air cleaner cover retaining clips and where applicable, undo the cover retaining screw. Lift the cover from the main body to allow access to the air filter element (photo).

3   Take out the air cleaner element and discard it (photos).

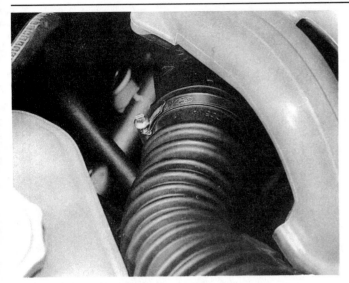

5C.1 Air intake hose connection to the inlet manifold (Fiesta)

5C.2 Release the air cleaner cover retaining clips (Fiesta)

5C.3A Air cleaner element removal (Fiesta)

5C.3B Air cleaner element removal (Escort/Orion)

5C.7A Air cleaner casing nut (arrowed) (Fiesta)

5C.7B Air cleaner casing nut (arrowed) (Fiesta)

5C.8A Releasing the air cleaner casing from a fixing stud (Fiesta)

5C.8B Releasing the air cleaner casing from fixing studs (arrowed) (Escort)

4   Wipe out the new casing and fit the new element into position.

5   Refit the cover and connect the air duct.

Air cleaner casing – removal and refitting

6   The location of the air cleaner unit is dependent on model, but will either be on the right or left-hand side of the engine compartment. The removal procedures for both are much the same. Raise and support the bonnet, loosen the retaining clip(s) and detach the air intake duct and the air outlet duct (to the manifold) from the air cleaner casing.

7   Unscrew the air cleaner securing nuts (photos).

8   Disengage the casing from the fixing studs and withdraw it from the vehicle (photos).

9   Refit in the reverse order of removal.

Idle speed – adjustment

Checking   all systems
Note: *Refer first to Chapter 3, Section 5, paragraphs 1 to 3. The pump's adjustments should only be disturbed if the idle speed is unreliable, or significantly above or below the specified range.*

Adjustment   Bosch system
10   If the idle speed recorded was incorrect, reset to 850 rpm using the idle speed adjusting screw ('B' Fig. 8.19). Once the idle speed is correct, insert a spacer 0.5 mm thick between the throttle lever and the residual capacity adjusting screw ('A', Fig. 8.19); the idle speed should not alter. If the speed does alter, carry out the basic idle setting procedure described in paragraphs 11 and 12 below. If the speed does **not** alter remove the spacer and replace it with one 1.0 mm thick, whereupon the speed should increase very slightly, by about 10 or 20 rpm. If the speed does increase, check the fast idle speed as described in paragraph 13 below; if it does **not** increase, carry out the basic idle setting procedure described in paragraphs 11 and 12 below.

11   Using the idle speed adjusting screw ('B', Fig. 8.19), set the idle speed to 850 rpm, release the fast idle waxstat device cable end stop and reposition it at the end of the cable so that it can have no effect. Insert a spacer 0.5 mm thick between the throttle lever and the residual capacity adjusting screw ('A', Fig. 8.19), then slacken its locknut and turn the screw anti-clockwise (away from the throttle lever) one full turn. Readjust the idle speed to 850 rpm using the idle speed adjusting screw; repeat the procedure until turning the residual capacity adjusting screw has no effect on the idle speed (to ensure that the engine is not idling on the residual capacity adjusting screw).

12   Remove the 0.5 mm spacer and replace it with one 1.0 mm thick, then adjust the residual capacity adjusting screw to give an engine

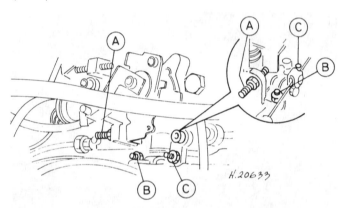

Fig. 8.19 Adjustment screws – Bosch fuel injection pump – 1.8 litre engine (Sec 5)

H.20633

A   Residual capacity (anti-stall) adjusting screw

B   Idle speed adjusting screw
C   Fast idle adjuster screw

speed of 860 to 870 rpm and tighten the screw's locknut. Remove the 1.0 mm spacer and note the idle speed, then replace the spacer with the 0.5 mm thick one; the idle speed should not change. If the idle speed **does** change, repeat the full procedure (paragraphs 11 and 12). When the basic idle setting is correct, reset the fast idle waxstat device cable and stop to give a 1.0 mm gap between the idle lever and the fast idle adjuster screw ('C', Fig. 8.19) when the engine is hot (waxstat in hot mode), then proceed to check the fast idle speed as described in paragraph 13 below.

13   To check the fast idle, ensure that the engine is thoroughly hot, then ensure that there is a gap of 1.0 mm between the idle lever and the fast idle adjuster screw ('C', Fig. 8.19); adjust if necessary by repositioning the stop on the end of the fast idle waxstat device cable. With the engine idling, move the idle lever against the fast idle adjuster screw and check that speed rises to 1180 to 1200 rpm; adjust if necessary by turning the fast idle adjuster screw.

Adjustment – CAV RotoDiesel system
Note: *A special tool, the spacer 23-016, will be required for this task. If not available, the tool can be replaced by the (careful) use of spacer(s) – see Fig. 8.16.*

14   Fit the special tool or alternative(s) and a 1.0 mm thick feeler blade (to a total thickness of 4.0 mm) between the anti-stall screw and the throttle lever, as shown in Fig. 8.16.

5C.24A Lower belt cover screw

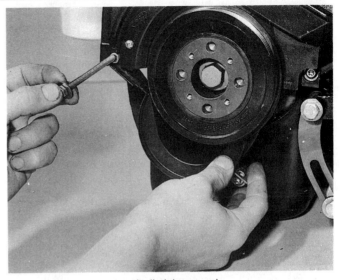

5C.24B Belt lower cover swivelled downwards

5C.26A Fuel feed line banjo bolt

5C.26B Fuel return union at pump

15   Using a 20.0 mm thick spacer, hold the idle speed lever (A) away from the adjusting screw, as shown in Figs. 14, 15 and 16.

16   Slacken the locknut (D), and turn the anti-stall adjustment screw (E) to give an engine idle speed of 900 ± 100 rpm.

17   Remove the 20.0 mm thick spacer. The idle speed stop lever must return and contact the adjuster screw (B).

18   Remove the special tool and the feeler gauge. Slacken the idle speed adjuster screw locknut and turn the screw to obtain an idle speed of between 840 and 870 rpm.

19   Should any problems of slow deceleration or stalling be evident, recheck the preceding adjustment. If the faults persist, then stalling may be corrected by turning the throttle lever anti-stall screw (by a **maximum of** a quarter of a turn) clockwise. To eliminate slow deceleration, turn the throttle lever anti-stall screw (again, by **no more than** a quarter turn) anti-clockwise.

Bosch injection pump – removal and refitting
20   Open the bonnet and disconnect the battery.

21   Slowly release the coolant expansion tank cap, and then disconnect the air bleed tube from the tank.

22   Release the fixing clips and bolt from the timing belt upper cover.

23   Raise the front of the car, remove the under-wing splash shield from the right-hand side.

24   Unscrew the lower timing belt cover fixing bolt, release the cover pivot bolt, and allow the cover to swing downwards (photos).

25   Lower the car, and remove the belt upper cover.

26   Disconnect the fuel feed and return hoses from the injection pump. Banjo type unions are used. Plug, or cap, the openings to prevent the entry of dirt. Disconnect the injector high pressure pipes (photos).

27   Disconnect the electrical connections from the fuel shut-off solenoid device and (where fitted) the upspeed control system cables waxstat fast idle and the cold start device.

28   Carefully identify the two vacuum hoses, and then disconnect them from the vacuum regulator valve (EGR system only).

29   Disconnect the throttle cable from the operating arm on the injection pump, and then remove the cable bracket.

30   Remove the bolts from the injection pump rear support bracket,

5C.41 Tightening a fuel injection pump fixing screw

and then slacken the bolts which hold the bracket to the cylinder block.

31   Engage 4th gear, raise the right-hand front roadwheel and turn it, while at the same time observing the injection pump timing pin slot. When the slot is at the 11 o'clock position, stop turning the roadwheel.

32   Remove the alternator protective cover.

33   Remove the crankshaft TDC gauge pin plug from the cylinder block, and screw in the pin (refer to Chapter 1, Section 9).

34   Using the roadwheel, slowly turn the crankshaft in its normal direction of rotation, until the crankshaft web contacts the TDC pin.

35   Insert the camshaft timing peg (refer to Section 3, Part B of this Supplement, paragraph 10).

36   Slacken the injection pump timing belt tensioner, and secure the tensioner away from the belt.

37   Unscrew and remove the injection pump belt sprocket bolts, and slide off the sprocket and belt.

38   Support the weight of the pump, remove the fixing screws, and remove it from the engine.

39   Before fitting a new pump, remove the blanking plugs and prime it with clean fuel, poured in through the return port.

40   Align the peg cut-outs of the pump body and drive flange.

41   Bolt the pump into position, making sure that the mounting surfaces are clean (photo).

42   Bolt the pump rear support bracket into position.

43   Locate the belt sprocket on the pump flange, but leave the fixing bolts slack (photos).

44   Insert the timing peg so that is passes through the sprocket, flange and pump body.

45   Centralise the sprocket bolts in the centres of their elongated slots by rotating the sprocket. Nip up the bolts.

46   Slide the toothed belt onto the pump sprocket, making sure that the slack side of the belt is on the tensioner side.

47   Slacken the pump sprocket bolts.

48   Release the tensioner, and allow it to snap against the belt to take up the slack.

49   Tighten the tensioner bolt, but check that they are not at the ends of their slots. If they are, adjust the belt tension to correct the situation.

50   Tighten the sprocket bolts to the specified torque, and remove the timing peg.

51   Remove the TDC pin from the crankcase.

52   Turn the crankshaft through two complete revolutions, until the injection pump sprocket peg slot is at the 11 o'clock position.

53   Refit the TDC pin, and then continue turning the crankshaft slowly until the crankshaft web contacts the TDC pin.

54   Now check that the timing peg will enter the pump sprocket and pass into the pump body. If the cut-outs are not in alignment, slacken the sprocket bolts and turn the pump flange until they are.

55   Tighten the sprocket bolts, and remove the peg.

56   Remake the electrical and hose connections and connect the fast idle and upspeed cables.

57   Reconnect the injector high-pressure pipes, but do not fully tighten

5C.43A Fitting fuel injection pump sprocket

5C.43B Inserting a fuel injection pump sprocket bolt

the connections at the injectors yet. Prime the system (as far as possible) as described in part A of this Section.

58   Remove the TDC pin, and fit the plug to the crankcase.

59   Fit the alternator cover.

60   Reconnect the throttle cable, making sure that the idle and full-throttle positions can be obtained.

61   Refit the belt covers and the splash shield.

62   Reconnect the expansion tank hose, and top up the coolant.

63   Reconnect the battery, and disengage 4th gear.

64   Operate the starter until fuel is seen to be ejected from the untightened injector pipes, then tighten the pipes.

65   Start the engine, and bring it to operating temperature. Check and adjust the idle speed as described earlier in this Supplement, then (where appropriate) check the adjustment of the EGR system vacuum regulator valve as described later in this Supplement.

CAV RotoDiesel injection pump – removal and refitting

66   Carry out the operations described in paragraphs 20 to 27, 29 and 32 for the Bosch type pump, but note that only the electrical wiring for the fuel shut-off solenoid need be disconnected.

67   Remove the bolts from the injection pump rear support bracket, and then slacken the bolts which hold the bracket to the cylinder block.

68   Engage 4th gear, raise the right-hand front roadwheel and turn it, while at the same time observing the injection pump sprocket timing pin slot. Stop turning when it is at 12 o'clock. The camshaft sprocket timing pin slot will be at 8 o'clock.

69   Now turn the crankshaft anti-clockwise until the pump timing slot is at the 11 o'clock position.

70   Remove the plug and screw in the crankcase TDC pin. Rotate the crankshaft slowly until the crankshaft web contacts the TDC pin.

71   Insert the timing pegs into the camshaft and the injection pump sprockets.

72   Slacken the pump drivebelt tensioner bolt, relieve the tension on the belt, and lock the tensioner away from the belt.

73   Unscrew and remove the bolts from the injection pump belt sprocket. Withdraw the sprocket and belt from the pump.

74   Unscrew the T40 Torx bolts, and remove the fuel injection pump.

75   Before fitting a new pump, remove the blanking plugs and prime it by pouring in clean diesel fuel.

76   Align the timing peg holes in the pump body and the drive flange.

77   Insert a timing peg through the flange hole into the body hole. If it is tight, it is permissible to use a 5.5 mm drill bit.

78   Fit the pump and tighten the Torx bolts to the specified torque.

79   Locate the pump sprocket and screw in the fixing bolts finger-tight. Make sure that the timing peg passes through all three holes (sprocket, flange and pump body).

80   Centralise the sprocket bolts in the middle of their elongated slots.

81   Engage the drivebelt with the pump sprocket, so that the slack side is towards the tensioner.

82   Release the tensioner so that it snaps against the belt and takes up any slackness.

83   Tighten the tensioner bolt.

84   Tighten the pump sprocket bolts to the specified torque.

85   Remove both timing pegs and the TDC pin.

86   Using the roadwheel, turn the crankshaft through two complete revolutions until the injection pump sprocket timing peg hole is at 12 o'clock, and the one in the camshaft sprocket is at 8 o'clock.

87   Now turn the crankshaft anti-clockwise until the pump timing hole is at the 11 o'clock position.

88   Refit the crankcase TDC pin, and then turn the crankshaft slowly, until the crankshaft web contacts the pin.

89   Refit the pump and camshaft sprocket pegs. If necessary, slacken the pump sprocket bolts and adjust the mounting flange to enable the peg to be inserted fully into the pump body. Should this adjustment of the flange position have to be carried out, then repeat the operations described in paragraphs 84 to 89.

90   Remove the timing pegs and TDC pin. Screw in the crankcase plug.

91   Refit the injection pump bracket.

92   Reconnect the injector high-pressure pipes (do not tighten yet), and also the fuel hoses, using new copper sealing washers.

93   Reconnect the throttle cable and (if fitted) the upspeed cable and the fuel shut-off solenoid wiring.

94   Refit the timing belt covers and splash shield.

95   Reconnect the battery. Disengage 4th gear.

96   Using the hand primer on the fuel filter, prime the system as described in Part A of this Section.

97   Reconnect the expansion tank hose, and top up the coolant.

98   Crank the engine by operating the starter motor until fuel is seen to be ejected from the untightened injector pipes, then tighten the pipes.

99   Start the engine and bring it to operating temperature. Check and adjust the idle speed as described earlier.

Fuel injectors – removal and refitting
100   Refer to Chapter 3, Section 10.

Draining water from fuel filter
101   Refer to Part A of this Section.

Fuel filter (element) renewal
102   Refer to Part A of this Section.

Fuel filter assembly – removal and refitting
103   Refer to Part A of this Section.

Bleeding air from fuel system
104   Refer to Part A of this Section.

Fuel shut-off solenoid – removal and refitting
105   Refer to Chapter 3, Section 11, or to Part B of this Section, according to the system fitted.

Glow plug relay and fuse – removal and refitting
106   Refer to Chapter 3, Section 14, but note that the glow plug relay location on later models is either located under the jack stowage position or on models fitted with an engine upspeed system, attached to a bracket on the left-hand inner wing panel in the engine compartment. The glow plug circuit fuse is in the additional fuse block located in front of the battery (photos).

5C.106A Fuel system glow plug relay location (arrowed) (later Fiesta)

5C.106B Fuel system glow plug relay location (arrowed) (later Escort fitted with engine upspeed system)

5C.106C Glow plug fuse location (later models)

Exhaust Gas Recirculation (EGR) system

General description
107   This system is fitted to some models to ensure that the vehicle complies with the appropriate emission control legislation. Only vehicles with the Bosch fuel injection system are so equipped.

108   By recirculating a controlled amount of exhaust gases back through the inlet manifold to be burned in the combustion chamber, combustion chamber temperatures are reduced, also the amount of surplus oxygen in the intake air, thus minimising the generation of oxides of nitrogen (NO_x).

109   The system consists of the following components:

(a)   *The Thermal-Operated Vacuum Switch – fitted to the thermostat housing, this is closed until the coolant temperature reaches 60°C, thus preventing the system from operating while the engine is warming up*

(b)   *The Vacuum Regulator Valve– mounted on the top of the fuel injection pump, this regulates according to throttle opening the amount of vacuum applied to the EGR valve*

(c)   *The Vacuum Delay Valve – fitted in the vacuum line to control the rate at which vacuum is applied to the EGR valve*

(d)   *The Exhaust Gas Recirculation (EGR) Valve– bolted to the inlet manifold and connected by a supply pipe to the exhaust manifold, this opens under the control of the vacuum switch,*

regulator and delay valves, using the depression created by the vacuum pump. This allows a proportion of the exhaust gases to flow up into the inlet manifold and into the combustion chamber

EGR system - checking
110   The system requires no maintenance except for the regular check of all hoses, pipes, etc.

111   Whenever the fuel injection pump is removed the vacuum regulator valve setting must be checked and, if adjusted necessary, as described below.

112   To check the system's operation, warm the engine up to normal operating temperature and allow it to idle. Disconnect and reconnect several times the vacuum pipe from the top of the EGR valve; the valve should be heard to operate each time.

113   If the EGR valve does not operate and vacuum can be felt at the pipe end, first check the setting of the vacuum regulator valve as described below.

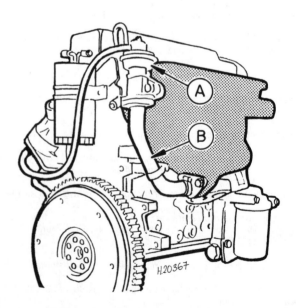

Fig. 8.20 Location of Exhaust Gas Recirculation system EGR valve (A) and supply pipe (B) (Sec 5)

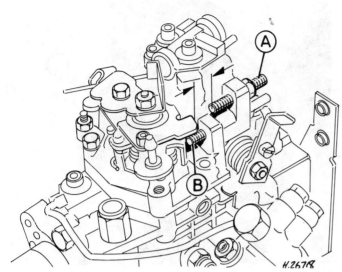

Fig. 8.21 EGR system vacuum regulator valve adjustment (Sec 5)

A Third stop screw – insert   B Maximum speed adjusting screw
   spacers in location shown

114   If the vacuum regulator valve is functioning correctly, the fault must be in the EGR valve, which must then be renewed. If the valve is to be renewed, it is always worth first trying the effect of cleaning any carbon build-up from its passages to check whether this is the reason for the failure. If the valve's diaphragm has failed, on the other hand, there is no alternative to the renewal of the complete valve unit.

115   If no vacuum can be felt, check back through the system until the leak or blockage is found and rectified.

Thermal-operated vacuum switch – removal and refitting
116   This unit is screwed into the vacuum pump side of the thermostat housing and can be identified by the two vacuum pipes connected to it.

117   Drain the cooling system, either completely or down as far as the thermostat (Chapter 2).

118   Disconnect the vacuum pipes and unscrew the switch.

119   On fitting the new switch, either ensure that a new sealing washer is used or apply a smear of suitable sealant to its threads, as applicable. Tighten the switch securely.

120   Refill the cooling system as described in Chapter 2.

Vacuum regulator valve – adjustment
121   Checking and adjustment of the vacuum regulator valve is only possible if a hand-operated vacuum pump/gauge is available.

122   Connect the pump/gauge to the inlet port (the one nearest the engine) of the regulator valve.

123   Hold the throttle in the fully open position, and operate the hand pump continuously. Note the vacuum reading on the gauge, which should be around 0.6 bar (8.7 lbf/in^2).

124   Fit an 11.8 mm (0.46 in) thick spacer between the throttle lever and third stop screw (A) – Fig. 8.21.

125   Push the throttle lever against the spacer and then operate the vacuum pump. The recorded vacuum pressure should be as previously noted.

126   Change the spacer for one 12.1 mm (0.48 in) thick. This spacer should hold the regulator valve open, so that no vacuum reading can be obtained when the vacuum pump is operated.

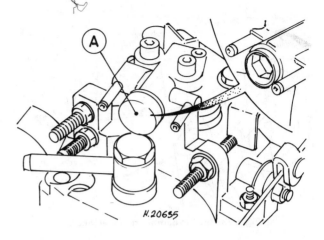

Fig. 8.22 EGR system vacuum regulator valve adjustment screw under tamperproof cap 'A' (Sec 5)

127   If the regulator valve does not behave as indicated, remove the tamperproof cover (A) – Fig. 8.22.

128   Hold the throttle lever hard against the maximum speed adjusting screw – Fig. 8.21.

129   Using the vacuum pump, the vacuum pressure should be between 0.6 and 0.7 bar (8.7 and 10.2 lbf/in^2).

130   Fit a 12.0 mm (0.47 in) thick spacer between the throttle lever and the third stop screw. Retain the throttle in this position, and operate the vacuum pump.

131   Turn the regulator adjuster screw to set the vacuum pressure to 0.35 bar (5.1 lbf/in^2).

132   Now recheck the vacuum readings using the 11.8 mm and 12.1 mm spacers as previously described.

133   Fit a new tamperproof cap, remove the pump and refit the original hose connections.

Vacuum regulator valve – removal and refitting
134   Note that the valve's inlet pipe (from the vacuum pump) is connected to the union nearest the engine. The valve's outlet union (to the EGR valve) is the union nearest the radiator; on later models this pipe will be marked with a yellow tracer.

135   If no identifying mark can be found, use paint or similar to make your own before disconnecting either pipe.

136   Unbolt and remove the regulator valve.

137   Refitting is a reversal of removal, but if a new valve is being fitted, it must be adjusted as described above.

Vacuum delay valve – removal and refitting
138   At the time of writing, no information was available concerning the precise location of this unit, or whether it is available separately from the vacuum pipes. See your local Ford dealer for details.

139   Note that valves of this type are usually clearly marked to show which way round they are to be fitted; note any such markings, or other identifying details of this unit, before disturbing it. Ensure that the valve is fitted the correct way round, as noted on removal, and that the vacuum pipes are securely fastened to each end.

Exhaust gas recirculation (EGR) valve – removal and refitting
140   Disconnect the battery earth (negative) terminal.

141   Disconnect the vacuum pipe from the top of the valve.

142   Unscrew the two bolts securing the supply pipe to the valve's underside; withdraw and discard the gasket.

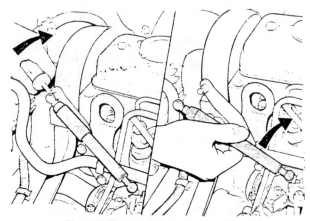

Fig. 8.23 Throttle damper removal (Sec 5)

143 Unbolt the EGR valve from the inlet manifold and withdraw it; again, withdraw and discard the gasket.

144 If the supply pipe is ever disturbed, always renew the gaskets at its upper and lower ends. Tighten the bolts to the torque wrench setting specified and ensure that the securing clamps are securely fastened on reassembly.

145 On refitting, always renew the gaskets and tighten the bolts to their specified torque wrench settings. Connect the vacuum pipe to the valve, start the engine and check that the system is operating correctly, as described above.

Throttle damper – Escort/Orion models (Bosch injection system)

146 A revised throttle damper unit can be fitted to these models, where the vehicle is regularly used under low speed and light throttle application, to help prevent vehicle shake and power 'on/off' effect at low engine speeds.

147 The damper is detached by prising free the top balljoint and moving the damper up so that the lower joint disconnects from the throttle end (Fig. 8.23). When refitting the damper, press it into position on the top and bottom end joints but ensure that the large diameter end joint is fitted to the top.

Idle upspeed control system (Escort/Orion) – general

148 An idle upspeed device may be fitted to these models to automatically raise the engine speed and prevent stalling when reverse gear is selected. The unit is attached to a bracket on the left-hand inner wing panel in the engine compartment. The glow plug relay moved

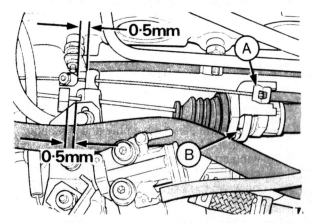

Fig. 8.24 Idle upspeed control system cable adjustment – Bosch injection system shown (Sec 5)

A Upspeed cable clip– on fast idle waxstat device cable bracket

B Slot in bracket for cable removal/refitting

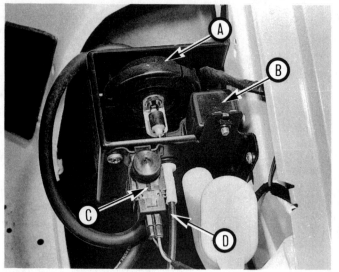

5C.148 Idle upspeed control system components   Escort with CAV RotoDiesel fuel injection system

A Vacuum diaphragm
B Glow plug relay
C Reverse light switch circuit connector
D Upspeed operating cable

from its original position and is now secured to the upspeed unit bracket (photo).

149 The control unit operates in conjunction with the reversing light circuit and the brake vacuum system. It differs according to the fuel injection type (CAV RotoDiesel or Bosch).

150 To check the idle upspeed system for satisfactory operation, first check that the system wiring and vacuum hoses are in good condition and securely connected.

151 Check that the operating cable adjustment is as follows according to system (photos).
   CAV RotoDiesel system: Ensure that the idle operating cable is fully released and there is no vacuum in the servo, then check that there is a clearance of 0.5 to 1.0 mm between the idle upspeed operating cable clamp and the idle lever. If necessary, loosen off the adjuster clamp screw and move the clamp to set the clearance as specified, then retighten the screw.
   Bosch system: Fully extend the waxstat operating cable by switching on the 'ignition' and leaving it in position 'II' for a period of three minutes, then check that the clearance between the cable clamp and the idle lever is 0.5 mm (Figs. 8.24 and 8.25).
If adjustment is required on either system, loosen off the cable clamp screw and set the clamp as required.

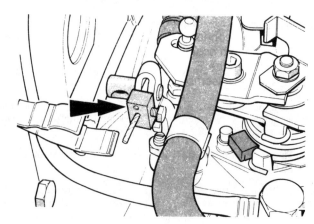

Fig. 8.25 Idle upspeed control system – Bosch injection system showing steel end stop (arrowed) for fast idle waxstat device cable (Sec 5)

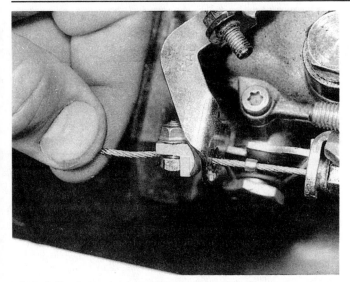

5C.151A Check that the upspeed operating cable is free

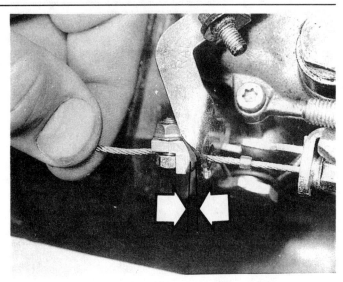

5C.151B Adjust to allow the required clearance between the clamp and lever

152   Start the engine and allow it to idle for a period of 5 minutes, then engage reverse gear. The idle speed should rise and then level off within three seconds of reverse gear being engaged. Now disengage reverse gear and check that the idle speed drops and levels off within three seconds of disengagement.

Inlet manifold – removal and refitting
153   Loosen off the clip securing the air intake duct to the filter unit section. Detach the duct from its connection to the filter.

154   Undo the retaining bolts, lift the plastic upper section clear of the inlet manifold and collect the four O-ring seals from the grooves in the mating face (photo). If required, the connector can be detached from the upper section by unscrewing the four retaining bolts.

155   Detach the crankcase breather hose and unbolt, (where applicable), the EGR valve from the manifold end face, then undo the retaining bolts and withdraw the manifold from the cylinder head. Collect the gasket.

156   Refitting is a reversal of the removal procedure. Ensure that the mating faces are clean. Ensure that a new gasket is fitted between the manifold and the cylinder head and tighten the retaining bolts to the specified torque wrench setting (photo). Securely locate new ring seals into the grooves in the plastic upper section prior to fitting it into position.

Exhaust manifold – removal and refitting
157   Refer to Chapter 3, Section 17 and Fig. 3.18 (photo). While the fasteners and tightening sequence remain essentially as described for the 1.6 litre engine, note that the 1.8 litre engine does not have a gasket fitted on production and that there is a plastic sleeve fitted around the stud (location 7, Fig. 3.18).

158   When the manifold is first removed, a gasket must be obtained and fitted on reassembly; it must then be renewed as a matter of course whenever the manifold is disturbed after that.

159   The plastic sleeve is fitted to ensure the correct clearance exists to allow for expansion when the manifold gets hot; check it whenever the manifold is disturbed and renew it if there is any doubt about its condition.

160   On models so equipped, note that the EGR valve must be unbolted from the manifolds before they can be removed.

Catalytic converters – general information and precautions
161   The exhaust gases of any internal combustion engine (however efficient or well-tuned) which burns hydrocarbon-based fuel consist largely (approximately 99%) of nitrogen (N_2), carbon dioxide (CO_2),

oxygen (O_2) and other inert gases and water vapour (H_2O). The remaining 1% is made up of the noxious materials which are currently seen (CO_2) apart as the major polluters of the environment; carbon monoxide (CO), unburned hydrocarbons (HC), oxides of nitrogen (NO_x) and some solid matter, including a small lead content.

162   Left to themselves, most of these pollutants are thought

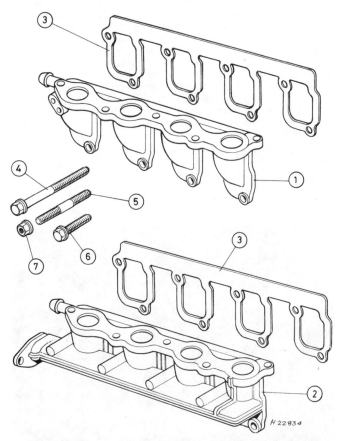

Fig. 8.26 Inlet manifold and fasteners– 1.8 litre engine (Sec 5)

1	Inlet manifold – Fiesta	4	Bolt– 4 off
2	Inlet manifold – Escort/Orion	5	Stud – 2 off
3	Gasket	6	(Hexagon-headed) screw 2 off
		7	Nut – 2 off

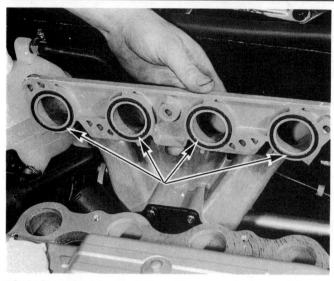

5C.154 Removing inlet manifold plastic upper section - note O-ring seals (arrowed)

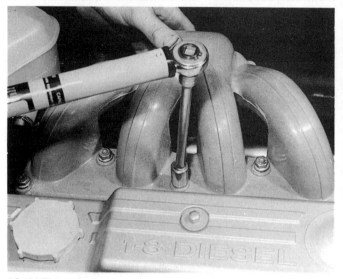

5C.156 Tightening bolts securing inlet manifold plastic upper section

eventually to break down naturally (CO and NO_x, for example, break down in the upper atmosphere to release CO_2) having first caused ground-level environmental problems, but the massive increase world-wide in the use of motor vehicles and the current popular concern for the environment has caused the introduction in most countries of legislation, in varying stages of severity, to combat the problem.

163   The device most commonly used to clean up vehicle exhausts is the catalytic converter. It is fitted into the vehicle's exhaust system and consists of an element (or 'subtrate') of ceramic honeycomb coated with a combination of precious metals in such a way as to produce a vast surface area over which the exhaust gases must flow; the whole being mounted in a stainless-steel box. The simple 'oxidation' (or 'two-way') catalytic converter fitted to Diesel engines uses platinum and palladium as catalysts to speed up the reaction between the pollutants and the oxygen in the vehicle's exhaust gases, CO and HC being oxidised to form H_2O and CO_2. **Note:** *The catalytic converter is not a filter in the physical sense; its function is to promote a chemical reaction, but it is not itself affected by that reaction.*

164   The catalytic converter is a reliable and simple device which needs no maintenance in itself, but there are some facts of which an owner should be aware if the converter is to function properly for its full service life.

   (a)   *There is no need to worry about using leaded/unleaded fuel in a*

vehicle equipped with a catalytic converter and a Diesel engine no Diesel fuel has added lead.

   (b)   *Always keep the fuel system well-maintained in accordance with the manufacturer's schedule (Routine maintenance) particularly, ensure that the air cleaner filter element and the fuel filter are renewed at the correct interval – if the intake air/fuel mixture is allowed to become too rich due to neglect, the unburned surplus will enter and burn in the catalytic converter, overheating the element and eventually destroying the converter.*

   (c)   *If the engine develops a misfire, do not drive the vehicle at all (or at least as little as possible) until the fault is cured - the misfire will allow unburned fuel to enter the converter, which will result in its overheating, as noted above. For the same reason, do not persist if the engine ever refuses to start (either trace the problem and cure it yourself or have the vehicle checked immediately by a qualified mechanic) and never allow the vehicle to run out of fuel.*

   (d)   *DO NOT push-or tow-start the vehicle   this will soak the catalytic converter in unburned fuel, causing it to overheat when the engine does start – see (b) above.*

   (e)   *Try to avoid repeated successive cold starts with short journeys if the converter is never allowed to reach its proper working temperature it will gather unburned fuel, allowing some to pass into the atmosphere and the rest to soak the element in unburned fuel, causing it to overheat when the engine does start see (B) above.*

   (f)   *DO NOT use fuel or engine oil additives – these may contain substances harmful to the catalytic converter.*

   (g)   *NEVER use silicon-based sealants on any part of the air intake/inlet manifold, or any kind of sealant on exhaust system joints forward of the catalytic converter; if pieces of sealant (however small) should break off, they will be carried into the converter and cause it to overheat locally.*

   (h)   *DO NOT continue to use the vehicle if the engine burns oil to the extent of leaving a visible trail of blue smoke -- the unburned carbon deposits will clog the converter passages and reduce its efficiency; in severe cases the element will overheat.*

   (i)   *Remember that the catalytic converter operates at very high temperatures – hence the heat shields on the vehicle's underbody – and the casing will become hot enough to ignite combustible materials which brush against it. DO NOT, therefore, park the vehicle in dry undergrowth, over long grass or piles of dead leaves.*

   (j)   *Remember that the catalytic converter is FRAGILE do not strike it with tools during servicing work, take great care when working on the exhaust system, ensure that the converter is well clear of any jacks or other lifting gear used to raise the vehicle and do not drive the vehicle over rough ground, road humps, etc., in such a way as to 'ground' the exhaust system.*

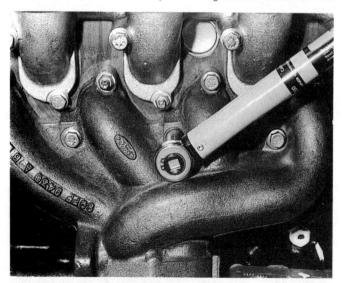

5C.157 Tightening bolts securing exhaust manifold

5C.166 Flexible balljoint on exhaust downpipe permits removal of catalytic converter

(k)   The catalytic converter, used on a well-maintained and well-driven vehicle, should last for between 50 000 and 100 000 miles from this point on, careful checks should be made at all specified service intervals to ensure that the converter is still operating efficiently if the converter is no longer effective it must be renewed.

Catalytic converter - removal and refitting

165   The exhaust system of a catalytic converter-equipped vehicle is similar in layout to that outlined in Chapter 3 except that the catalytic converter is located to the rear of the downpipe's lower end.

166   To remove the catalytic converter, undo the nuts securing its front and rear ends. Prise away the exhaust system centre section until the converter and downpipe can be swung down on the downpipe's balljoints (photo); collect the gasket (where fitted). Carefully separate the converter from the downpipe; see paragraph 158, note (j) above.

167   On refitting, clean carefully the mating surfaces, fit a new gasket (where applicable as noted above, never use exhaust sealants upstream of the converter) and offer up the converter. On early models, ensure that the arrow on the converter's body points to the rear, in line with the exhaust gas flow; on later models, the converter will fit correctly only one way, as the front and rear flanges are either of different sizes or have offset studs to prevent incorrect installation (this fact must be remembered when renewing separately any of the affected parts of the system).

168   Tighten the nuts to their specified torque wrench settings.

169   If renewing the rubber mountings, ensure that the mounting nearest the converter is of the correct type: due to the converter's high operating temperatures, this mounting must be of high-temperature resistant material.

170   When working on any other part of the system, note that the underbody of the vehicle is protected by heat shields from the very high operating temperatures of a catalytic converter; these may have to be unbolted before the exhaust system itself can be removed from the vehicle.

6   Clutch, transmission and driveshafts

Clutch release lever

1   On late 1.6 litre engines and all 1.8 litre units, the clutch release lever is separate from the release fork, being located by splines on the fork's upper end and secured by a pinch-bolt (photo).

6.1 Clutch release arm located on release fork upper end by splines (arrowed)

2   To remove the lever, disconnect the cable, then unscrew the nut and remove completely the pinch-bolt; withdraw the lever off the fork splines.

3   Refitting is the reverse of the removal procedure; the lever can be fitted only the correct way as it has a (wider) master spline which will engage only in the fork's wider groove.

Clutch release lever damper

4   On all models with the separate clutch release lever (see above), a damper may be fitted to the lever end to prevent engine noises and vibration being transmitted along the clutch cable and into the passenger compartment; the damper being secured by a single screw to the end of a revised release lever (visible in photo 3C.32B).

5   Cable and release lever removal and refitting procedures are unaffected by the presence of the damper.

6   The revised lever/damper assembly can, if required, be fitted to vehicles which did not have it fitted on manufacture; see your local Ford dealer for details.

Clutch assembly - 1.8 litre engines

7   The clutch cover assembly/pressure plates and clutch discs/driven plates fitted to these engines are marked 'Low-lift'. This is to identify them as being of a modified design which, by altering the pressure plate's internal ratio, increases the clutch's torque-handling capabilities without increasing pedal travel/effort; this results in reduced pressure plate lift, hence the designation.

8   Clutch cover assembly/pressure plates and clutch discs/driven plates marked in this way must never be mixed with unmarked components or the clutch take-up may be faulty; it is possible that such a mixture may even result in a clutch that cannot release. **Always** use only a pressure plate and driven plate that are correctly marked when renewing these components.

9   To minimise gear rattle at idle speed, a revised clutch disc/driven plate is available; see your local Ford dealer for details.

Transmission removal and refitting   1.8 litre engines

10   In addition to the comments made in Chapter 4, Section 3, note the following points.

11   On Escort/Orion models, remove the duct from the air cleaner to the inlet manifold, unbolting its support bracket.

12   On some models a speed sensor is fitted, the cable for which will have to be disconnected.

Fig. 8.27 Power-assisted steering pump fluid pressure and return hose unions (arrows) – seen from centre-line of vehicle (Sec 7)

A   *Pressure hose support bracket on oil pump*

7 Suspension and steering

Power-assisted steering

General
1   Power-assisted steering may be fitted to some of the revised (September 1990-on) range of Escort/Orion models. The system is essentially the same as that fitted to the petrol-engined vehicles and covered in the appropriate manual, except for a slightly different fluid pump and drivebelt installation.

2   This Section covers **only** those aspects of the system that are different on Diesel-engines models; for all other information refer to the relevant Chapter of the petrol-engine manual.

Drivebelt check, renewal and adjustment
3   Refer to the appropriate sub-section of Section 4 of this Chapter.

Power-assisted steering pump – removal and refitting
4   The pump and alternator are both mounted on a bracket that is bolted to the front right-hand end of the cylinder block.

5   Before any pump servicing operations can be undertaken, adequate access must first be gained by jacking up the front right-hand side of the vehicle and supporting it on axle stands placed at the points shown in the appropriate manual for petrol-engined vehicles.

6   Disconnect the battery earth (negative) lead.

7   Detaching the shield(s) and/or cover(s) as necessary, remove the alternator/pump drivebelt as described in Section 4 of this Chapter.

8   Disconnect the fluid pressure and return hoses (Fig. 8.27) from the pump and allow the fluid to drain into a suitable container. Plug or cap hoses and unions to keep dirt out.

9   Insert a 9 mm Allen key into the centre of the pump drive spindle to prevent it from turning, then unscrew and remove the three pump pulley retaining bolts. Withdraw the pulley from the pump.

10   Unscrew the three retaining bolts (Fig. 8.28) and withdraw the pump.

11   Refitting is the reverse of the removal procedure, noting the following points:

(a)   *Tighten all fasteners to the torque wrench settings specified – if not given in this Chapter, they will be the same as those given in the manual for the petrol-engined vehicle*
(b)   *Remove the plugs when reconnecting the hoses, ensure no dirt*

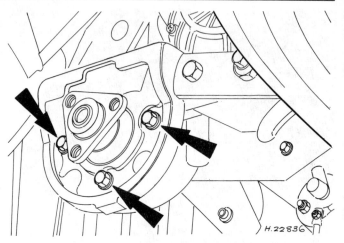

Fig. 8.28 Power-assisted steering pump retaining bolts (arrows) (Sec 7)

is allowed to enter the system and check that both hoses are correctly routed, well clear of any adjacent components
(c)   *Refit and adjust the alternator/pump drivebelt as described in Section 4 of this Chapter*
(d)   *Refill the system with the specified type of fluid, then bleed any air from it as described in the manual for the petrol-engined vehicle*

8 Electrical system

Starter motor – removal and refitting
1   Refer to Chapter 7, Section 6.

Starter motor – brush renewal

All types
2   Remove the starter motor from the vehicle as described in Chapter 7 and clean it thoroughly, then unscrew the nuts securing the tail bracket and withdraw it (if still fitted).

Bosch EV
3   Undo the two retaining screws and remove the end cap.

4   Wipe clean the end of the armature shaft, then prise the C-washer from the groove in the shaft's end. Remove the plain washer(s).

5   Unscrew the two through-bolts, then remove the commutator end cover.

6   Unscrew the nut and disconnect the brush link lead from the solenoid's terminal stud.

7   Withdraw the thrustplate assembly (taking care to release the spring pressure from each brush before disturbing the assembly so as not to damage the brushes), then release the brushes from their holders in the brushplate.

8   Clean and inspect the brush assemblies. If any of the brushes have worn down to, or beyond, the specified minimum length they must be renewed as a set. To renew the brushes, their leads must be unsoldered from the brushplate terminals, then the new brush leads soldered in their place.

9   Before refitting the brushes, check the condition of the commutator face on which they run. Wipe the commutator with a petrol-moistened cloth. If the commutator is dirty, it may be cleaned with fine glass paper, then wiped with the cloth.

10   Position the brushplate over the commutator and refit the brush holders, springs and brushes onto the brushplate, ensuring that the

Fig. 8.29 Exploded view of Bosch (DW) reduction gear starter motor (Sec 8)

1   Solenoid yoke
2   Spring
3   Solenoid plunger
4   Operating arm
5   Drive end housing
6   Pinion and clutch assembly
7   Thrustwasher
8   Ring gear
9   Planet gear shaft
10 Circlip
11 Through-bolt
12 Armature end cap
13 C-washer
14 Plain washer
15 Commutator end cover
16 Brushplate
17 Field winding yoke
18 Rubber plug
19 Armature
20 Armature retaining plate
Note: Refer to Chapter 7 for details of this motor

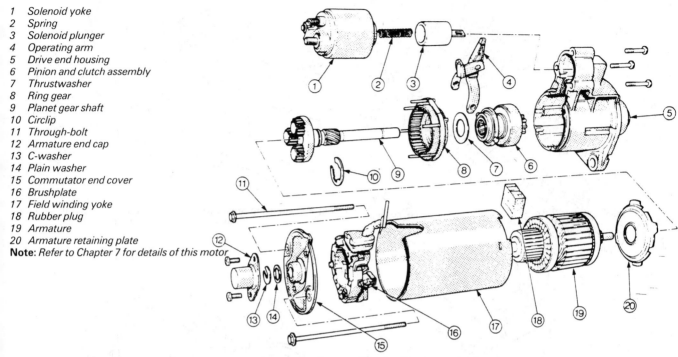

holders' securing lugs are positively located. Make sure that the brushes move freely in their holders.

11   Refit the commutator end cover and secure it with the through-bolts. Connect the brush link lead to the solenoid's terminal stud and secure it with the nut.

12   Refit the plain washer(s) to the end of the armature shaft and secure with the C-washer. Apply some grease to the shaft, then refit and secure the end cap. Finally, refit the tail bracket, tightening its retaining nuts only lightly at first.

Lucas/Magneti Marelli M80R
13   Undo the two nuts and withdraw the support bracket, then undo the two screws and remove the commutator end cover and the plastic insulator.

14   Unscrew the retaining nut and disconnect the brush link lead from the solenoid's terminal stud.

15   Withdraw the brushplate assembly (taking care to release the spring pressure from each brush before disturbing the assembly so as not to damage the brushes), then release the brushes from their holders in the brushplate.

16   Clean and inspect the brush assemblies. If any of the brushes have worn down to or beyond the minimum length specified, they must be renewed as a set.

17   Before refitting the brushes, check the condition of the commutator face on which they run. Wipe the commutator with a petrol-moistened cloth. If the commutator is dirty, it may be cleaned with fine glass paper, then wiped with the cloth.

18   Fit the new brushes and reassemble the motor using a reversal of the dismantling procedure. Make sure that the brushes move freely in their holders.

19   Refit the plastic insulator, the commutator end cover and the support bracket, securing them with the screws and nuts. Connect the brush link lead to the solenoid's terminal stud and secure it with the nut. Finally, refit the tail bracket, tightening its retaining nuts only lightly at first.

Starter motor – overhaul

All types
20   With reference to the notes in Chapter 7, Section 8, paragraph 1, **always** check first exactly what replacement component parts are available and their cost, before deciding whether to overhaul the existing unit or to replace it with a new or reconditioned one.

21   Remove the starter motor from the vehicle as noted above, then clean it thoroughly and unbolt the tail bracket (if still fitted).

22   Remove the brushgear as described in the relevant paragraphs above.

Bosch EV
23   With the brushgear removed, carefully withdraw the complete field winding yoke and armature assembly from the drive end housing, noting how the armature retaining plate is located.

24   Unscrew the solenoid mounting screws and withdraw the solenoid yoke.

25   Withdraw the complete planet gear shaft assembly, with the operating arm and solenoid plunger and the pinion and clutch assembly, from the drive end housing. Dismantle and clean these components, unhooking the solenoid plunger from the operating arm and removing the pinion and clutch from the planet gear shaft as described in paragraph 6 (and accompanying photos) of Chapter 7, Section 8.

26   Clean and check all components as described in Chapter 7, Section 8; renewing as necessary any that are worn or damaged.

27   Check the bearings and bushes for excessive wear and damage. New bushes may be fitted if necessary but they should be soaked in engine oil for 30 minutes before fitting.

28   Check that the one-way clutch only allows the pinion to rotate in one direction.

29   Refitting is a reversal of the removal procedure but lubricate all moving parts as they are assembled.

30   On reassembly, fit the pinion and clutch to the planet gear shaft as

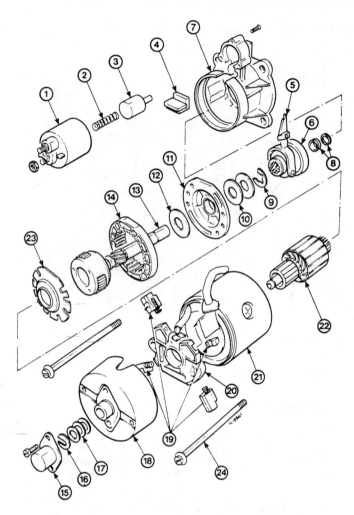

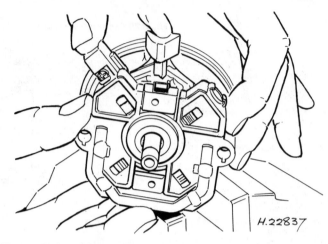

Fig. 8.31 Refitting brushplate to commutator – Bosch (EV) reduction gear starter motor (Sec 8)

Fig. 8.30 Exploded view of Bosch (EV) reduction gear starter motor (Sec 8)

1　Solenoid yoke	12　Thrustwasher
2　Spring	13　Planet gear shaft
3　Solenoid plunger	14　Ring gear
4　Rubber plug	15　Armature end cap
5　Operating arm	16　C-washer
6　Pinion and clutch	17　Plain washers
assembly	18　Commutator end cover
7　Drive end housing	19　Brushes
8　Thrust collar and spring	20　Brushplate
clip	21　Field winding yoke
9　Circlip	22　Armature
10　Thrustwashers	23　Armature retaining plate
11　Cover plate	24　Through-bolt

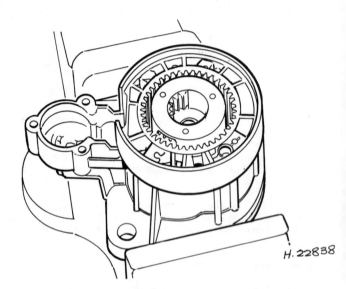

Fig. 8.32 Correct location of ring gear – Bosch (EV) reduction gear starter motor (Sec 8)

described in paragraph 15 (and accompanying photos) of Chapter 7, Section 8.

31　Apply a smear of lithium-based grease to the solenoid plunger 'hook' and engage it on the operating arm, then refit the complete planet gear shaft assembly to the drive end housing, ensuring that the ring gear is correctly located as shown in Fig. 8.32.

32　Do not forget the spring when refitting the solenoid yoke.

33　Ensure that the armature retaining plate is correctly located before refitting the armature/field winding yoke assembly to the drive end housing (Fig. 8.33).

34　Refit the brushgear as described in the relevant paragraphs above.

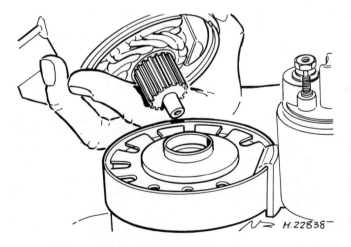

Fig. 8.33 Correct location of armature retaining plate – Bosch (EV) reduction gear starter motor (Sec 8)

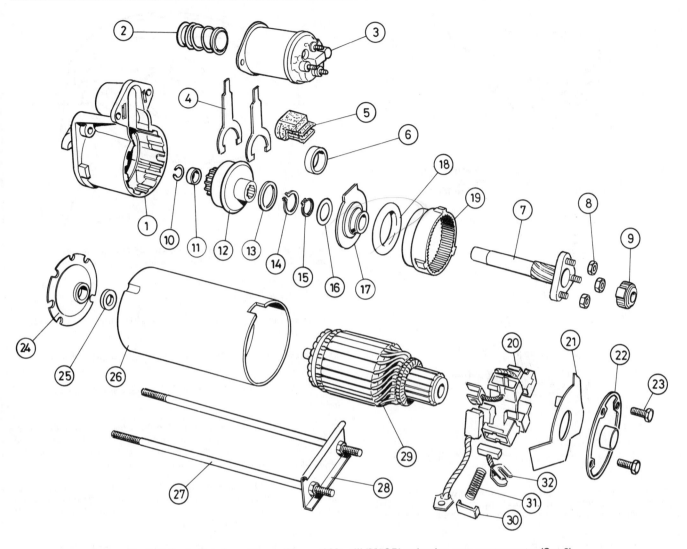

Fig. 8.34 Exploded view of Lucas/Magneti Marelli (M8OR) reduction gear starter motor (Sec 8)

1	Drive end housing
2	Solenoid plunger with spring
3	Solenoid yoke
4	Operating arm
5	Rubber plug
6	Carrier
7	Planet gear shaft
8	Planet gears
9	Sun gear
10	Spring clip
11	Thrust collar
12	Pinion and clutch assembly
13	Washer
14	Circlip
15	Circlip
16	Washer
17	Bearing support plate
18	Seal
19	Plastic support cup
20	Brushplate
21	Insulator
22	Commutator end cover
23	Screws
24	Armature retaining plate
25	Spacer
26	Field winding yoke
27	Through-studs
28	Support bracket
29	Armature
30	Brush clip
31	Brush spring
32	Brush

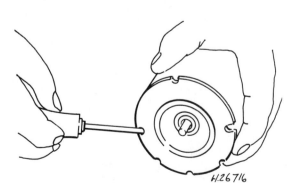

Fig. 8.35 Removing armature retaining plate   Lucas/Magneti Marelli (M80R) reduction gear starter motor (Sec 8)

Lucas/Magneti Marelli M80R

35   With the brushgear removed, unscrew the mounting screws and withdraw the solenoid yoke, then unhook and remove the solenoid plunger and spring.

36   Carefully withdraw the complete field winding yoke and armature assembly from the drive end housing, then remove the armature retaining plate (Fig. 8.35) and withdraw the spacer. When extracting the armature from the yoke against the pull of the magnets, take care not to allow either to be damaged.

37   Withdraw the complete planet gear shaft assembly, with the operating arm and rubber plug and the pinion and clutch assembly, from the drive end housing.

38   Remove the pinion and clutch from the planet gear shaft as described in paragraph 6 (and accompanying photos) of Chapter 7, Section 8. Remove the circlip and washer (Fig. 8.36) to separate the

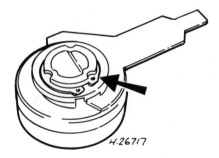

Fig. 8.36 Remove circlip (arrowed) to release washer, operating arm and carrier from pinion and clutch assembly – Lucas/Magneti Marelli (M80R) reduction gear starter motor (Sec 8)

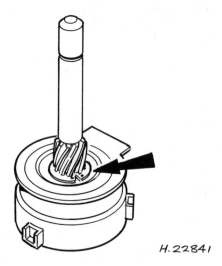

Fig. 8.37 Remove circlip (arrowed) to release washer, bearing support plate, seal and plastic support cup from planet gear shaft – Lucas/Magneti Marelli (M80R) reduction gear starter motor (Sec 8)

operating arm and carrier from the pinion and clutch assembly, then withdraw the operating arm members from the carrier and remove the rubber plug.

39   Remove the circlip and washer (Fig. 8.37) from the planet gear shaft and withdraw the bearing support plate, the seal and the plastic support cup.

40   Clean and check all components as described in Chapter 7, Section 8; renewing as necessary any that are worn or damaged.

41   Check the bearings and bushes for excessive wear and damage.

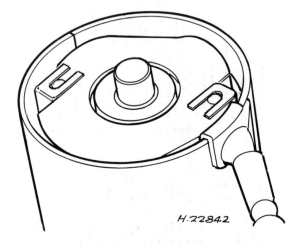

Fig. 8.38 Correct location of insulator and brush connections Lucas/Magneti Marelli (M80R) reduction gear starter motor (Sec 8)

New bushes may be fitted if necessary but they should be soaked in engine oil for 30 minutes before fitting.

42   Check that the one-way clutch only allows the pinion to rotate in one direction.

43   Refitting is a reversal of the removal procedure but lubricate all moving parts as they are assembled.

44   On reassembly, ensure that the seal is correctly located in the support cup.

45   Fit both operating arm members to the carrier, then refit the carrier to the pinion and clutch assembly, securing it with the washer and circlip. Fit the pinion and clutch to the planet gear shaft as described in paragraph 15 (and accompanying photos) of Chapter 7, Section 8.

46   Refit the rubber plug to the operating arm and refit the complete planet gear shaft assembly, with the operating arm and rubber plug and the pinion and clutch assembly, to the drive end housing; ensure that the rubber plug is correctly located.

47   Lubricate the reduction gears with lithium-based grease.

48   Insert the armature into the field winding yoke, ensuring that the through-studs are correctly located, then refit the spacer and retaining plate and refit the assembly to the drive end housing, ensuring that it is correctly aligned.

49   Apply a smear of lithium-based grease to the solenoid plunger 'hook' and engage it on the operating arm, then refit the solenoid yoke; do not forget the spring.

50   Refit the brushgear as described in the relevant paragraphs above.

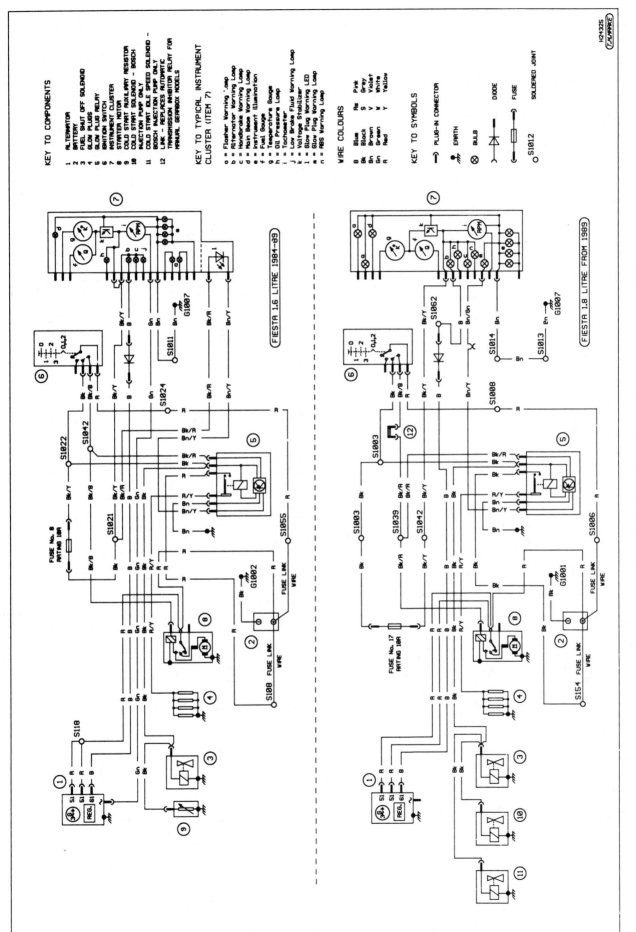

KEY TO COMPONENTS

1 ALTERNATOR
2 BATTERY
3 FUEL SHUT OFF SOLENOID
4 GLOW PLUGS
5 GLOW PLUG RELAY
6 IGNITION SWITCH
7 INSTRUMENT CLUSTER
8 STARTER MOTOR
9 COLD START AUXILIARY RESISTOR
10 COLD START SOLENOID - BOSCH INJECTION PUMP ONLY
11 COLD START IDLE SPEED SOLENOID - BOSCH INJECTION PUMP ONLY
12 LINK - REPLACES AUTOMATIC TRANSMISSION INHIBITOR RELAY FOR MANUAL GEARBOX MODELS

KEY TO TYPICAL INSTRUMENT CLUSTER (ITEM 7)

a = Flasher Warning Loop
b = Alternator Warning Loop
c = Handbrake Warning Loop
d = Main Beam Warning Loop
e = Instrument Illumination
f = Fuel Gauge
g = Temperature Gauge
h = Oil Pressure Loop
i = Tachometer
j = Low Brake Fluid Warning Loop
k = Voltage Stabilizer
l = Glow Plug Warning LED
m = Glow Plug Warning Loop
n = ABS Warning Loop

WIRE COLOURS

B   Blue   Rs   Pink
Bk   Black   S   Grey
Bn   Brown   V   Violet
Gn   Green   W   White
R   Red   Y   Yellow

KEY TO SYMBOLS

—) PLUG-IN CONNECTOR
⊣⊢ EARTH
⊗   BULB
▷| DIODE
▭   FUSE
O   SOLDERED JOINT   S1012

FIESTA 1.6 LITRE 1984-89

FIESTA 1.8 LITRE FROM 1989

Starting, charging and general engine wiring diagram – 1.6/1.8 litre Fiesta models

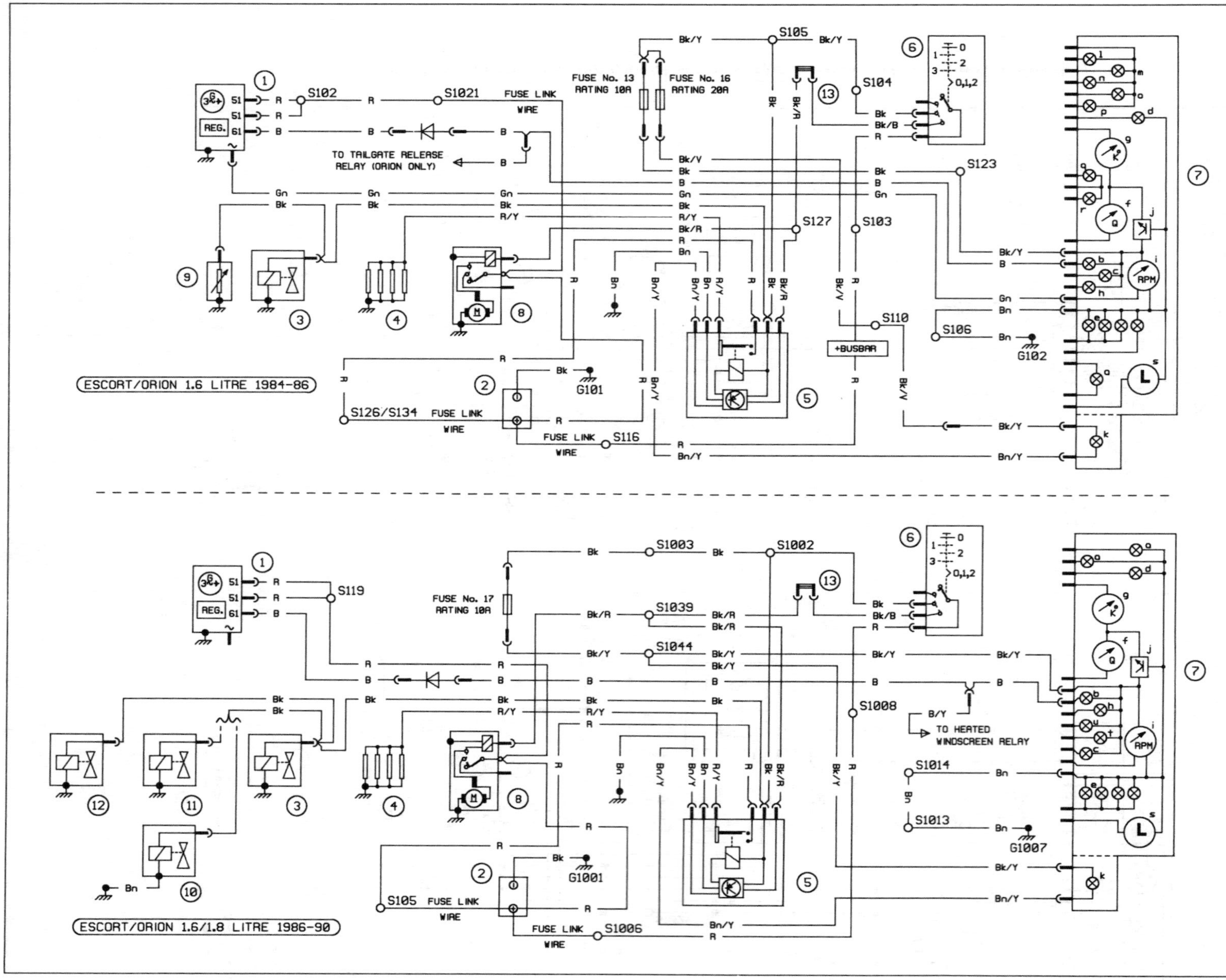

H24326 *HAYNES*

KEY TO COMPONENTS

1 = ALTERNATOR
2 = BATTERY
3 = FUEL SHUT OFF SOLENOID
4 = GLOW PLUGS
5 = GLOW PLUG RELAY
6 = IGNITION SWITCH
7 = INSTRUMENT CLUSTER
8 = STARTER MOTOR
9 = COLD START AUXILIARY RESISTOR
10 = COLD START SOLENOID
11 = COLD START SOLENOID - BOSCH INJECTION PUMP ONLY
12 = COLD START IDLE SPEED SOLENOID - BOSCH INJECTION PUMP ONLY
13 = LINK - REPLACES AUTOMATIC TRANSMISSION INHIBITOR RELAY FOR MANUAL GEARBOX MODELS

KEY TO TYPICAL INSTRUMENT CLUSTER (ITEM 7)

a = Flasher Warning Lamp
b = Alternator Warning Lamp
c = Handbrake Warning Lamp
d = Main Beam Warning Lamp
e = Instrument Illumination
f = Fuel Gauge
g = Temperature Gauge
h = Oil Pressure Lamp
i = Tachometer
j = Voltage Stabilizer
k = Glow Plug Warning Lamp
l = Brake Pad Wear Warning Lamp
m = Low Washer Fluid Warning Lamp
n = Low Oil Level Warning Lamp
o = Low Coolant Level Warning Lamp
p = Low Fuel Level Warning Lamp
q = Econolight Amber
r = Econolight Red
s = Clock
t = ABS Warning Lamp
u = Choke Warning Lamp

WIRE COLOURS

B = Blue	Rs = Pink
Bk = Black	S = Grey
Bn = Brown	V = Violet
Gn = Green	W = White
R = Red	Y = Yellow

KEY TO SYMBOLS

PLUG-IN CONNECTOR
EARTH
BULB
DIODE
FUSE
S1012 SOLDERED JOINT

ESCORT/ORION 1.6 LITRE 1984-86

ESCORT/ORION 1.6/1.8 LITRE 1986-90

Starting, charging and general engine wiring diagram – 1.6/1.8 litre Escort/Orion models 1984-90

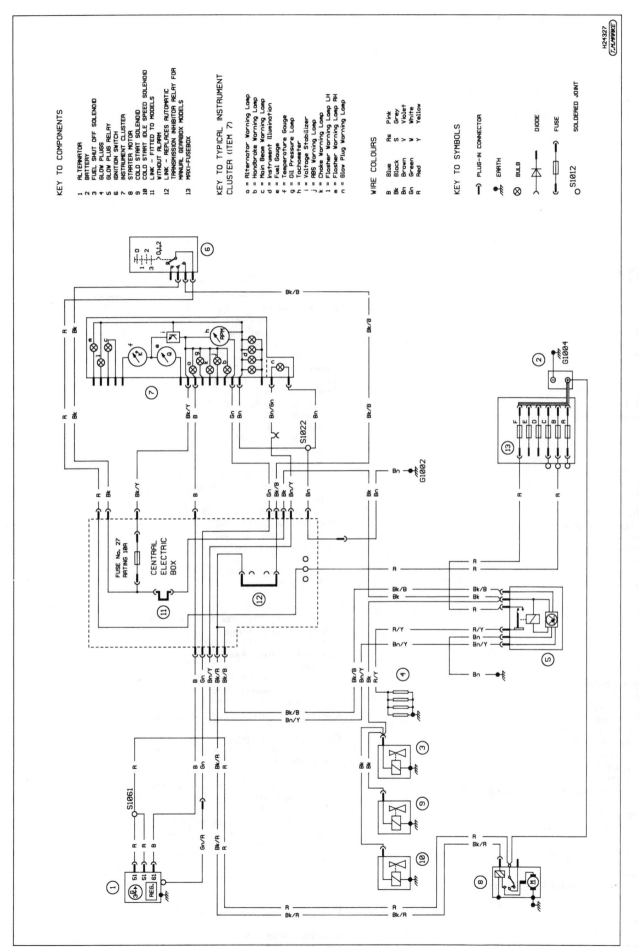

KEY TO COMPONENTS

1 ALTERNATOR
2 BATTERY
3 FUEL SHUT OFF SOLENOID
4 GLOW PLUGS
5 GLOW PLUG RELAY
6 IGNITION SWITCH
7 INSTRUMENT CLUSTER
8 STARTER MOTOR
9 COLD START SOLENOID
10 COLD START IDLE SPEED SOLENOID
11 LINK – FITTED TO MODELS WITHOUT ALARM
12 LINK – REPLACES AUTOMATIC TRANSMISSION INHIBITOR RELAY FOR MANUAL GEARBOX MODELS
13 MAXI-FUSEBOX

KEY TO TYPICAL INSTRUMENT CLUSTER (ITEM 7)

a = Alternator Warning Lamp
b = Handbrake Warning Lamp
c = Main Beam Warning Lamp
d = Instrument Illumination
e = Fuel Gauge
f = Temperature Gauge
g = Oil Pressure Lamp
h = Tachometer
j = Voltage Stabilizer
J = ABS Warning Lamp
k = Choke Warning Lamp
l = Flasher Warning Lamp LH
m = Flasher Warning Lamp RH
n = Glow Plug Warning Lamp

WIRE COLOURS

B Blue
Bk Black
Bn Brown
Gn Green
R Red
Rs Pink
S Grey
V Violet
W White
Y Yellow

KEY TO SYMBOLS

PLUG-IN CONNECTOR
EARTH
BULB
DIODE
FUSE
S1012 SOLDERED JOINT

Starting, charging and general engine wiring diagram – 1.8 litre Escort/Orion models from 1990

Index